I0812764

IMAGES
of America

MARSHALL COUNTY

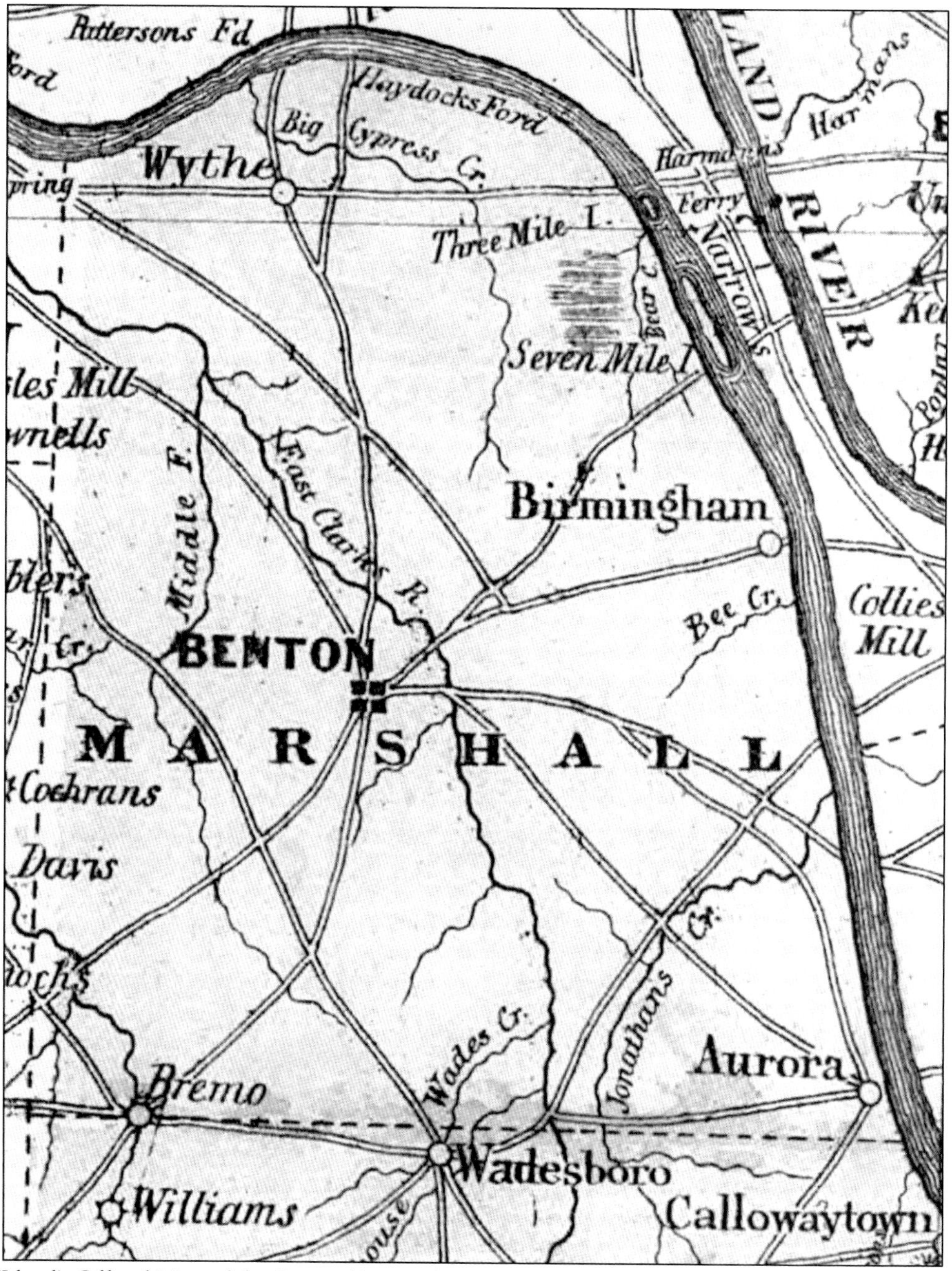

"Lloyd's Official Map of the State of Kentucky," dated 1863, shows few communities in the new county. James T. Lloyd was a commercial mapmaker and publisher during the mid-19th century. His early map of Marshall County shows only a few settlements.

ON THE COVER: Watkins Remedies agent Benjamin F. Johnson and his family posed beside their Fair Dealing home, *c.* 1900. Benjamin and his wife, Caroline (McLeod), raised two children, William and Augusta. Their extended family is believed to have also occupied this home. B. F. Johnson, besides being the Watkins dealer, was also a farmer. (Courtesy of Claude Nimmo.)

IMAGES
of America

MARSHALL COUNTY

Connie M. Huddleston, Carol Aldridge,
and Virginia Smith

ARCADIA
PUBLISHING

ISBN 978-0-7385-4284-3

Published by Arcadia Publishing
Charleston, South Carolina

Printed in the United States of America

Library of Congress Catalog Card Number: 2006923518

For all general information contact Arcadia Publishing at:
Telephone 843-853-2070
Fax 843-853-0044
E-mail sales@arcadiapublishing.com
For customer service and orders:
Toll-Free 1-888-313-2665

Visit us on the Internet at www.arcadiapublishing.com

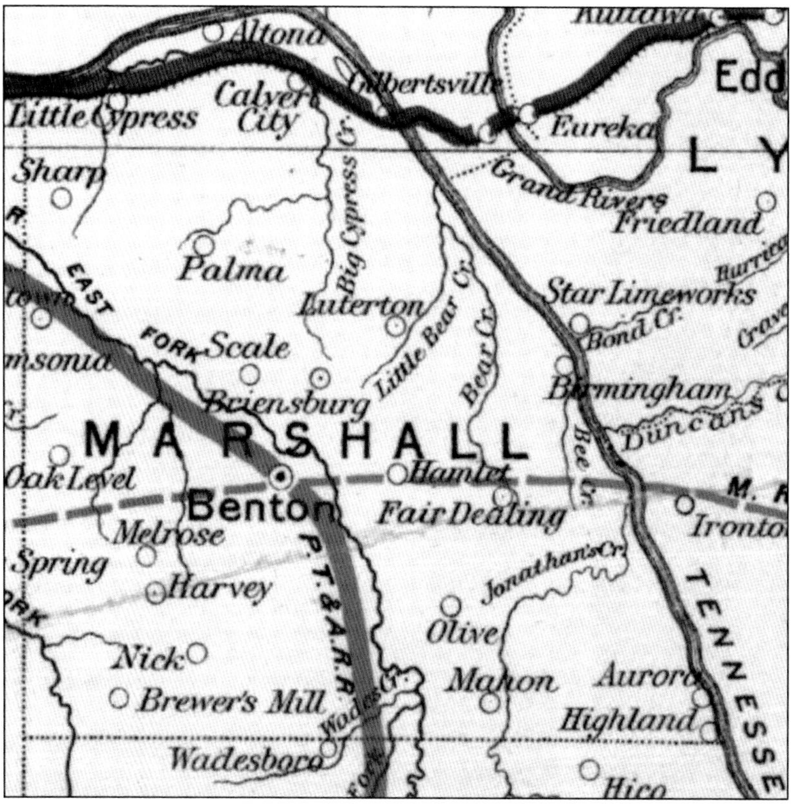

The "Kentucky Geological Survey Preliminary Map of Kentucky," dated 1891, illustrates how Marshall County's population had grown since the county was created in 1842.

Contents

Acknowledgments

Without family, old friends, new friends, and acquaintances in Marshall County, this book would not have been possible. Their sharing of treasured family photographs and memories allowed the telling of their stories on these pages. In particular, I wish to thank Elizabeth Harrell, Viola Collins, Mayme Ruth Brooks, Charles Hall, Harvey and Bobby Culp, Louise Wyatt, Howard Ivey, Marion Wade, Rivers Capps, and Claude Nimmo. Each of these special individuals shared more than just photographs—they shared their recollections of days gone by.

My coauthors, Virginia Smith and Carol Aldridge, spent countless hours telephoning old friends and relations. Their dedication to the project made it successful. Virginia also provided much of the research needed to add dates and names to many of the photographs. Her love of research and preserving history wins my greatest praise and gratitude.

The authors also wish to thank the Marshall County Genealogical and Historical Society for sharing their photographic collection for this publication. A treasure trove of documentation and history resides within their repository. The many volunteer hours that members dedicate to supporting this public collection are laudable.

Finally two editors who read every word of the manuscript and gave praise and suggestions along with their corrections must be noted. They are Charles V. Huddleston and Amy Davis. You are both greatly appreciated. Also thanks to Arcadia Publishing's editors. We began this project with Arcadia's Lauren C. Bobier and finished with Kendra L. Allen. Their help and guidance were both necessary and relied upon throughout this project.

INTRODUCTION

In the early 1800s, the area now encompassing Marshall County belonged to the Chickasaw Indians. After their departure in the early 1820s, settlers quickly moved west of the Tennessee River into the Jackson Purchase. These pioneers grew corn, oats, and wheat; established ferries across the Tennessee and the area's other rivers; made improvements to their land; and began to establish small communities. Population grew because of cheap land prices and the new nation's lust for westward expansion. In 1825, land prices were $1 an acre; however, by 1829, the price had dropped to 25¢ per acre for those who actually planned to settle on and improve the land.

Settlers arrived by foot, by wagon, and by boat. They carried with them the few provisions and tools they owned, often no more than an axe, a rifle, a kettle, and a frying pan. As the purchase became more populated, neighbors welcomed any new family by helping to raise their cabin. Then the farmer cleared a few acres and planted corn. While tending the children, cooking, and washing, his wife planted a garden. Days bounded by, full of labor and fresh, wholesome food. Neighbors established churches and schools and visited and aided others in distress.

Some ambitious settlers opened gristmills and sawmills. Blacksmith shops flourished, as they shod horses, repaired wagons and buggies, and made tools of all kinds. Storekeepers opened general merchandise shops at crossroads and furnished surrounding farming families with the items they could not grow, such as cloth, shoes, and household implements. Hucksters traveled the county in wagons selling goods door-to-door.

Marshall County, named for Chief Justice John Marshall, was established out of Calloway County on June 1, 1842. The new county commissioners chose a central location for the county seat and named it Benton to honor Thomas H. Benton, the famous U.S. senator from Missouri. The new county encompassed 209,920 acres. Rich farmlands along rivers, such as the three forks of Clarks River and the Tennessee, sat among hillsides covered with hickory, black and sweet gum, oak, white ash, and walnut trees.

The Civil War brought division as the county's young men joined units fighting for both sides. Confederates raised two companies, both of which were attached to the 3rd Kentucky Infantry. In 1861, a company was raised for the Union from both the state militia and other sources and was attached to the 20th Kentucky Infantry. Others joined the 1st Battalion, 16th Kentucky Calvary and other units formed in surrounding counties. Gangs of guerillas from both sides roamed the countryside, stealing and terrorizing the residents. Two skirmishes took place in the county, one near Sinkhole Hill and the other on the Hugh Arant farm. Those killed in these skirmishes were buried in the Gilbert Cemetery.

The years leading to the 20th century brought limited changes to Marshall County. Some of the small communities grew into small prosperous towns. Birmingham, a port on the Tennessee River, was founded on dreams of rivaling Birmingham, England, based on nearby iron industries. Birmingham grew into a bustling community—the county's largest with a population of about 350. Downriver Gilbertsville, surrounded by rich farming lands, enjoyed the proceeds of river traffic and rail transportation. Others, such as Hardin and Calvert City, also developed around rail stops. Yet the county continued to be mostly a collection of rural farms and farming communities.

World War I, the war to end all wars, called to many of the county's young men and at least one young woman. Approximately 535 of Marshall County's young men served in World War I; 19 never returned and are commemorated on our courthouse square. The county's Ruth Anna Malcolm served as an overseas nurse during the conflict. Others, mostly men, left for good wages in the munitions plants. Many never returned, and others would follow this footpath to promised prosperity in the first years of the new century and into the years of the Great Depression.

The Great Depression impacted all who resided in our great nation. Prosperity became a thing of the past. Jobs and opportunities were nonexistent. Yet farming families in areas not hit by the great drought of the 1930s survived. County residents listened weekly to Pres. Franklin D. Roosevelt's Fireside Chats on their radio. Those without radios learned the news from others on the courthouse steps, along country roads, and at the local store.

Modern innovations began to arrive slowly throughout the county in the early 20th century. Calvert City, Benton, and Birmingham had electricity. Others had telephone service. Rail transportation became more important than the river. Then automobiles arrived, and a trip to Paducah no longer took two days.

Nevertheless, Marshall County changed the most because of a series of natural disasters—floods! In particular, the great flood of 1937 and the country's economic recovery from the Great Depression pushed Marshall County into the 20th century. After the great flood of 1937, the Tennessee Valley Authority decided to dam the Tennessee River at Gilbertsville to prevent future flooding. Kentucky Dam brought electricity, telephones, new schools, new opportunities, and tourists to Marshall County.

One

Marshall County

Photographs capture moments that might otherwise be forgotten. In formal studio portraits, one can see images of people trying to impress friends and relations by dressing in their very best for the camera. Others might share moments of joy, like a marriage or the birth of a new baby. Some posed for photographs to be sent to loved ones far away.

Photographers also traveled, often from house to house or school to school. People posed beside their homes, carefully staged to show relationships, friendships, even servitude. Prized possessions sometimes were included in photographs, such as horses, buggies, bicycles, cars, dolls, and dogs. School classes posed year after year beside their school buildings, often making one year's class photograph look just like the last.

Yet the informal snapshot that came about with George Eastman's introduction of the $1 Brownie Camera in 1900 often brings us the greatest joy. Informal photographs began to capture everyday life rather than just staged scenes. People began to smile for the camera. Instead of the ordeal of dressing up and standing or sitting very still for a photograph, spontaneity sprang from the pictures that individuals snapped with their box cameras.

During the early part of the 20th century, government photographers documented landscapes, new buildings and bridges, and monumental events. This became especially true as Roosevelt's New Deal programs and the Tennessee Valley Authority (TVA) hired photographers to substantiate and support their public works. These photographs often snatched reflections of places and events that might not otherwise have been photographed.

Using all types of photographs, both professional and amateur, this book bestows upon the viewer images of rural Marshall County. Using private photographic collections from county residents, the Marshall County Genealogical and Historical Society's collection, and others from state and national archives, it tells stories of the county's residents, their homes, their livelihoods, and their pastimes. Drawing upon family reminiscences, the lives of common folks and county traditions spring from the pages for your enjoyment. This first chapter presents images from all over the county and is followed by chapters about individual towns and areas.

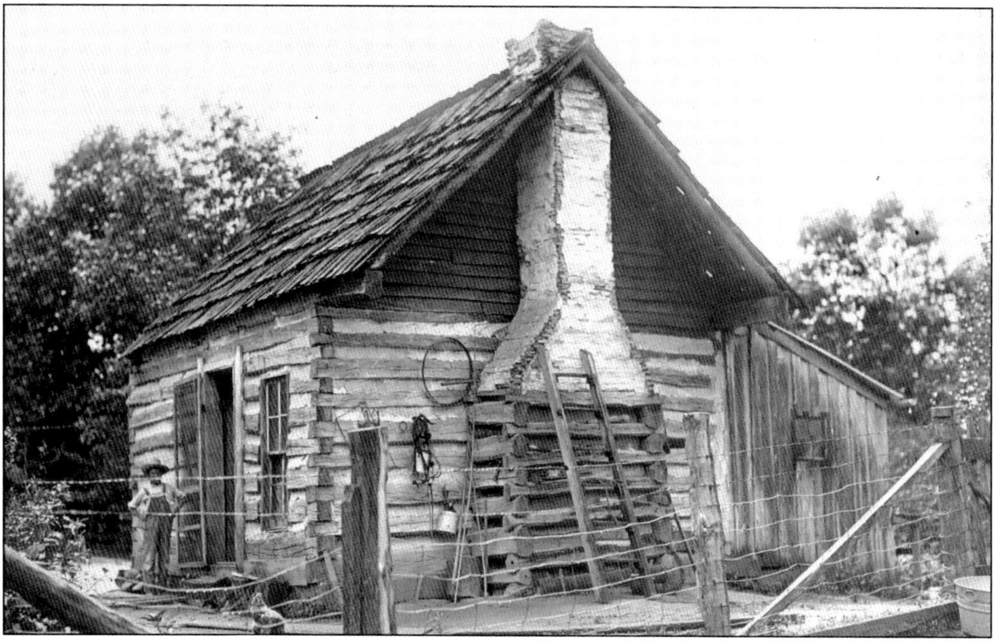

Log cabins housed many families during the county's formative years. Even large families often lived in one-room cabins constructed of hand-hewn logs with wood shake roofs. Furniture was limited, and children most often slept on floor pallets or in lofts. Mud and stick chimneys, such as this one, were designed to be pushed away from the cabin in case of a chimney fire. This often prevented loss of the entire cabin. Wire fencing kept small children, chickens, and other small livestock safe from predators. (Courtesy of the Kentucky Historical Society.)

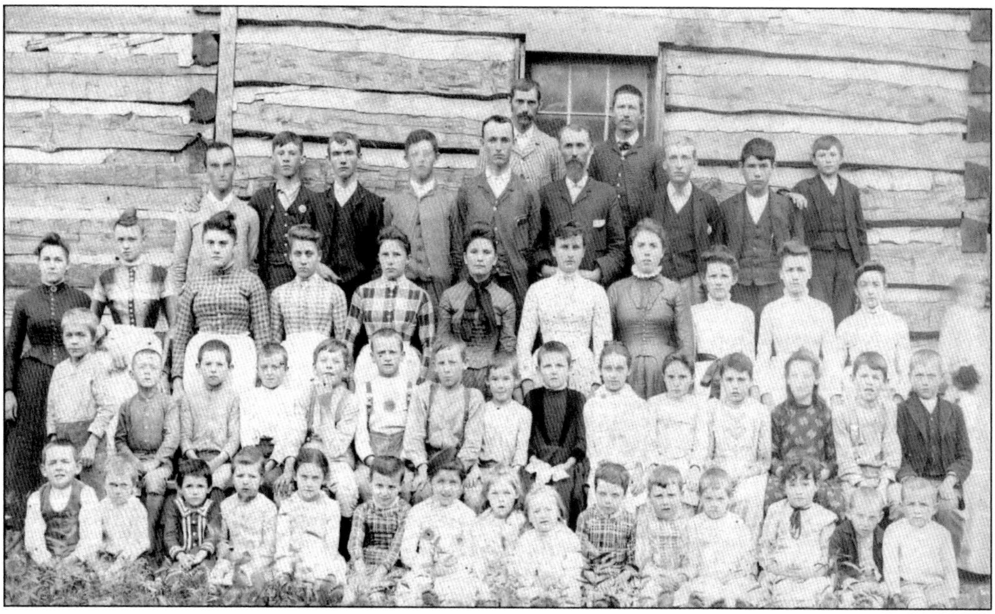

A school, a church, or a family gathering—those details are now lost to history. Yet this image portrays a bit of Marshall County's history. Based on the type of photograph and the women's clothing, it was probably taken in the 1880s. (Courtesy of the Marshall County Genealogical and Historical Society.)

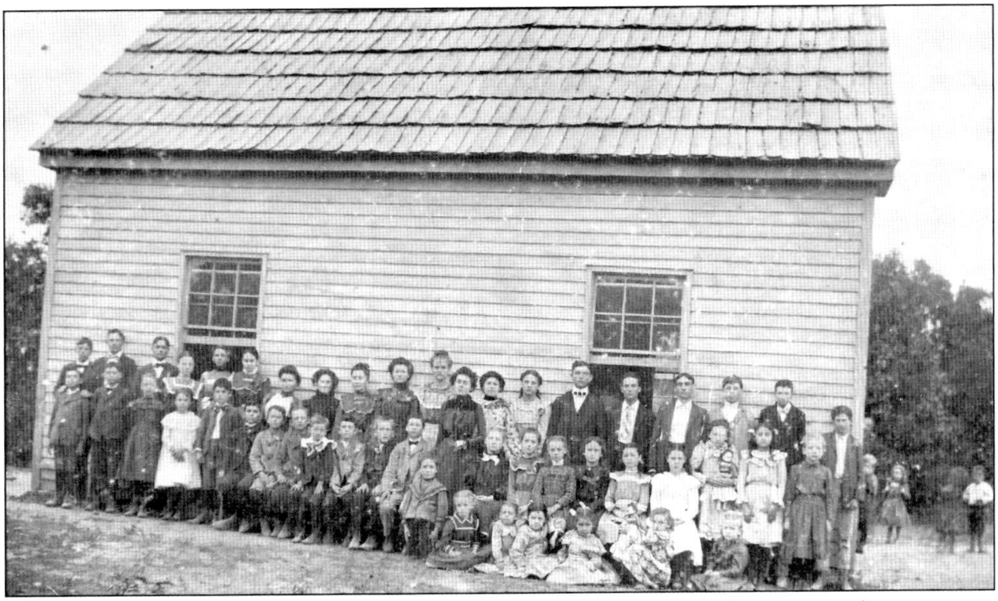

This Marshall County school photograph is undated and unidentified. Interestingly it contains images of two African American children peeking out from the right end of the building beside two Caucasian children. Based on clothing and the type of photograph, it is believed to date to the 1880s or 1890s. At that time, most of the county's African American residents lived in or near Birmingham. (Courtesy of the Marshall County Genealogical and Historical Society.)

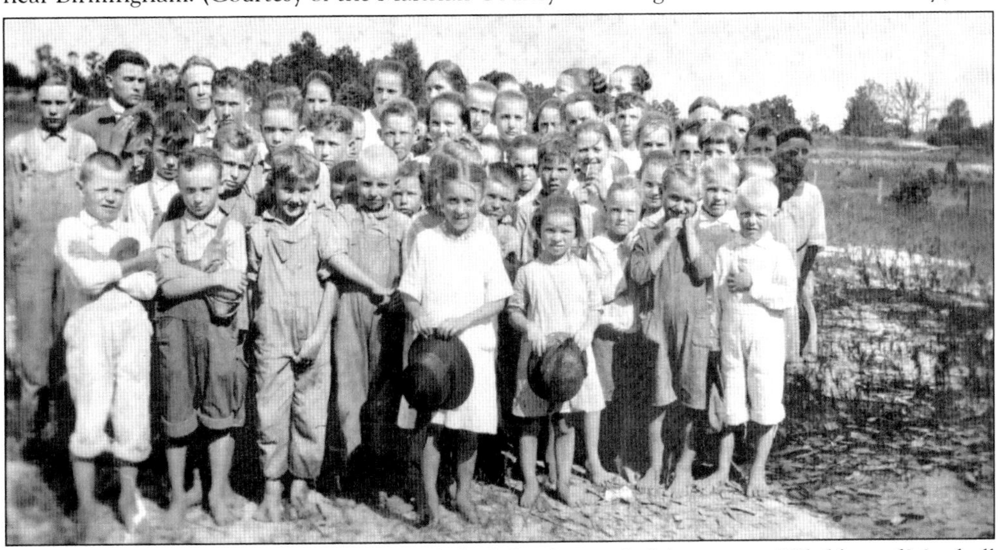

Cora Wilson Stewart, founder of the Moonlight Schools, entitled this picture "Children of Marshall County who will be better served of life because their parents even late in life are going to school." When the Moonlight Schools opened in 1911, adults were taught at night by volunteer teachers in the one-room schools where children learned by day. Adults attended only on moonlit nights when they could see to find their way to the school house. This photograph shows one African American student on the far right peeking out around the other children. African American adults were often taught in their homes by willing teachers as part of the Moonlight Schools. (©University of Kentucky, all rights reserved, Cora Wilson Stewart Photographic Collection, Special Collections and Digital Programs, University of Kentucky Libraries.)

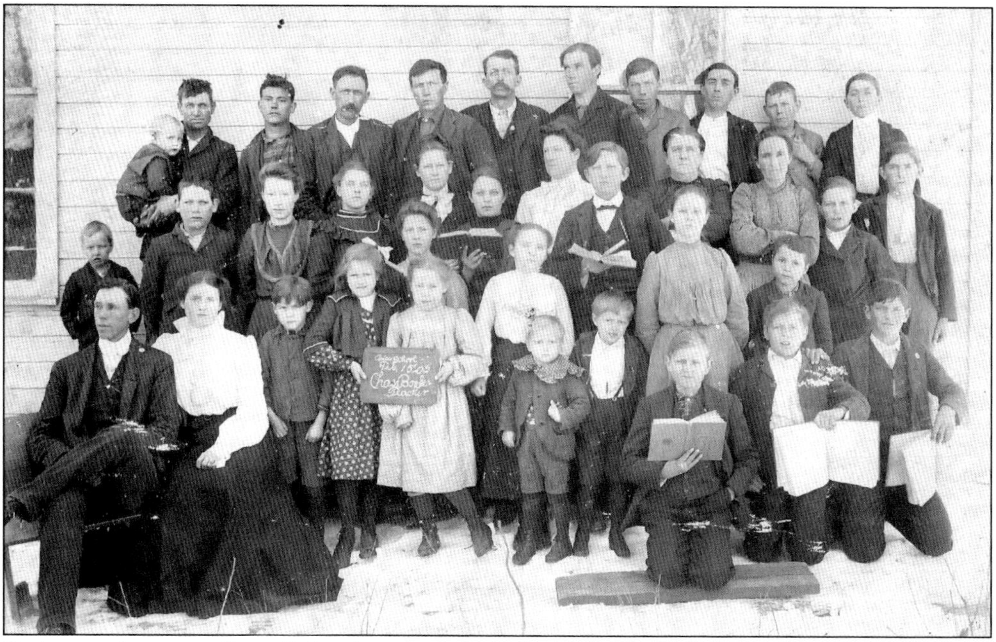

Posing in the snow, Price School students proudly showed off their work and textbooks on February 15, 1905. The presence of adults suggests the school allowed adults to attend, although the Moonlight Schools program did not yet exist. Another explanation is that as photographs were rare and expensive, the school invited families to be photographed with their children. Charles Booker, seated at the left, was the teacher. (Courtesy of Billy Hardison.)

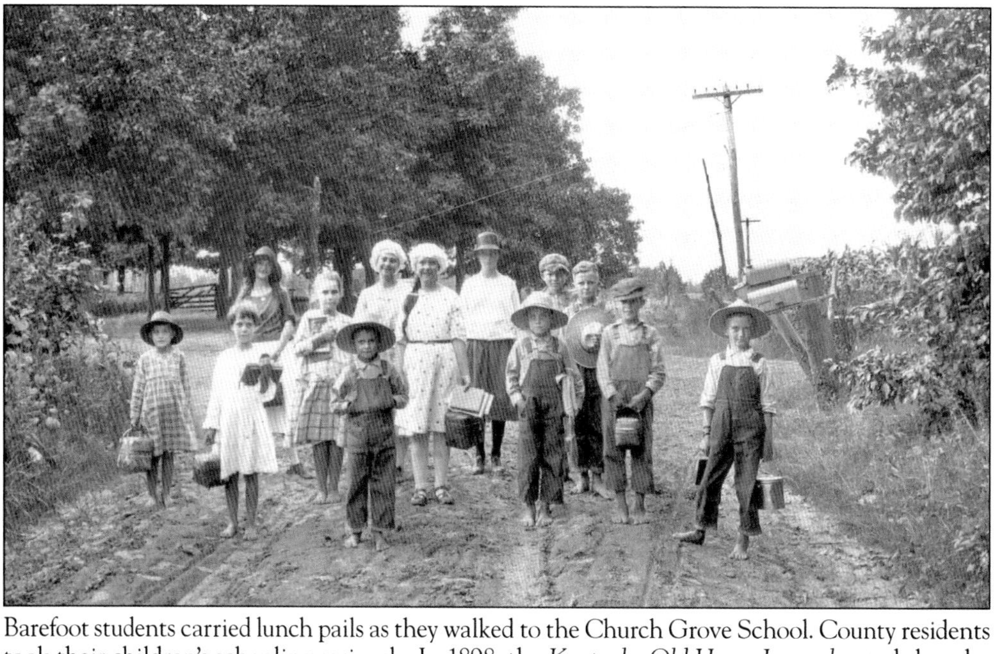

Barefoot students carried lunch pails as they walked to the Church Grove School. County residents took their children's schooling seriously. In 1898, the *Kentucky Old Home Journal* noted that the county contained 54 public school buildings. Public school was free for children between the ages of 6 and 20 for five months each year. Parents paid for the other four months of schooling. (Courtesy of the Kentucky Historical Society.)

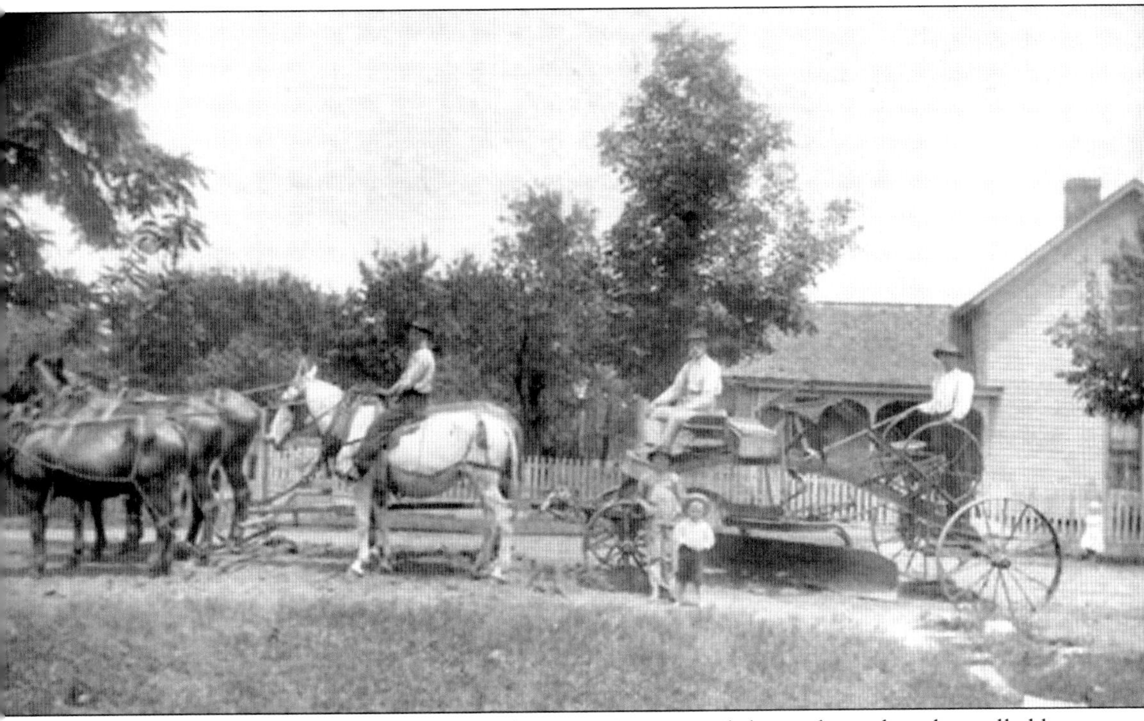

About 1899, William Harvey Penney, on the wagon's seat, used this early road grader, pulled by a five-mule hitch, to prepare the bed for the laying of rail tracks throughout the county. The grader was most likely an Austin Manufacturing Company reversible road machine. Frederick C. Austin of Illinois was a well-known manufacturer of graders in the late 19th and early 20th centuries. The *Kentucky Old Home Journal* also mentions its use to improve the area's roads. The two boys are believed to be his sons, James Clifford and Amos. The Penneys lived on the Egner Ferry Road in a one-room log cabin. (Courtesy of Claude Nimmo.)

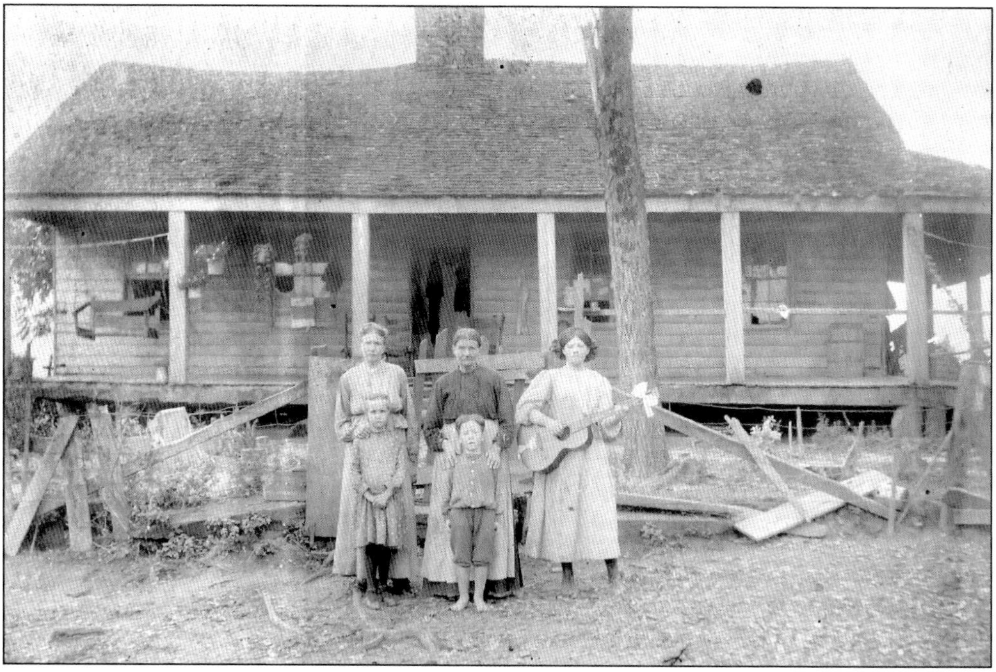

This saddlebag home's porch was part of its living space. Clothing hung from pegs just inside the front door. Some of the broken window panes were covered with cardboard. The yard was surrounded by a rustic wood and wire fence. Ida McGregor (far left) is pictured with, from left to right, (first row) her daughter, Pearl, and Dewey Lindsey; (second row) Mary Lindsey (Ida's mother) and May Lindsey around 1910. (Courtesy of Billy Hardison.)

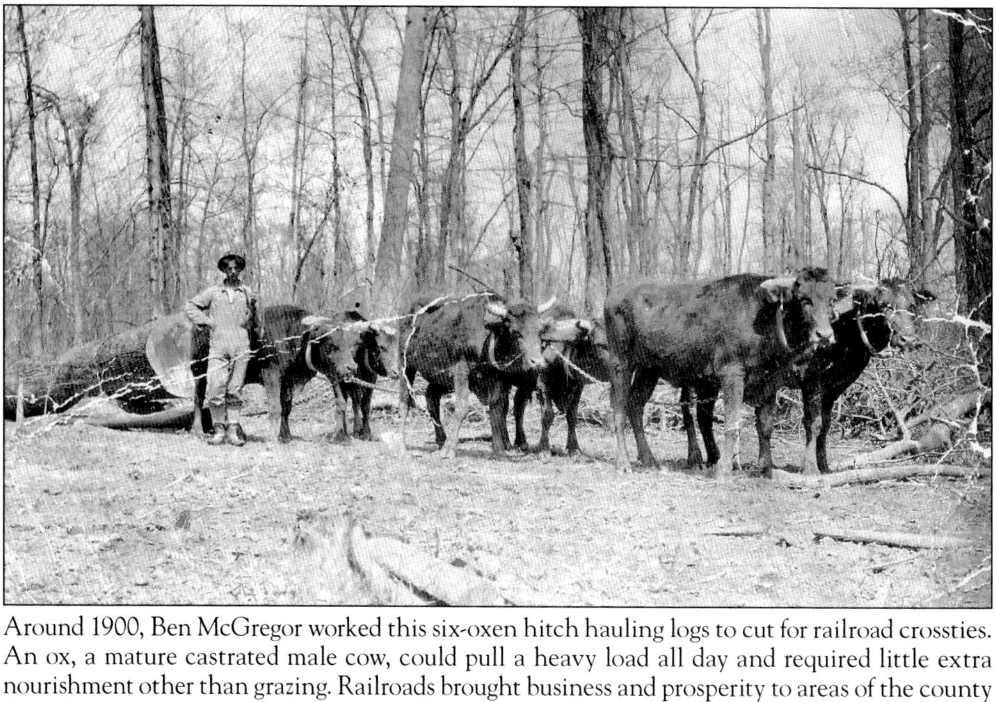

Around 1900, Ben McGregor worked this six-oxen hitch hauling logs to cut for railroad crossties. An ox, a mature castrated male cow, could pull a heavy load all day and required little extra nourishment other than grazing. Railroads brought business and prosperity to areas of the county that river transportation did not serve. (Courtesy of Billy Hardison.)

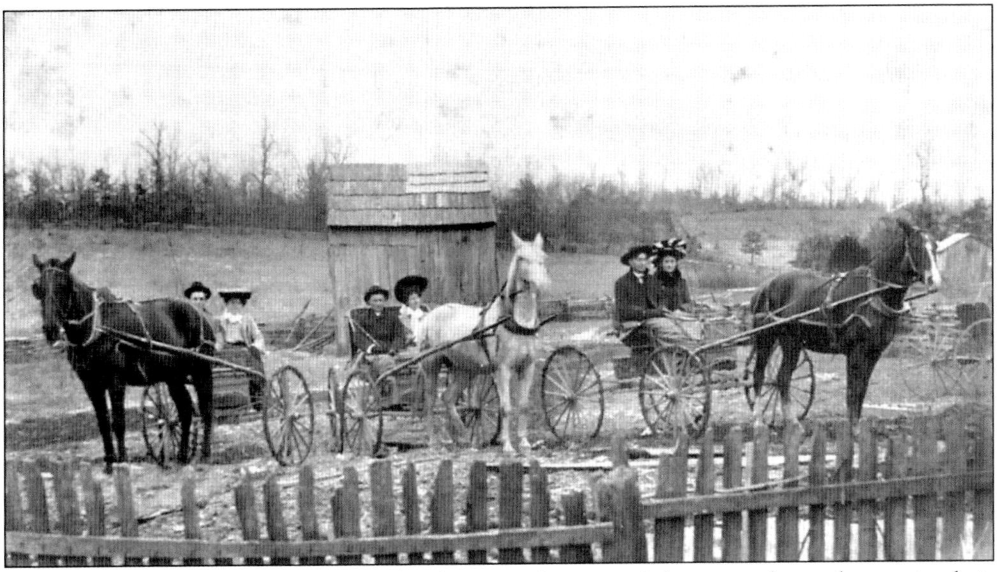

Rev. Richard F. Gregory, standing on his front porch, married three couples as they sat in their buggies on a cold January day in 1905. Richard Gregory lived in the Gilbertsville District and was a Baptist minister. One of these three couples is Fred Martin Franklin and May Riley. Their marriage lasted 62 years. They raised eight children. (Courtesy of the Marshall County Genealogical and Historical Society.)

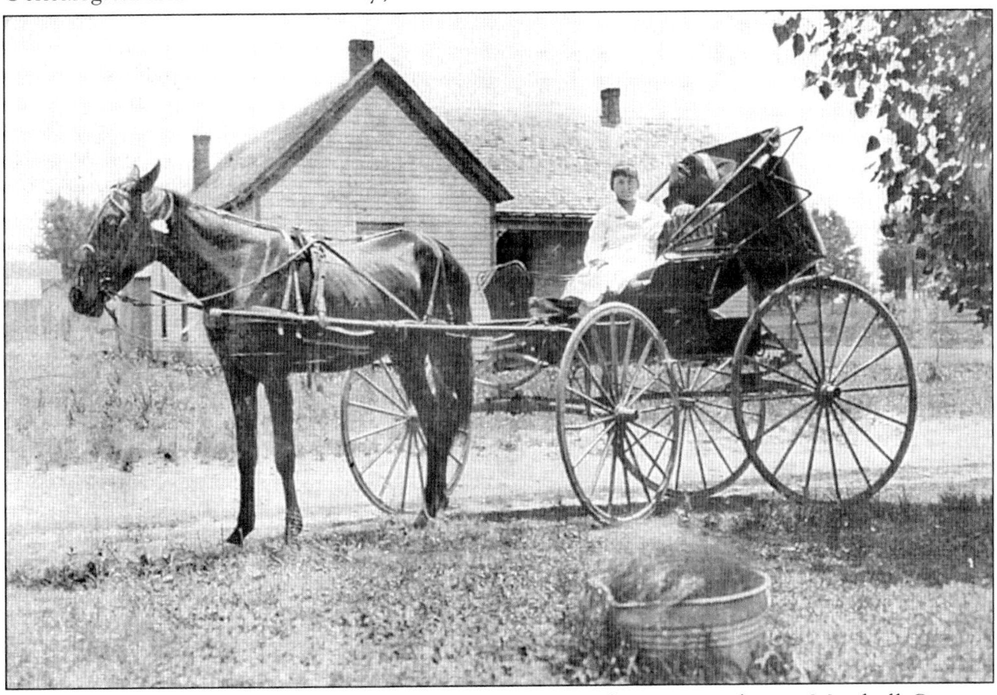

Buggies, weddings, and preachers named Gregory seemed to go together in Marshall County. Sitting in a buggy, Kathleen Owen awaited her soon-to-be-husband Cecil Donohoo on August 27, 1922, as he asked T. W. Gregory, a Birmingham minister, to perform the ceremony. Cecil Donohoo worked for the Illinois Central Railroad. He and Kate settled in Gilbertsville after their wedding. (Courtesy of the Donohoo and Capps families.)

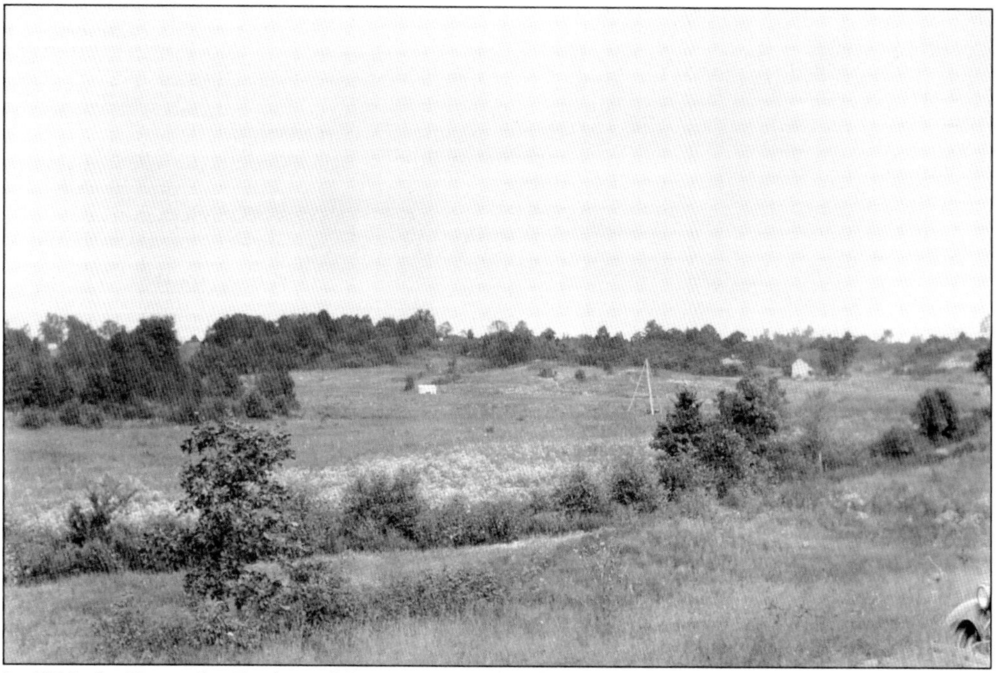

In 1920, the Kentucky Geological Survey mapped and photographed Marshall County. Big Spring Valley was typical of the farming lands found throughout the county. Most farmers owned between 50 and 200 acres. (Courtesy of the Kentucky Historical Society.)

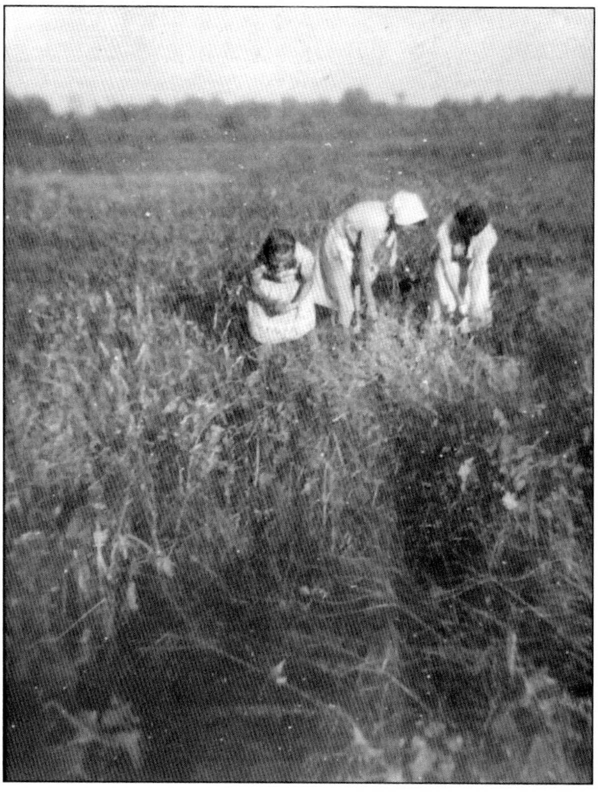

Picking produce, in this case peas, often fell to the women and children during harvest seasons. Truck gardens, farms where vegetables are grown for market, were common in Marshall County. Families grew enough vegetables for home canning to supply their winter needs. The remainder of the crop was sold at one of the area's larger farmers' markets, and the cash was used for necessities. (Courtesy of Louise Norton Wyatt.)

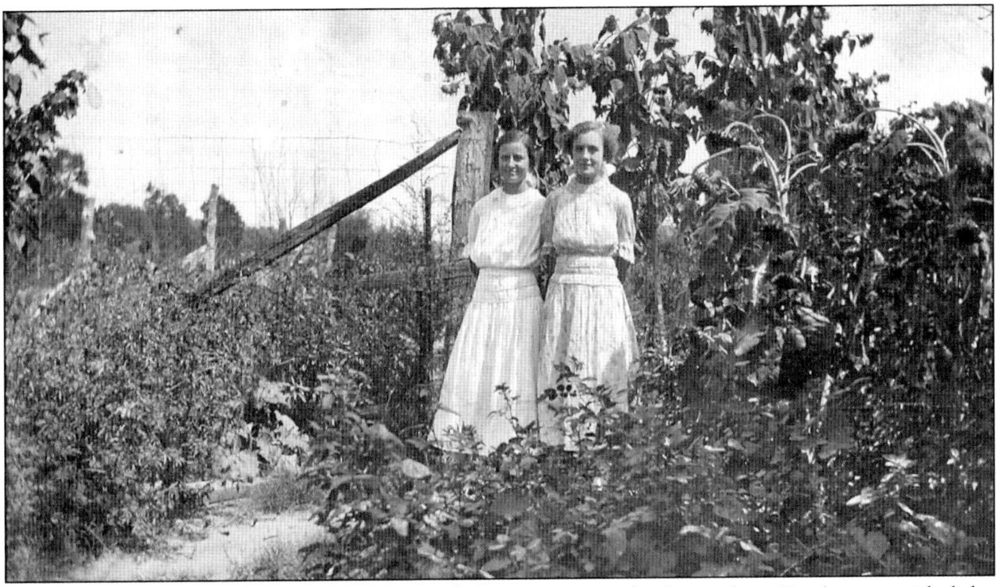

Whether families lived on farms or in a small town, everyone had a garden. Gardens provided the fresh vegetables needed by each family and often provided a bit of bartering material at the local grocery. Seldom was a garden that didn't contain flowers along the garden fence; friends Kate Owen (left) and Stella Shadwick posed in someone's garden, *c.* 1915. (Courtesy of the Donohoo and Capps families.)

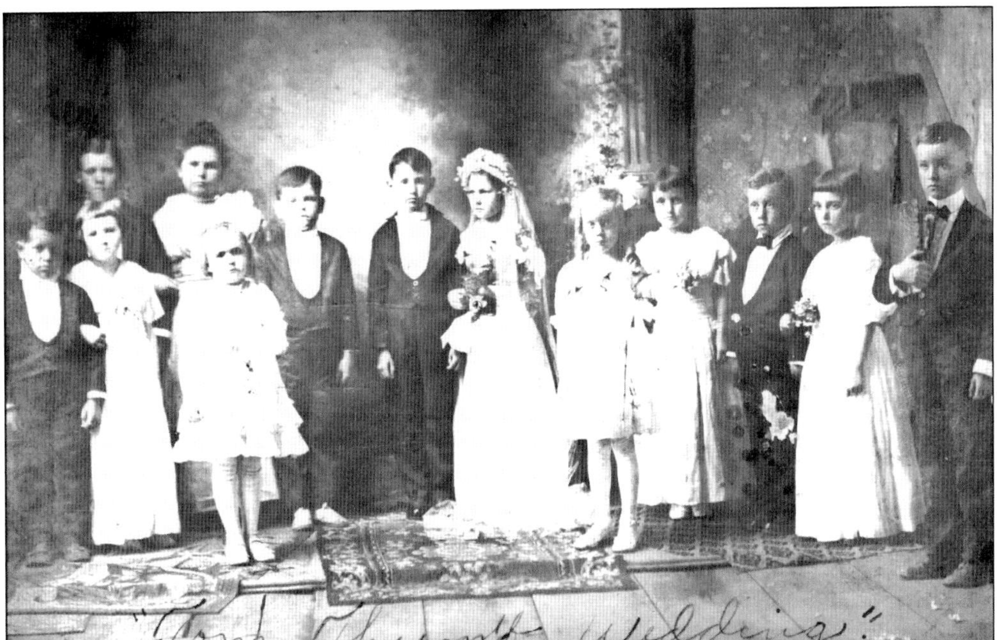

In the early 1900s, children performed *The Tom Thumb Wedding*, which portrayed the real wedding of Charles Stratton, a dwarf who entertained with the Ringling Brothers Barnum and Bailey Circus. In 1863, Stratton married Lavinia Warren, also a dwarf, in a highly publicized and lavish wedding. The humorous play was a spectacle that was often used a money-raising event. (Courtesy of the Mike McWane family.)

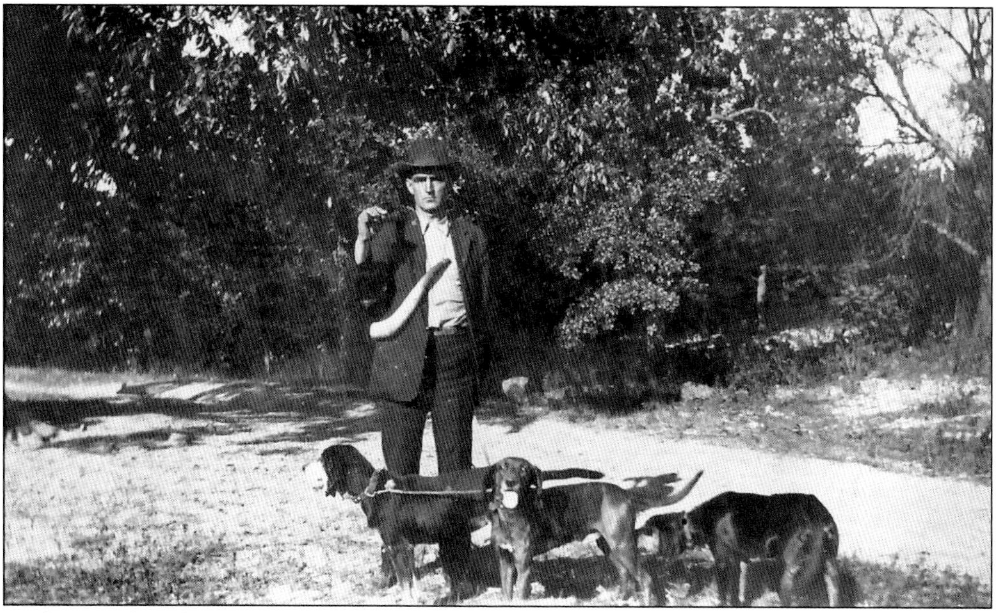

Andrew Taylor, like many men in the county, enjoyed fox hunting. In America, fox hunting was more often fox chasing, for the purpose is not to kill the fox, but to "chase it to ground" with a pack of trained dogs. To chase to ground means the fox would hide in its underground den. The sound of the foxhounds and horn could be heard for miles. (Courtesy of Bobbie Foust.)

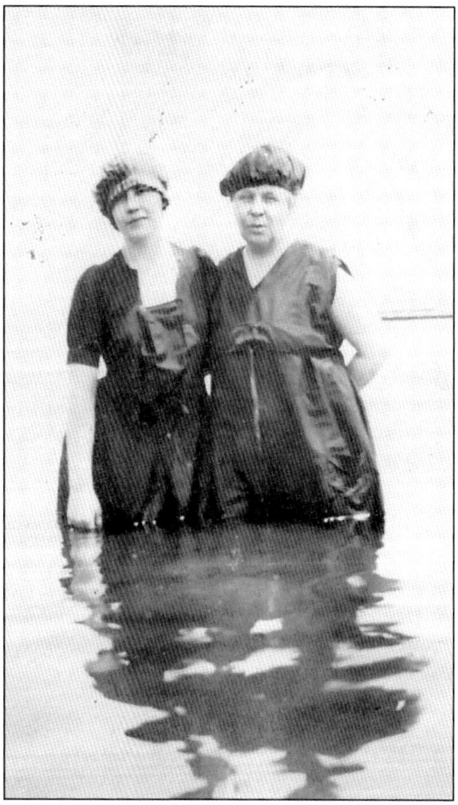

These two ladies enjoyed swimming despite the voluptuous swimming attire of the time. From the beginning, Marshall County residents have always enjoyed swimming, fishing, and boating in the county's many rivers, streams, and ponds. (Courtesy of Janet Copeland Wallace.)

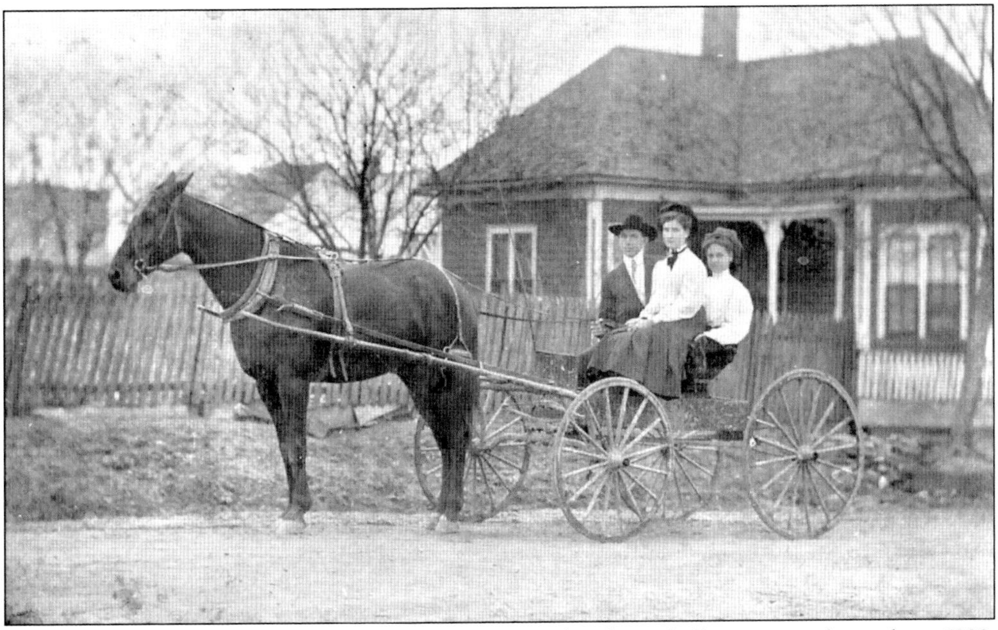

Dr. Luther E. Jones married Mary Lucinda May Strow, daughter of a Benton merchant about 1899. They first resided in Benton. Like most county doctors, Luther was a horse-and-buggy doctor. In 1894, twenty-three regular physicians were listed in the county; this number continued to grow as the new century progressed. The other young woman in the buggy is unidentified. (Courtesy of the Marshall County Genealogical and Historical Society.)

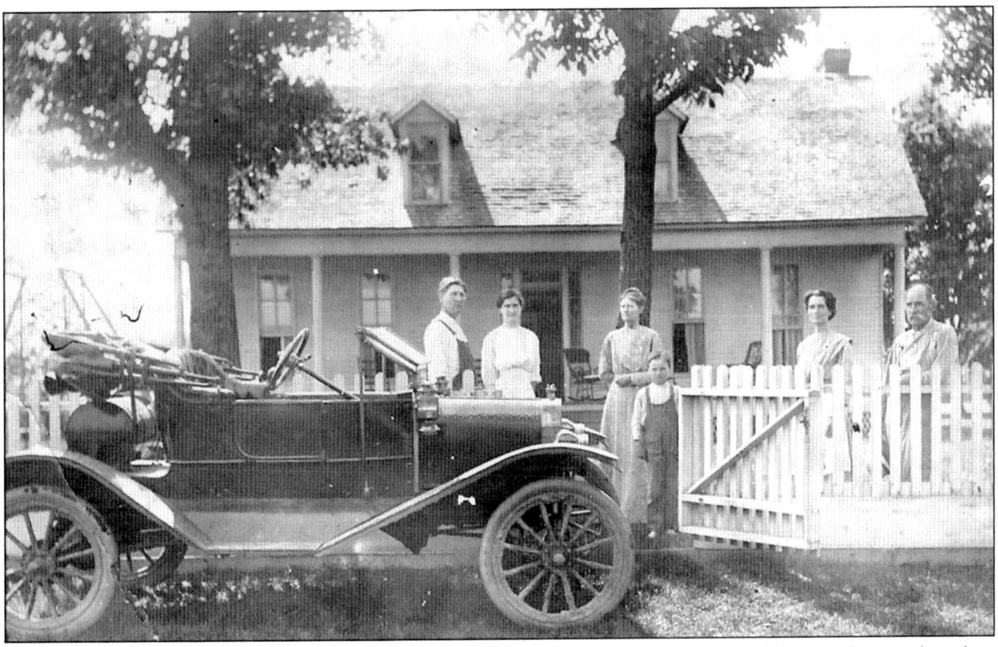

As times changed, so did Dr. Jones's transportation and his home. By 1915, he no longer lived in Benton but still practiced medicine in the county and made house calls. Dr. Jones is on the left next to his wife, May; the others are relatives of Dr. Jones. (Courtesy of the Marshall County Genealogical and Historical Society.)

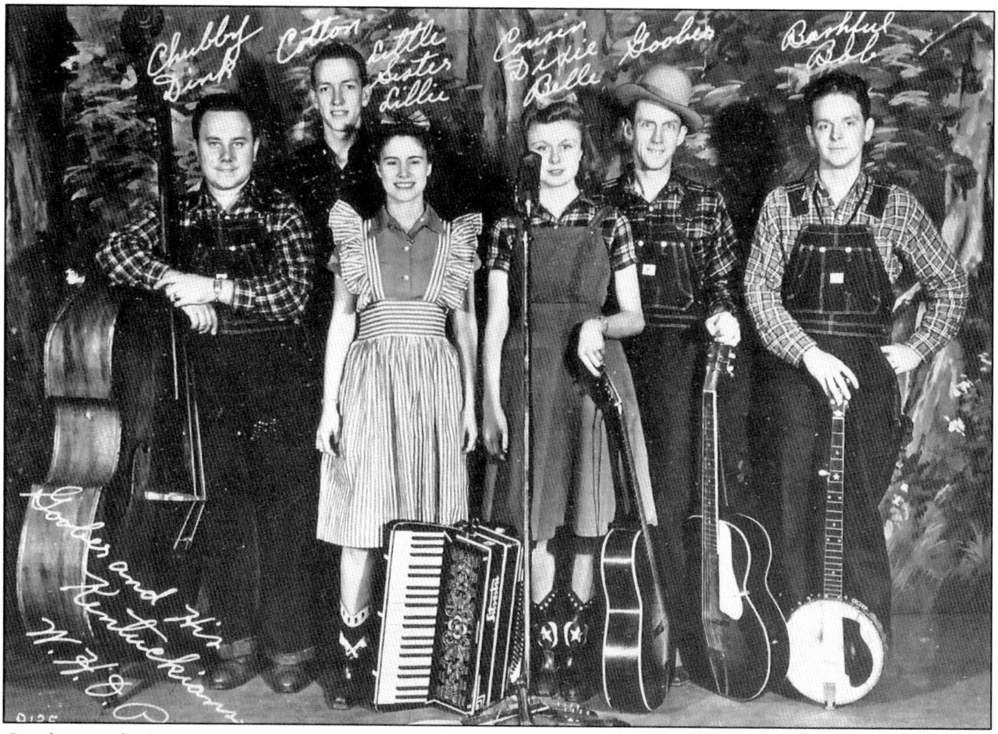

Goober and His Kentuckians toured the country presenting their own brand of country music. Autographed photographs, such as this one dated August 1935, promoted and advertised their shows and became a keepsake for a Marshall County resident. Goober's musicians often played Nashville's Grand Ole Opry at Ryman Auditorium. (Courtesy of Virginia Smith.)

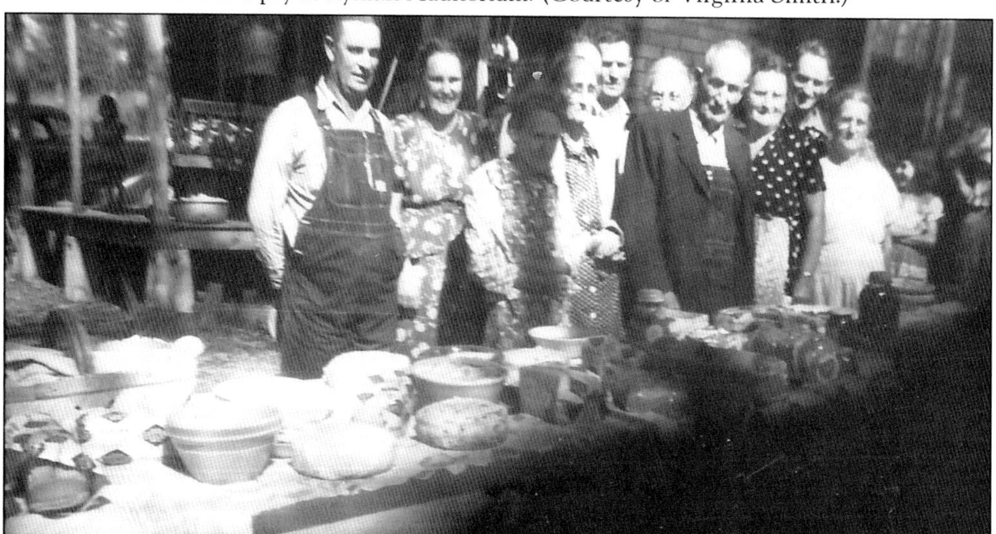

Summer family celebrations most often centered around a meal presented on linen-covered plank tables set up in the yard. Each woman brought her best and favorite dishes along with her finest cakes, pies, and preserves. While children gathered at a separate table, adults ate, talked, and caught up on family news. (Courtesy of Virginia Smith.)

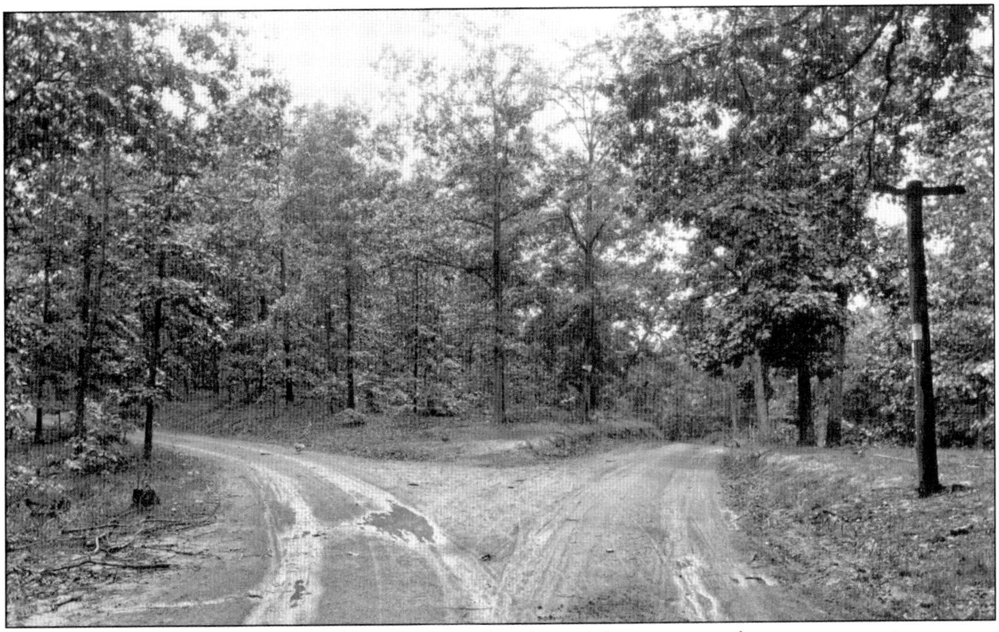

Dirt roads, sometimes running through dense hardwood forests, served as transportation routes throughout most of the county. This fork in the road was near Birmingham. Few paved roads existed before the arrival of Works Progress Administration (WPA) crews during the 1930s. However, the WPA's first priority was city streets, not rural roads. (Courtesy of the Kentucky Historical Society.)

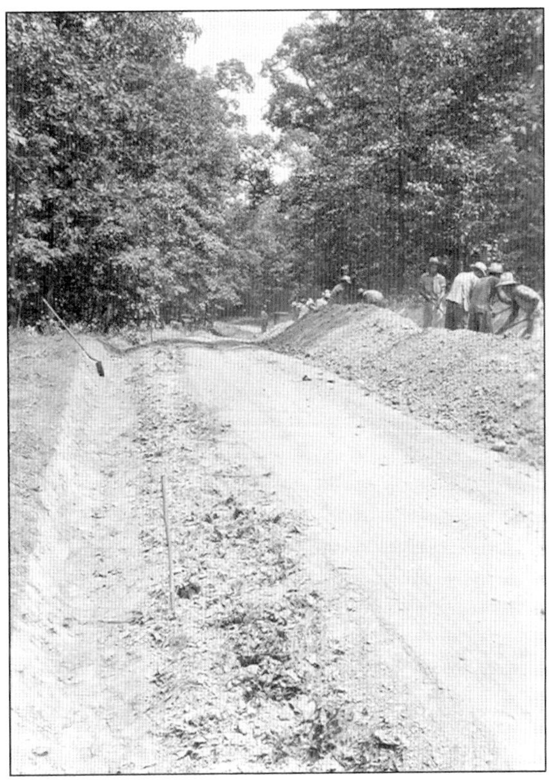

Shovels and manual labor, along with road graders, prepared for the construction of the Benton-to-Birmingham road by the WPA. In the 1930s and early 1940s, the WPA employed many of Marshall County's young men and women on a variety of projects, including building roads, schools, and bridges. (©University of Kentucky, all rights reserved, Goodman-Paxton Photographic Collection, Special Collections and Digital Programs, University of Kentucky Libraries.)

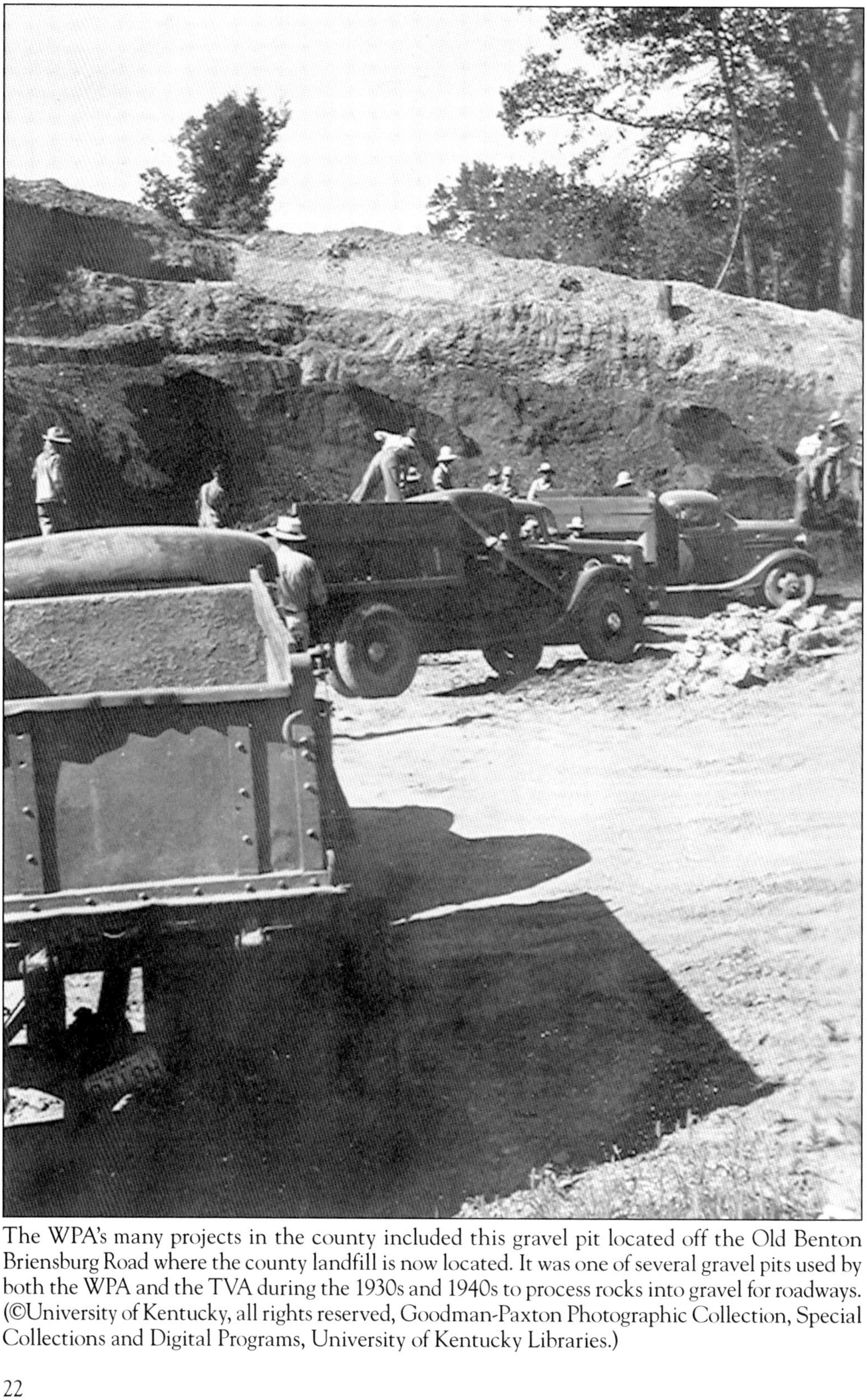

The WPA's many projects in the county included this gravel pit located off the Old Benton Briensburg Road where the county landfill is now located. It was one of several gravel pits used by both the WPA and the TVA during the 1930s and 1940s to process rocks into gravel for roadways. (©University of Kentucky, all rights reserved, Goodman-Paxton Photographic Collection, Special Collections and Digital Programs, University of Kentucky Libraries.)

Two

Benton

A 30-acre tract of land belonging to Francis Clayton was chosen for Marshall County's seat of government. The tract was located in almost the geographical center of the county. An adjoining tract of 50 acres was donated by John H. Beardon. Named for Thomas Hart Benton, Missouri senator and Jacksonian Democrat, Benton was incorporated on January 11, 1845. A plat, dated 1874 by P. Palmer, shows the town laid out with five streets running east and west and six streets running north and south. Barry's Addition was incorporated into the town in 1893.

As the town approached the beginning of the 20th century, its population had finally reached more than 1,000 persons. The Paducah, Tennessee, and Alabama Railway (later taken over by the Nashville, Chattanooga, and St. Louis Railway) had arrived in the early 1890s, greatly increasing the number of businesses and new homes. The 1890s saw the construction of a new, elegant depot. Town businesses included three churches (Methodist, Baptist, and Christian), two restaurants, four dry good stores, two drug stores, a hardware store, two shoe shops, two butcher shops, one paint store, and one hotel. Services included two livery stables, a photography studio, and two millinery shops. Industry included a tobacco warehouse, a planing mill, carding factory, printing office, and a flour mill. Business could be conducted at the Bank of Benton and with seven lawyers. Four doctors and three ministers serviced the community as well as a saloon.

The first Monday in April was and still is Tater Day in Benton. For over 150 years, that day was the traditional trading day when farmers would bring their seed sweet potatoes to town for sale. Everyone would gather and enjoy the fellowship of seeing their kinfolk and friends after the long weeks of winter. J. R. Lemon, publisher of the *Benton Tribune*, began the traditional Big Singing by calling a meeting of those who loved to sing in the old Southern harmony style. They met at the courthouse. Every year since, on the fourth Sunday in May, singers have gathered to sing from the old *Southern Harmony* songbook.

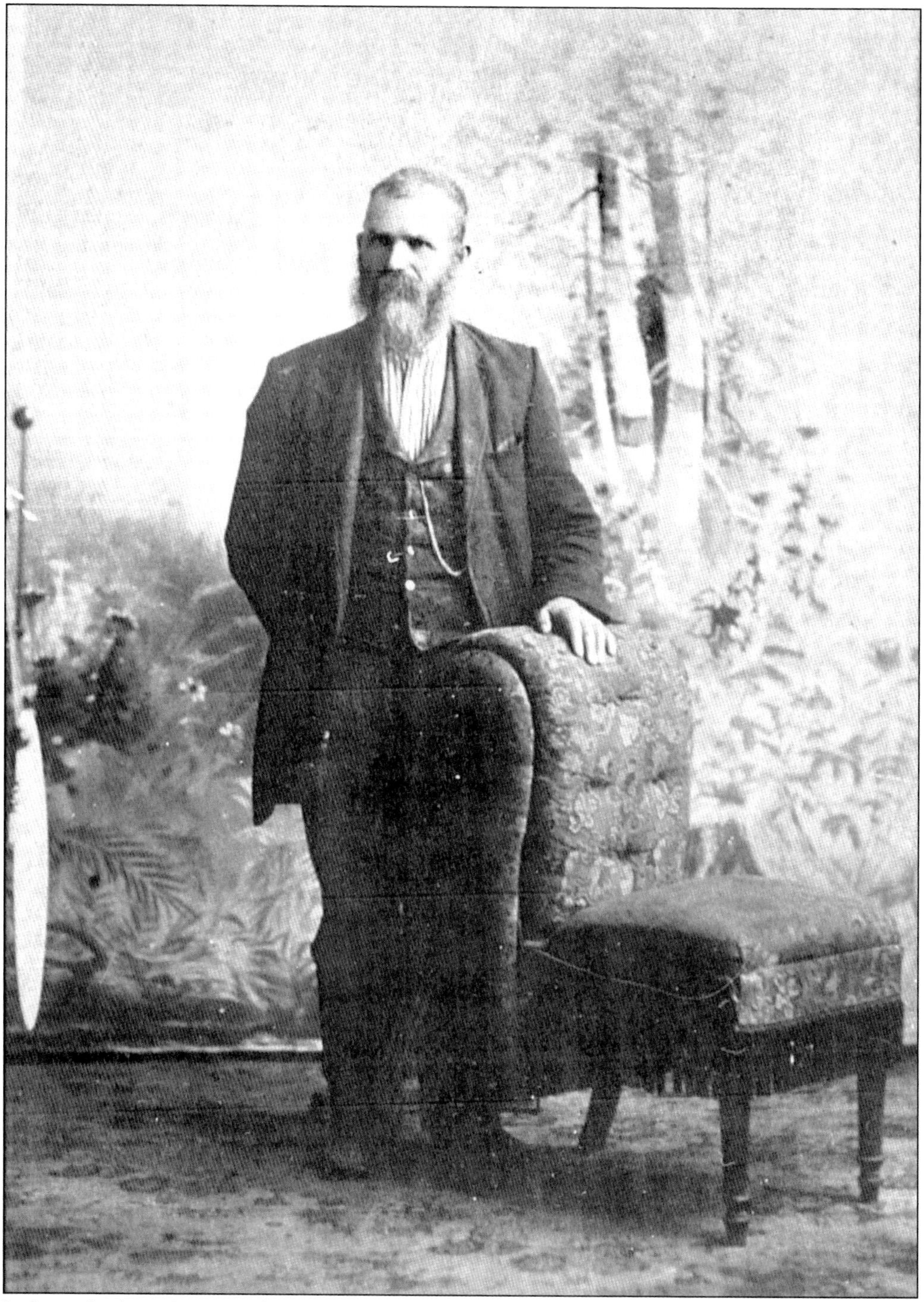

Jackson Andrew Cope was born in 1844 in Benton. He enlisted in the military in 1862 at age 18 and served one year with the U.S. Kentucky 15th Cavalry, Company D. This company mainly served garrison duty at Paducah. After the war, Jackson was employed as a farmer and sawmill worker. By 1880, he had married Mahala, fathered three sons and four daughters, and moved to Graves County. (Courtesy of the Marshall County Genealogical and Historical Society.)

Marshall County's first courthouse was built of logs by Francis Clayton in 1843. Built in 1847, the county's second courthouse cost $6,000 and stood until 1881. This third courthouse was designed by architect John McKinnon and built by M. Lewman and Company for $14,000. It burned on December 14, 1914. Citizens saved most of the records in the vault. (Courtesy of the Marshall County Genealogical and Historical Society.)

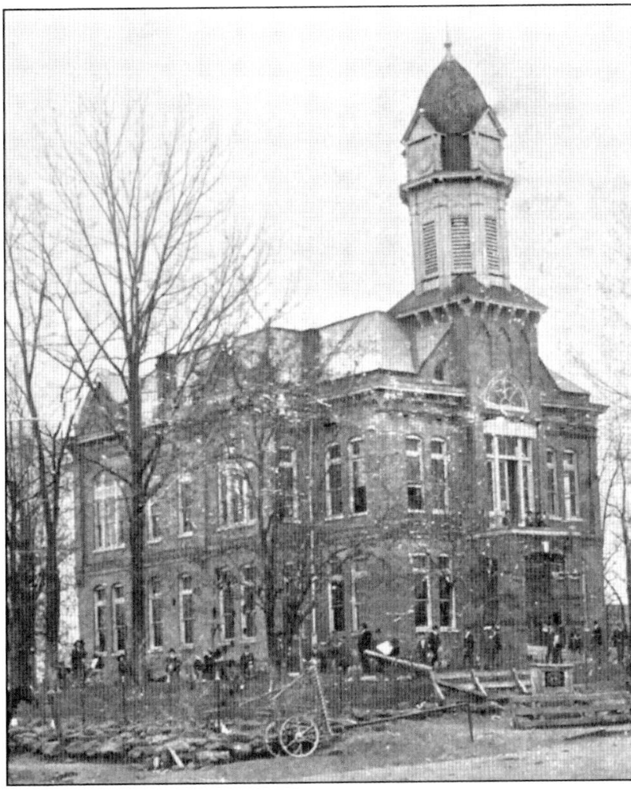

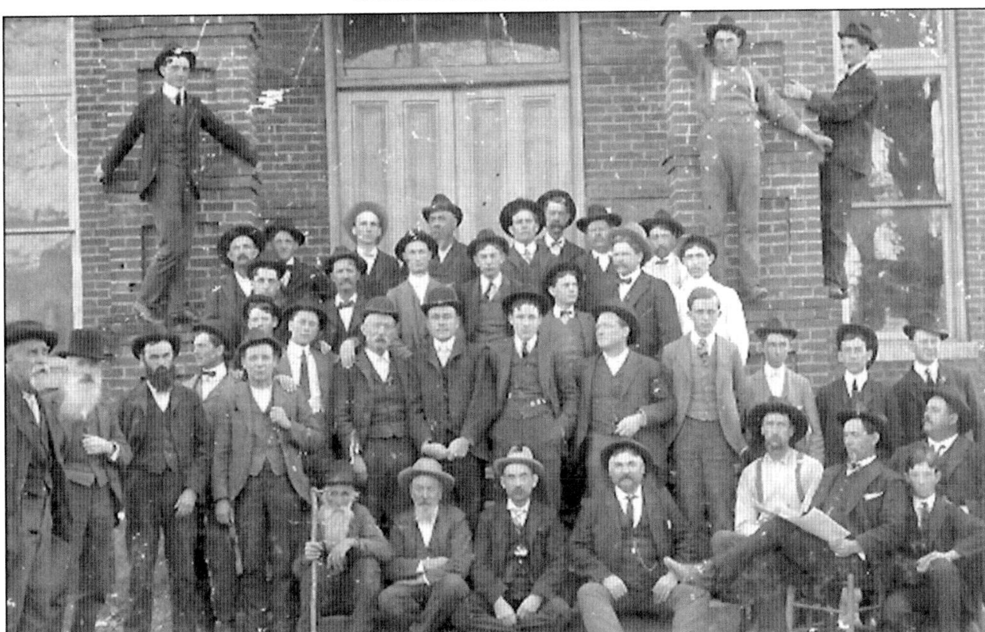

Who can say why these gentlemen posed in front of Marshall County's third courthouse? Yet sometime before the last month of 1914, forty men decided to have their photograph made at the door to the courthouse, including one who just happened to be sitting reading his paper and ignoring the hijinks of the others. (Courtesy of Coy Arnett and Ann King.)

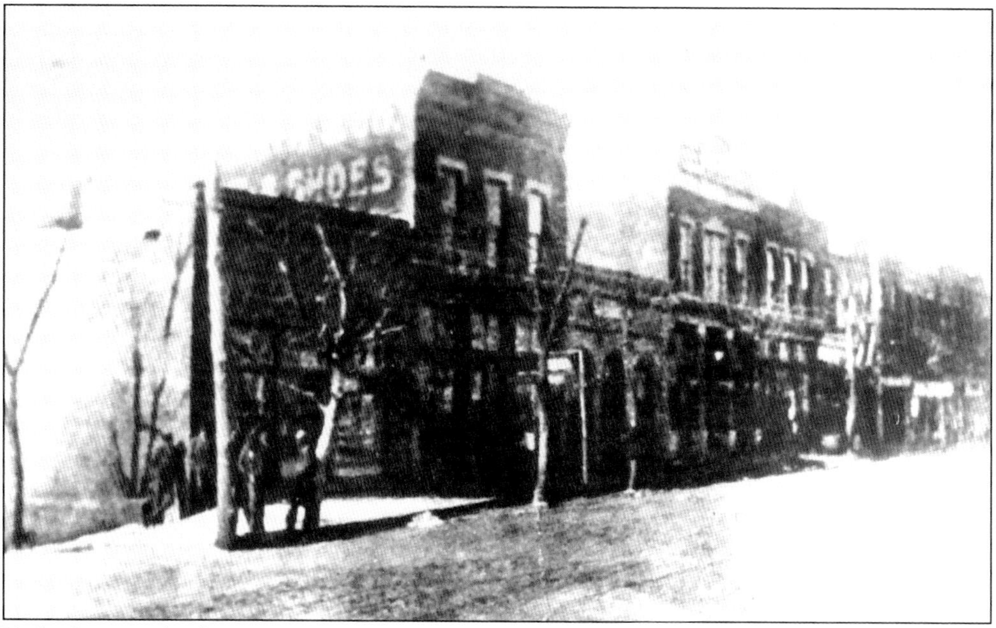

Early photographs show Benton's Main Street contained many of the same buildings we see today. Although businesses have come and gone, the buildings on this side of Benton's town square have changed little. (Courtesy of the Marshall County Genealogical and Historical Society.)

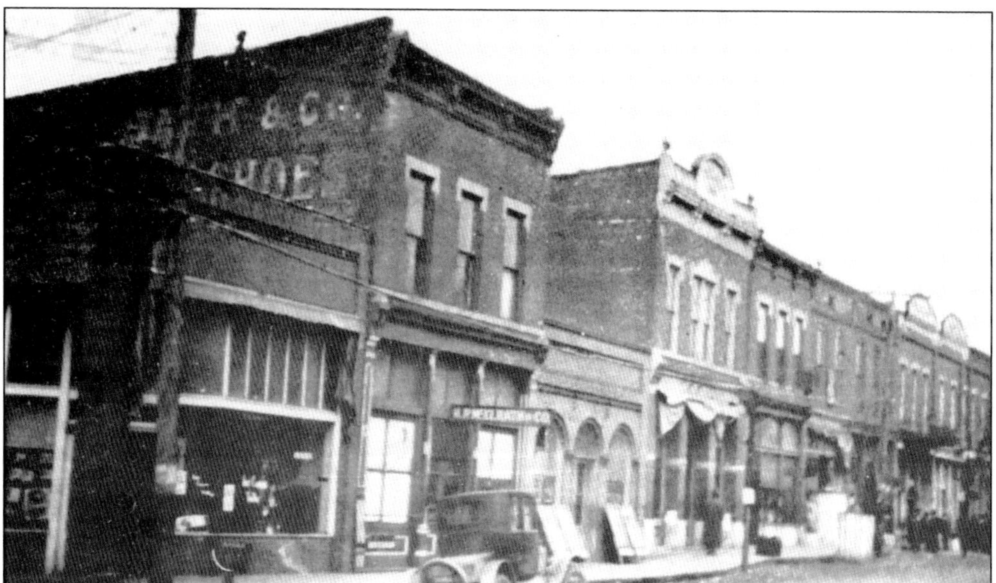

Oldsmobile debuted the large-scale production line manufacturing affordable automobiles in 1902. As Henry Ford made the automobile accessible to the general public in the 1910s, Benton's Main Street added parking and a few new buildings. This photograph was taken c. 1915. (Courtesy of the Marshall County Genealogical and Historical Society.)

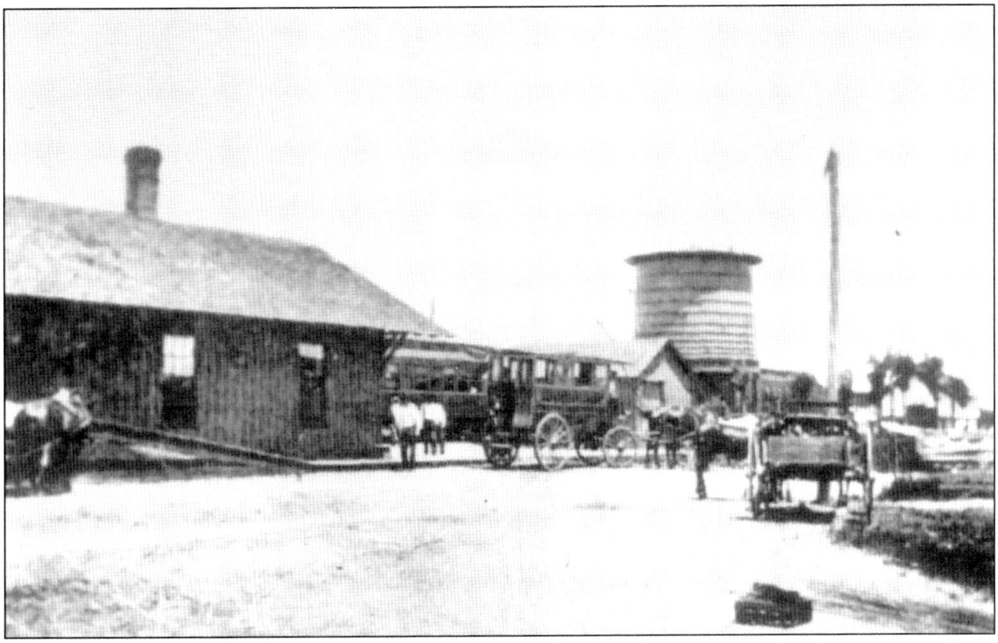

Benton's rail depot sat about one-half mile north of the courthouse on Poplar Street near where the Marshall County Co-op is today. Local residents could catch a passenger train, ship freight, or pick up supplies at the depot. Many passengers caught the train to Paducah and returned the following day. (Courtesy of the Marshall County Genealogical and Historical Society.)

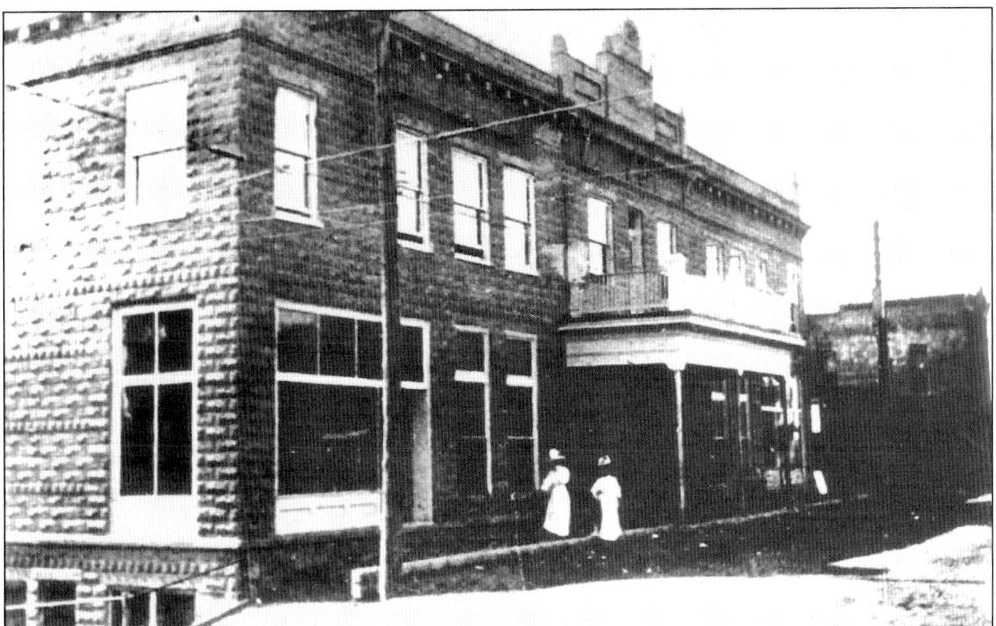

Located on Benton's courthouse square, the Benton Hotel, photographed before 1913, later became the National Store and prospered for years. Now it is an antique gallery. (Courtesy of the Marshall County Genealogical and Historical Society.)

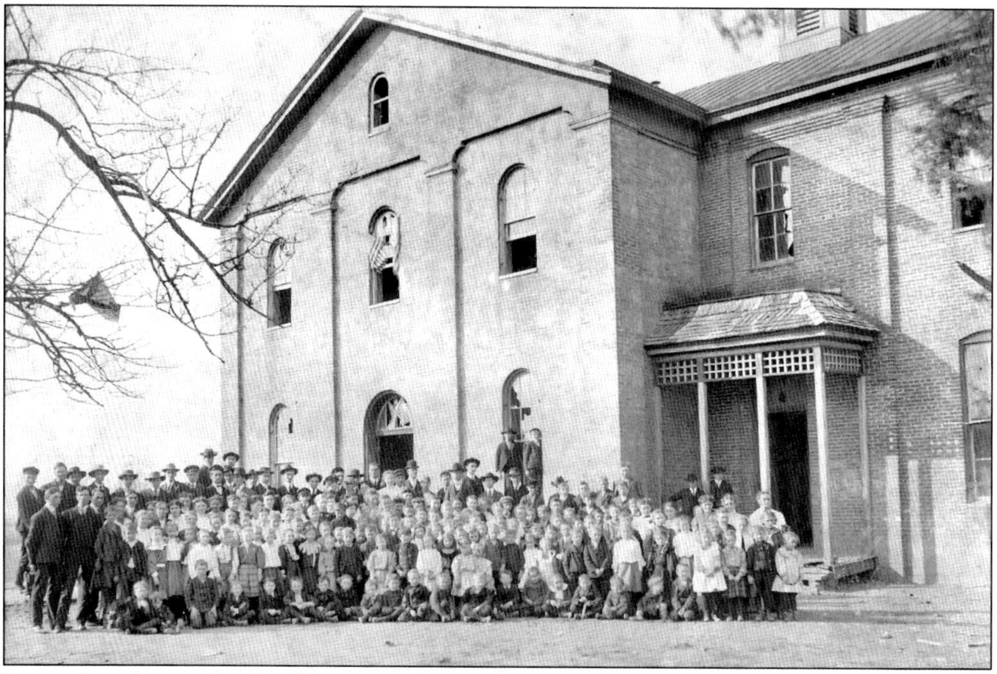

Located on the north side of Seminary Street, the Marshall County Seminary opened in 1868. It consolidated with the county school system in 1888. This photograph was taken in 1906. (Courtesy of the Marshall County Genealogical and Historical Society.)

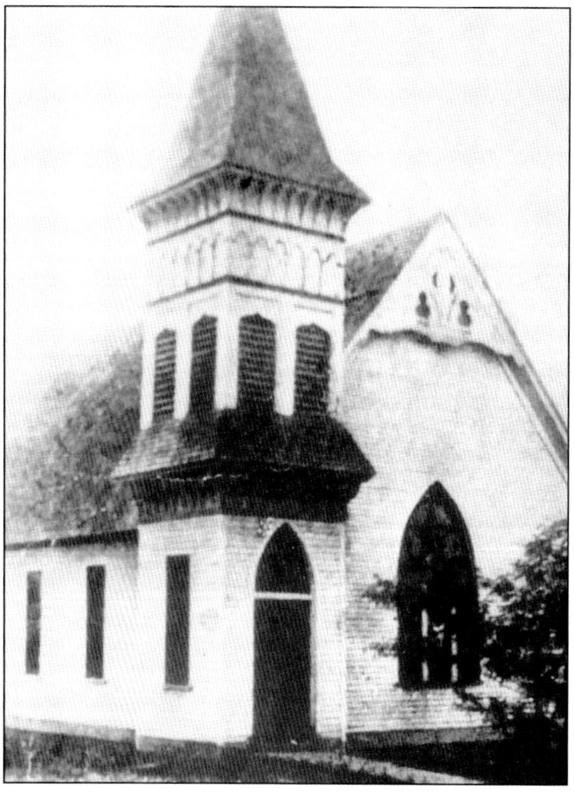

Benton's First Baptist Church sat at the corner of Tenth and Main Street. Organized in 1860, for 34 years, the congregation shared a building with the Union Christian Church and worshipped with them. Their first building was constructed and dedicated in 1894. (Courtesy of the Marshall County Genealogical and Historical Society.)

DeWitt Clinton Strow and his wife, Nina Ely, posed with one of their five children, probably the first, L. C., born in 1904. DeWitt attended the Marshall County Seminary and worked in his father's store as a young man. He attended the Bryant and Stratton Business College in Louisville. At the time of this photograph, Clinton was a merchant with J. L. Strow and Sons, a mercantile firm. (Courtesy of the Marshall County Genealogical and Historical Society.)

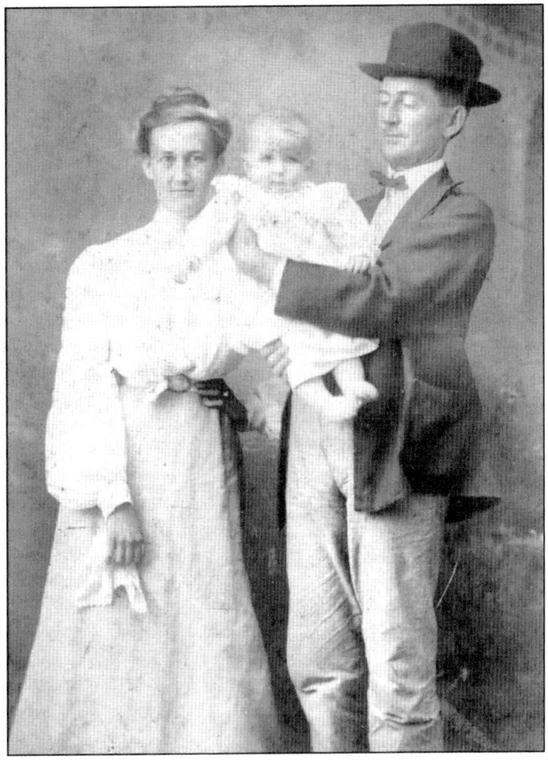

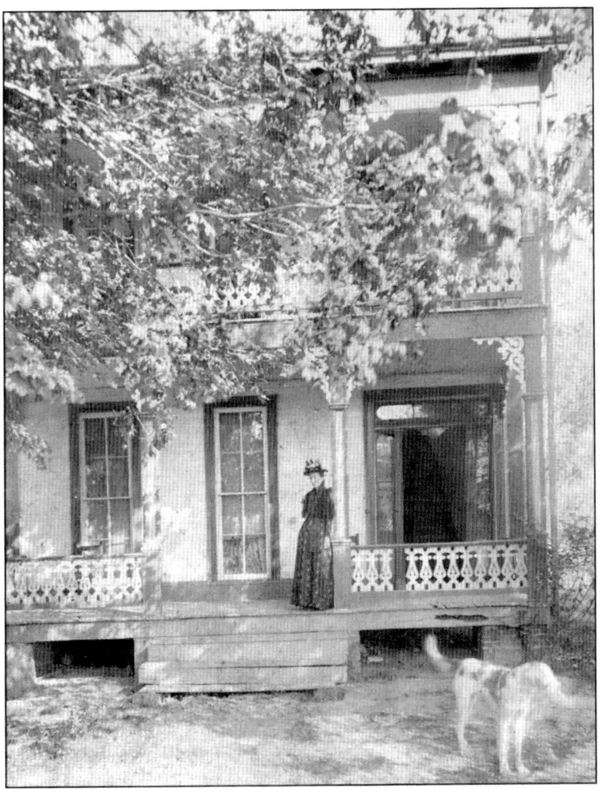

The Strow House sat at the northeast corner of Twelfth Street and the current Joe Creason Drive. The Strow name is an old one in Marshall County history and particularly in Benton, where the family owned a series of mercantile stores, specializing in men's clothing. This house is believed to be the home of DeWitt Clinton Strow. (Courtesy of the Marshall County Genealogical and Historical Society.)

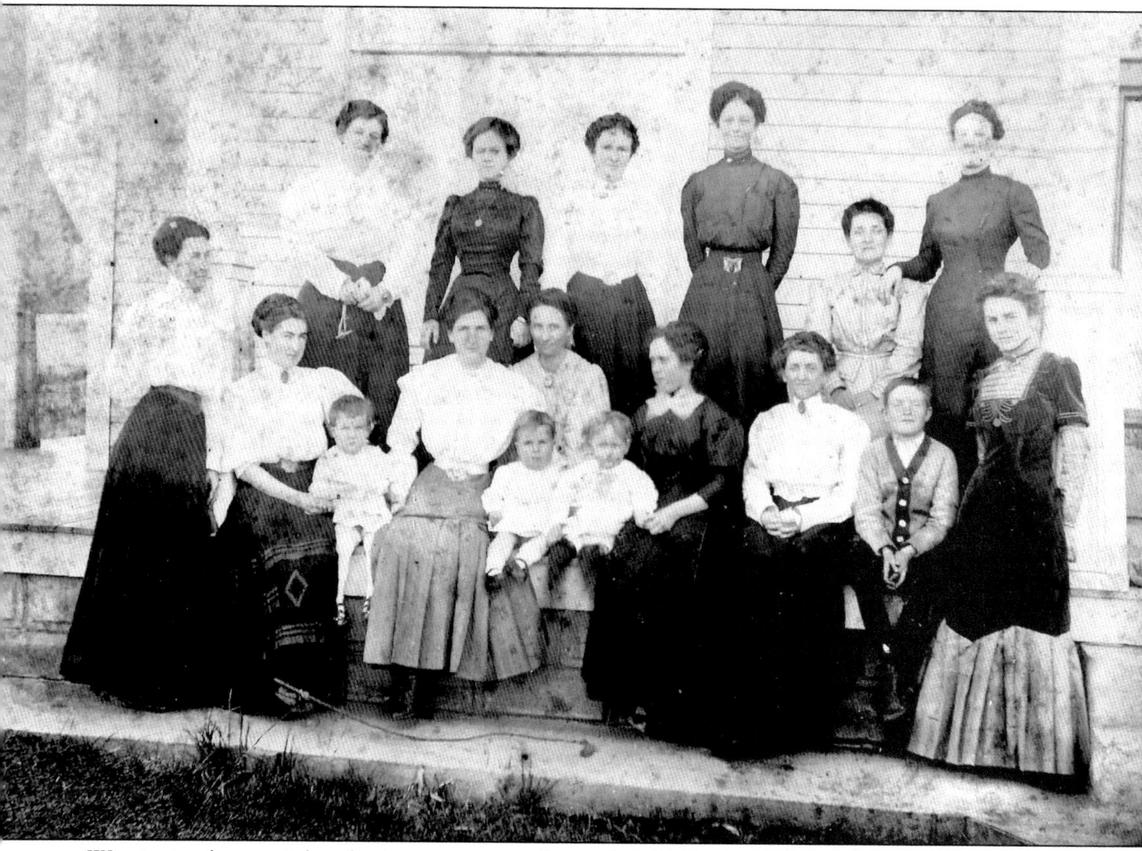

Was it simply a social gathering or an actual social club? Some of those photographed, *c.* 1915, are identified. From left to right are (first row) Annie Barnes Strow, Nell Barnes Strow Maddox with son Harry Jr.; May Strow Jones and Bruce Maddox; Bird Barnes Maddox; possibly Mrs. Bert Barnes and child; Mattie Jo Reeder; unidentified boy; and Lily Holland Hall; (second row) Virgie Ross Nelson; Willa May Maddox Yongue; Valeta Johnson Ely; and three unidentified. (Courtesy of the Marshall County Genealogical and Historical Society.)

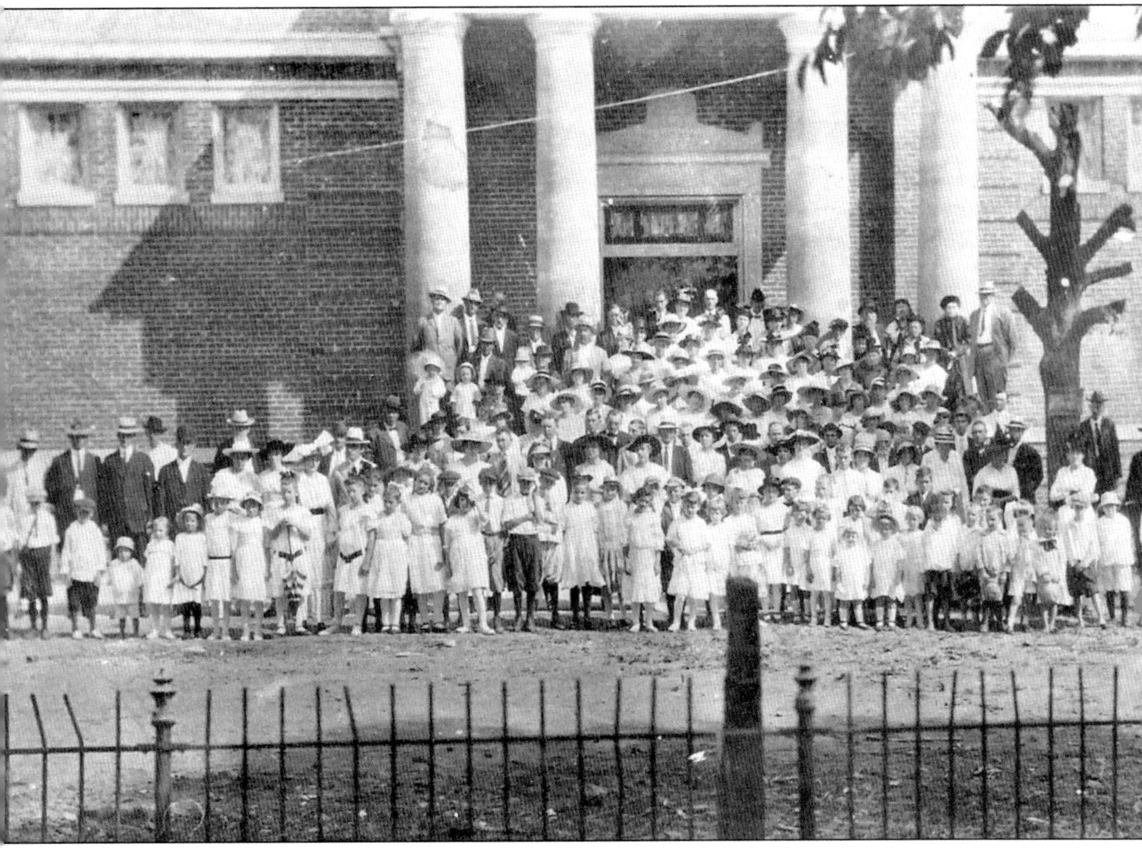

Organized in Benton's second courthouse in 1849, the First Methodist Church was given their first property by Dr. Smith in 1860. This first church sat at the corner of Eleventh and Olive Streets. On September 10, 1916, the congregation moved to a new building directly north of the courthouse. Its cornerstone, now embedded in the sidewalk, commemorates this building, which was donated by Walter Dycus in honor of his mother, Martha P. Ford. This portrait was taken about 1916. (Courtesy of the Marshall County Genealogical and Historical Society.)

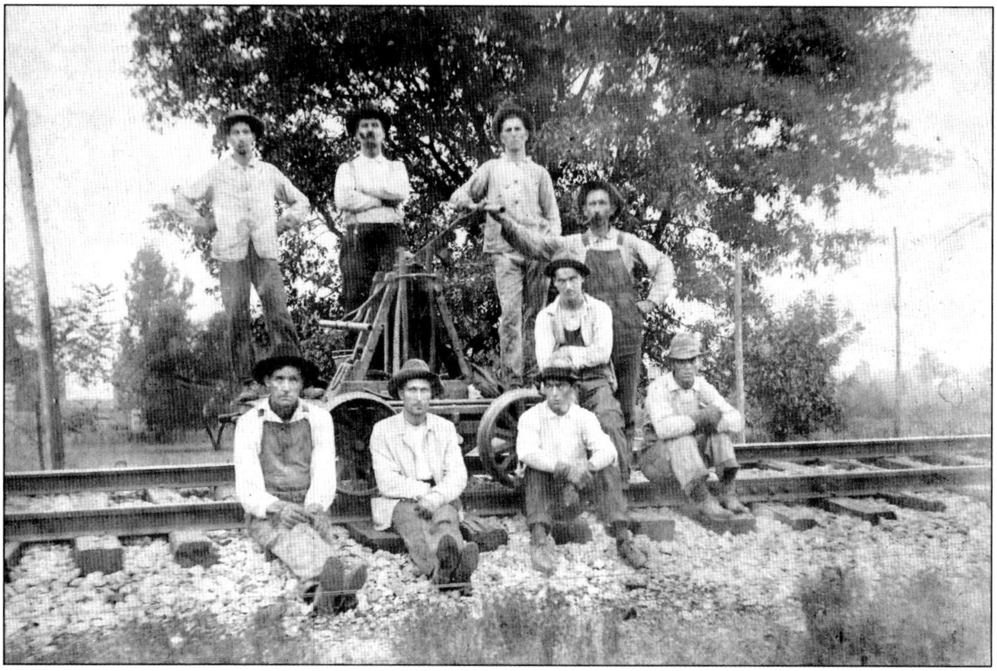

Ben McGregor, seated far left, worked with the railroad crew building the rail lines through Benton about 1910. This crew most likely served as tie hacks, which used broad axes to hand-hew railroad ties. A good tie hack could cut 50 ties a day. (Courtesy of Billy Hardison.)

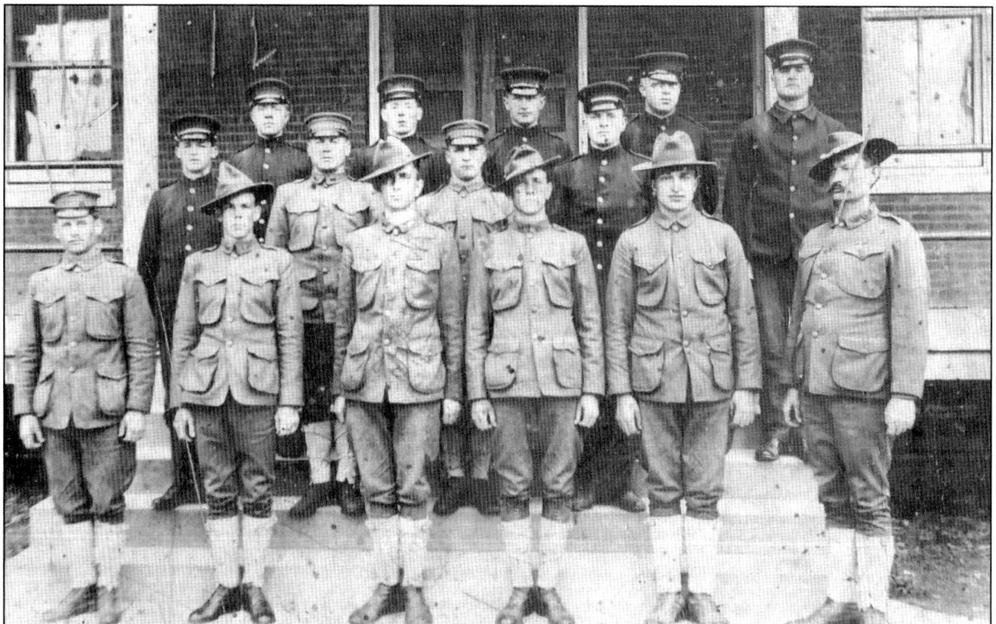

Some of Marshall County's young men left for military service in 1917 and 1918. Some sent back photographs of their units or of themselves from stateside camps and overseas operations. Frank Cooper Watson (first row, third from left) sent this photograph back home to his parents. (Courtesy of Charles Hall.)

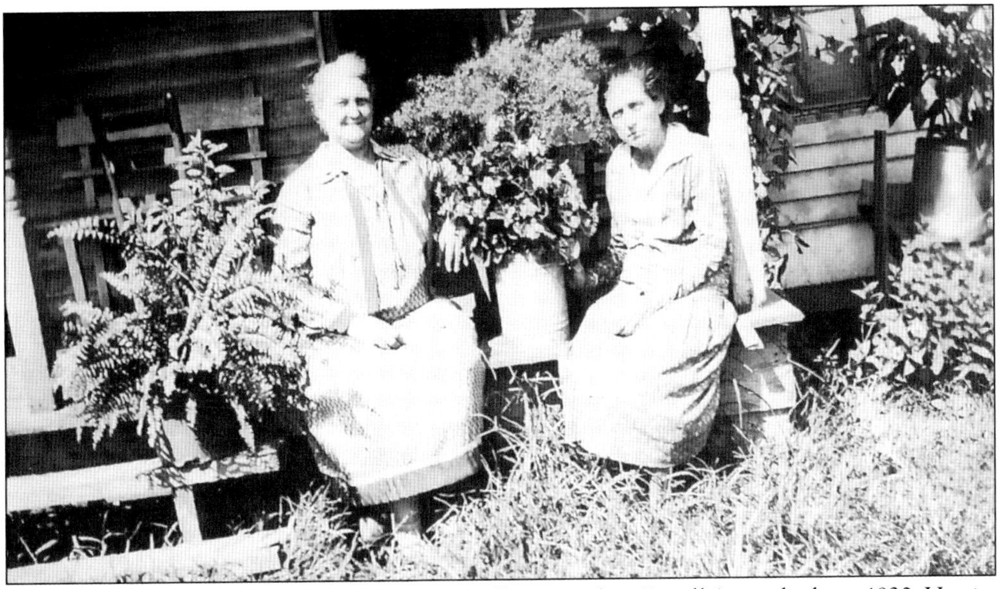

Half-sisters Hettie Morton (left) and Rosella Kelley visited on Rosella's porch about 1930. Hettie, a county native, was transplanted to St. Louis during the Civil War by the family caring for her during her father's absence. Hettie's father returned from military service and searched for the child he had left with neighbors as he marched off to war. Many years later, Hettie learned of her half sisters in Marshall County. She returned each summer to visit her long-lost family. Unfortunately, her father had passed away before she learned of this extended family. (Courtesy of Louise Norton Wyatt.)

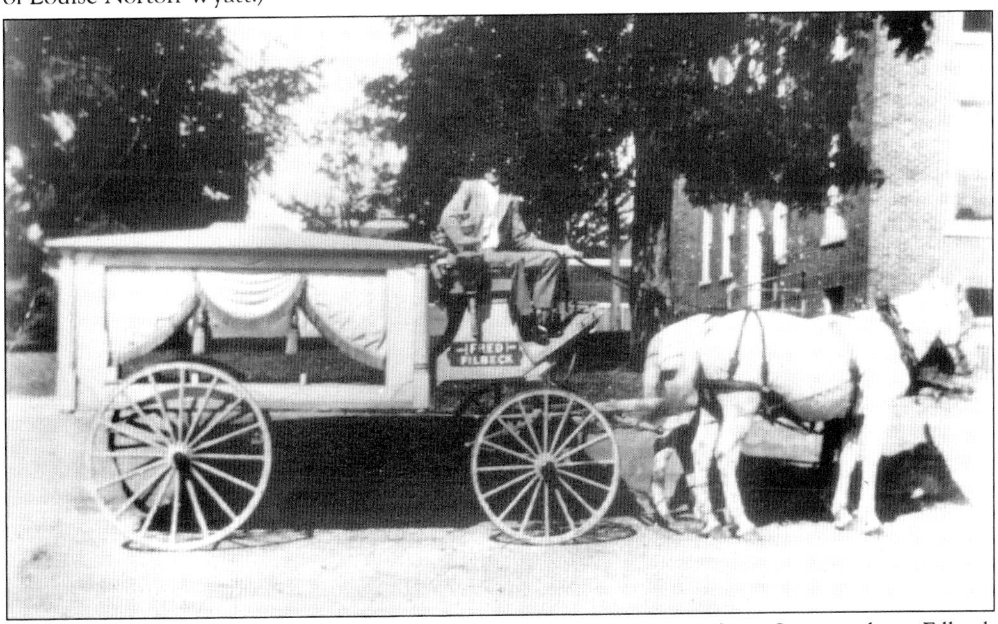

In 1924, Fred Filbeck clerked at J. D. Peterson and Company selling caskets. One year later, Filbeck bought into the casket division, earned his degree and his professional license, and opened his first funeral service business. He married Genoa Culp, who became the third woman in Kentucky to become a licensed funeral director. (Courtesy of the Marshall County Genealogical and Historical Society.)

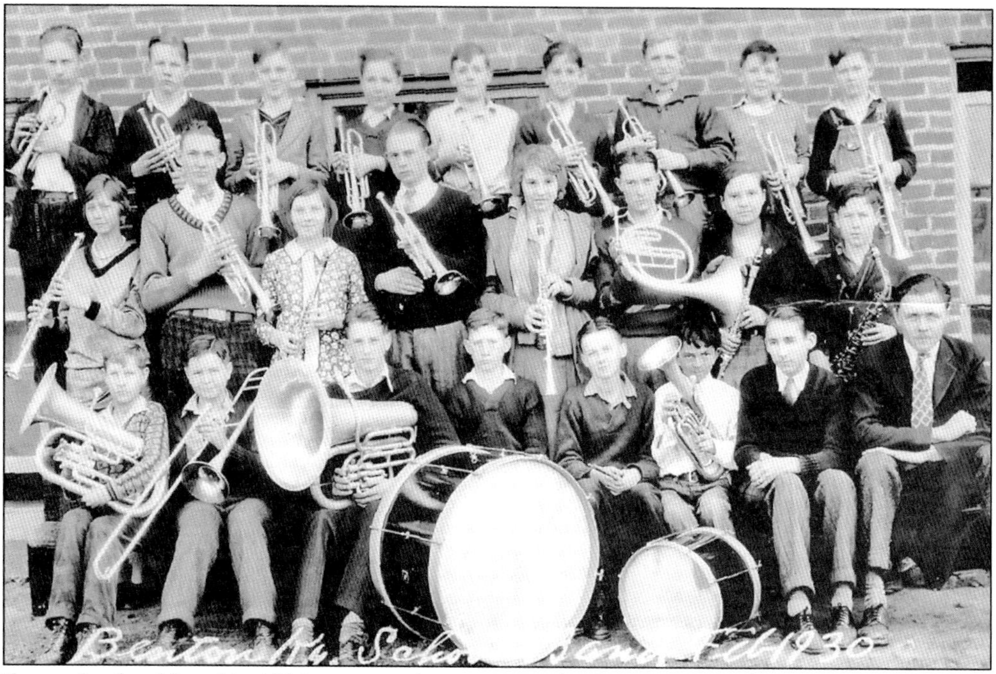

Benton's school band in 1930 contained one soon-to-be-famous Kentucky journalist, Joe Cross Creason. Creason once called Benton "the only Kentucky town where I was born." Joe is located on the first row, sixth from left. The director's name was Buyman. (Courtesy of the Marshall County Genealogical and Historical Society.)

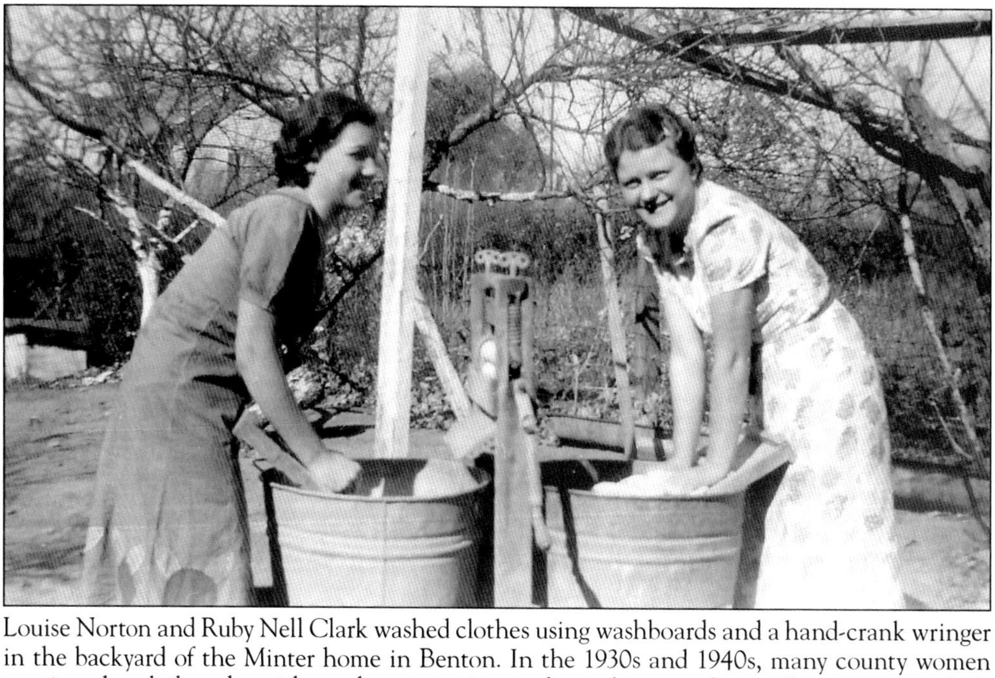

Louise Norton and Ruby Nell Clark washed clothes using washboards and a hand-crank wringer in the backyard of the Minter home in Benton. In the 1930s and 1940s, many county women continued to do laundry without the convenience of a washing machine. This was particularly true in areas of the county that did not have electricity until after Kentucky Dam was completed. (Courtesy of Louise Norton Wyatt.)

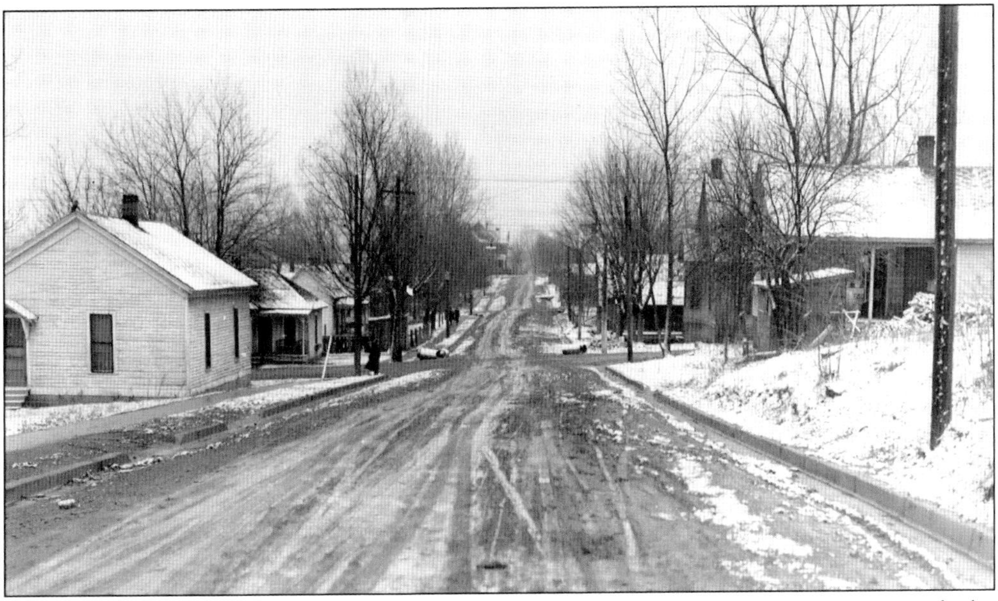

In 1928, Mayor Van Albert Strow led the vote to bring Benton into the 20th century with the installation of waterworks and sewers. The city received help in their undertakings under Pres. Franklin D. Roosevelt's New Deal Works Progress Administration, as curbs and gutters were extended throughout Benton in the late 1930s. (©University of Kentucky, all rights reserved, Goodman-Paxton Photographic Collection, Special Collections and Digital Programs, University of Kentucky Libraries.)

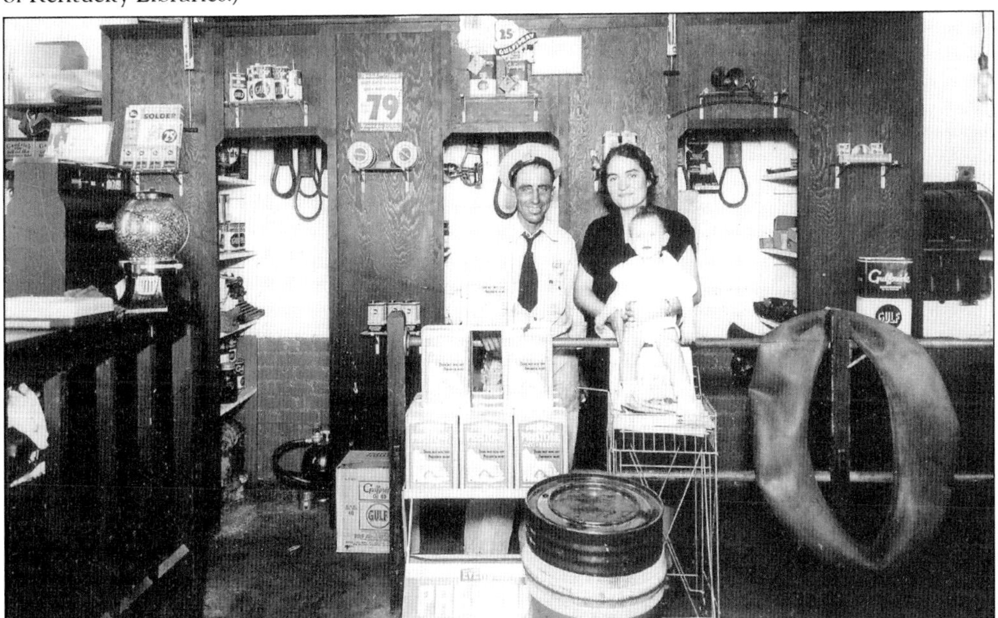

Thomas Galen Hiett served in World War I before returning to his home in Marshall County. He married Pauline in the early 1930s, and they operated a series of service stations located across from where Phillips Chevrolet is today. Ill health forced Galen to return to farming in 1949. Pauline lived on Olive Street in Benton at the time of her death in 2004 at the age of 97. (Courtesy of the Pauline Hiett Collection.)

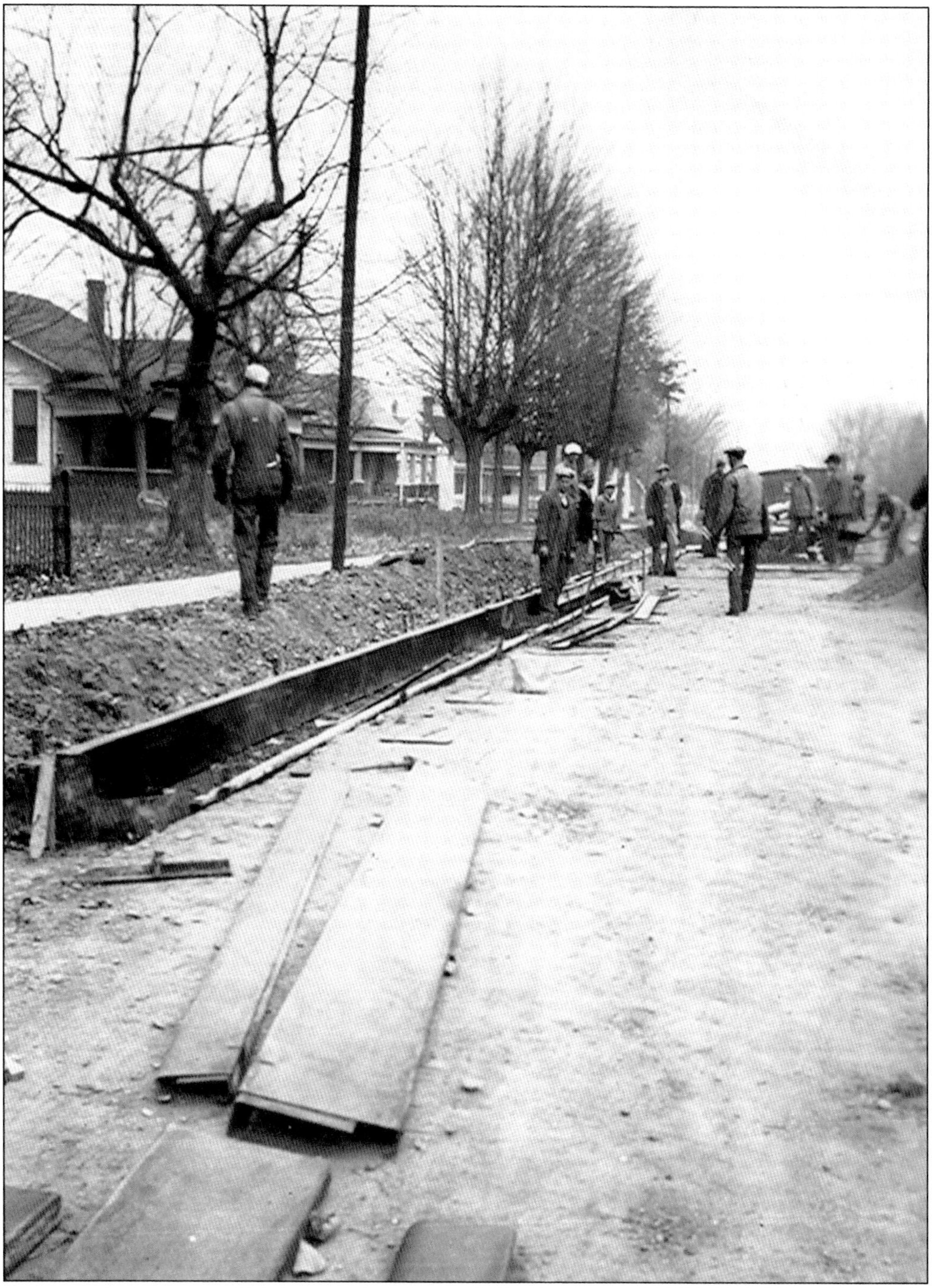

The Works Progress Administration employed a fair number of Marshall County men on projects such as the completion of Benton's streets. Other works of the WPA included reprinting, in its 1854 form, the *Southern Harmony* songbook, in use since 1884, when the citizens of Benton organized what came to be known as the "Big Singing." This annual event is now the only annual use of the *Southern Harmony*. (©University of Kentucky, all rights reserved, Goodman-Paxton Photographic Collection, Special Collections and Digital Programs, University of Kentucky Libraries.)

Three

BIRMINGHAM

The small town of Birmingham existed for slightly less than 100 years. John Stone and wife, Morning Crowe, of North Carolina, began farming near Birmingham about 1820, after walking to the area carrying their baby and household goods. In 1849, Thomas Love, a Scotsman, chose this spot on the Tennessee River as a likely place for shipping and commerce. In 1853, he laid out the town, naming it for Birmingham, England. Birmingham incorporated in 1860.

While Thomas Love bought, sold, and shipped goods, others swarmed into the area. Thomas A. Grubbs became a partner of Love. Laban and James Locker, both Englishmen, moved to town and opened one of the first stores; Laban became the first postmaster. James Love, Thomas's brother, settled in town and entered into the lucrative tobacco business. Frenchmen John and James Chaudet came to Birmingham where John settled in town, and James settled across the river, where he took up farming.

Birmingham's most financially successful years occurred between 1860 and 1870. Its status as a shipping point on the Tennessee River had developed rapidly. Depue and Brown's stave factory employed more than 150 men. The Love brothers opened the first tobacco stemmery in Kentucky. A tobacco stemmery redried tobacco to meet a customer's specifications. A warehouse built over the river made loading and unloading convenient. Farmers and merchants from surrounding towns shipped, bought, and sold goods in Birmingham. Two steam-powered, paddle-wheel passenger boats arrived frequently. First-class fare to Paducah was $1.50.

By the 1890s, the town had six streets and a population of 201. Two hotels, a bank, three white and two African American churches, two schools, four general stores, three grocers, a drug store, two millinery shops, two blacksmith shops, a doctor, and two dentists served the community. Nevertheless, the railroad had come to the county, and river transportation was no longer the only option for farmers and merchants.

The 1930s saw a Birmingham with six stores, three mills, a bank, a high school, three churches, a blacksmith shop, a garage, and three filling stations. Then came the flood of 1937.

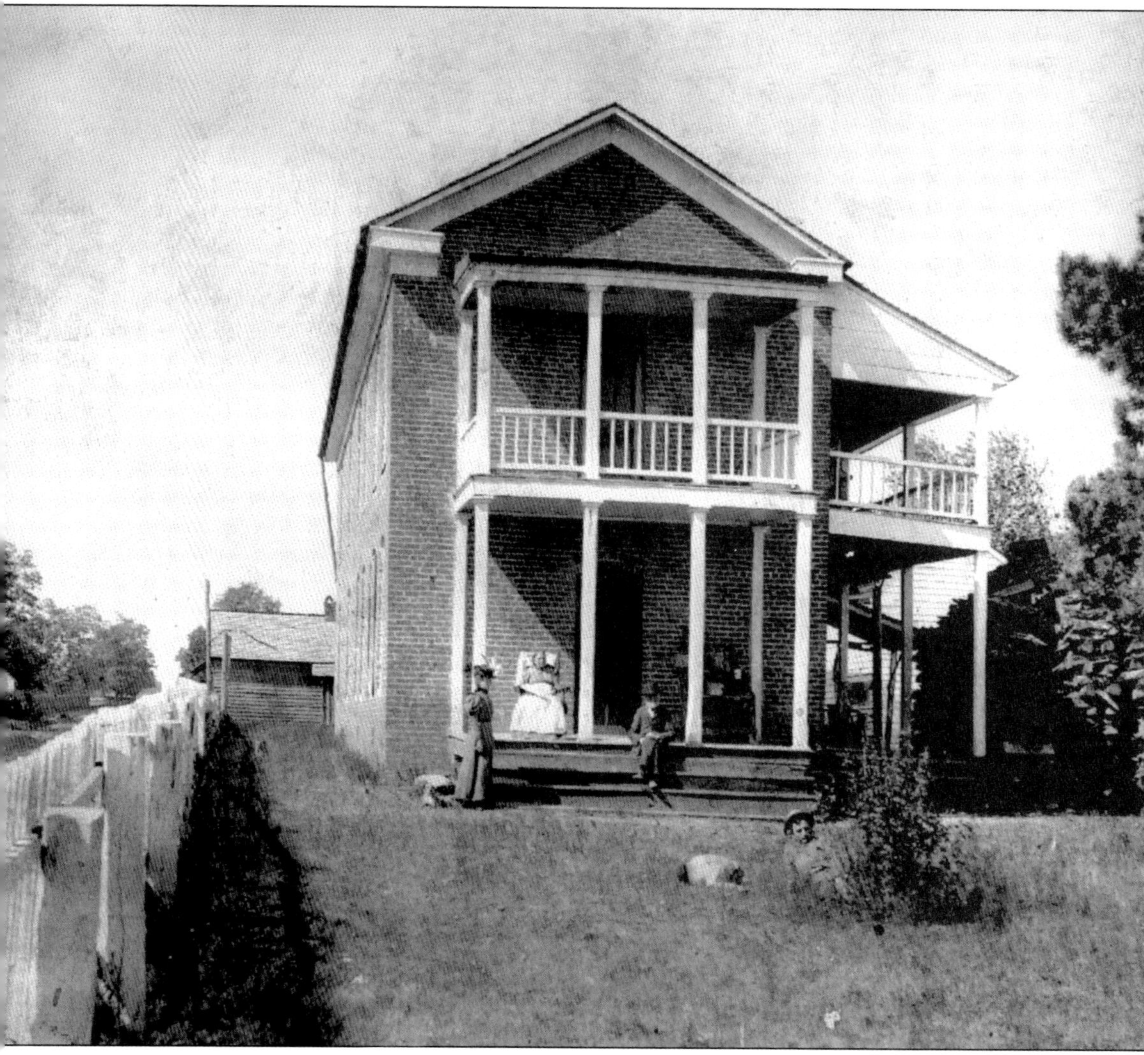

James Love built one of the only brick homes in Birmingham. He directed workers in the molding and firing of the brick. Love invested his money in a tobacco stemmery, which later burned. He had no insurance, so investors were repaid from his private funds. On the porch are James and his wife, Chynthilia. Daughter Meta, who ran a thriving millinery shop in the building behind the house, stands in the yard. Meta was an educated woman who had completed a degree in business in Evansville, Indiana. The boy is the Loves' son, Erle. (Courtesy of Madelle Sirls.)

In 1874, on their wedding day, Samuel J. Culp and Susan P. Lindsey posed for the photographer. Samuel and Susan settled on a farm off the Gilbertsville-to-Birmingham road. Susan and Samuel raised a large family, and many of their descendants continue to live in the county today. (Courtesy of Harvey Culp.)

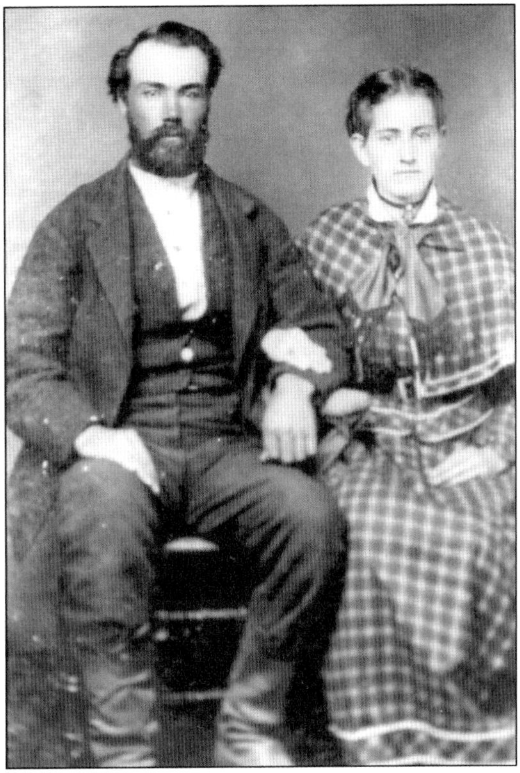

The Culp family gathered next to their log cabin, c. 1920. The Culps farmed near Birmingham. Samuel and Susan are seated. From left to right are (second row) Harvey Leander Culp and five of Samuel and Susan's children—Oddie, Roy, Genoa, Viamie, and Luella; (third row) Jessie, Charley, and Evan Culp. Charley was the oldest of Samuel and Susan's children. (Courtesy of Harvey Culp.)

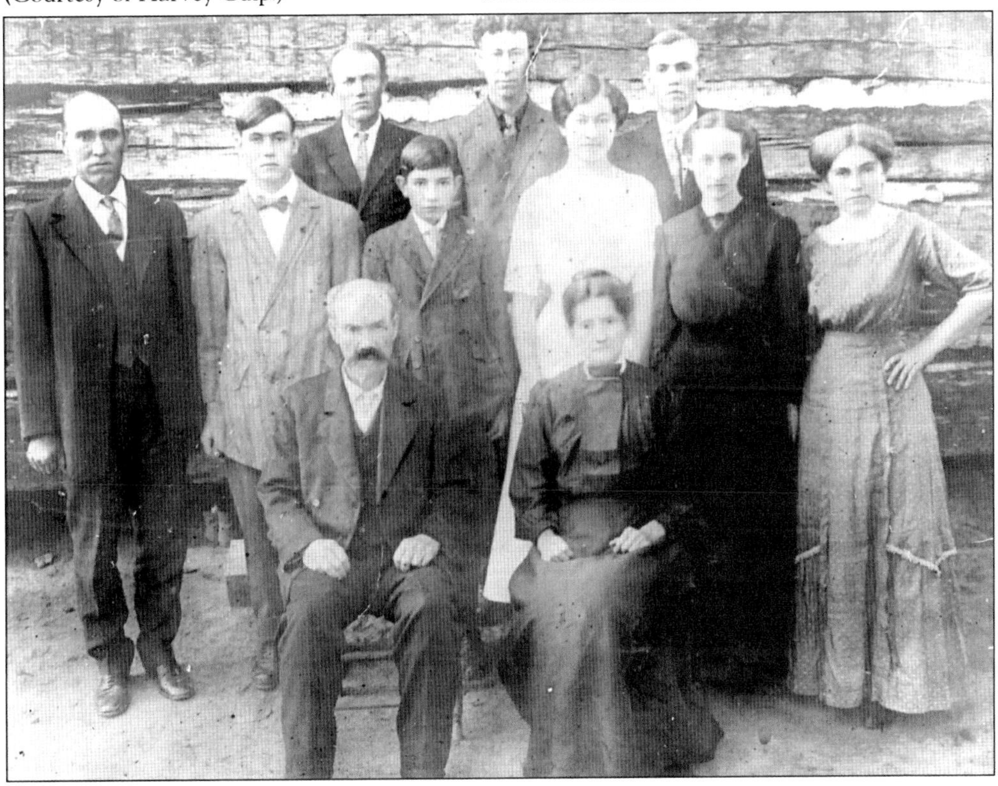

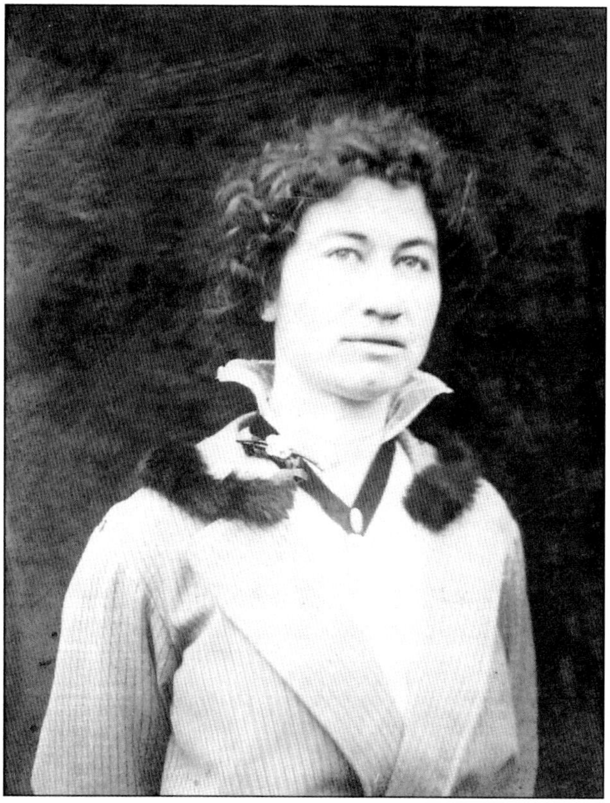

The fifth of seven children, Genoa Culp was born about 1893 to Samuel and Susan Culp. In 1920, she married Fred Filbeck and moved to Gilbertsville, where she lived with her husband's family and taught at the Pinnacle School. Teachers Ida (Canada School) and Reba (Davis Chapel School) Gallahan also lived with the Filbecks. Genoa served as the Pinnacle School's Moonlight teacher. (Courtesy of the Marshall County Genealogical and Historical Society.)

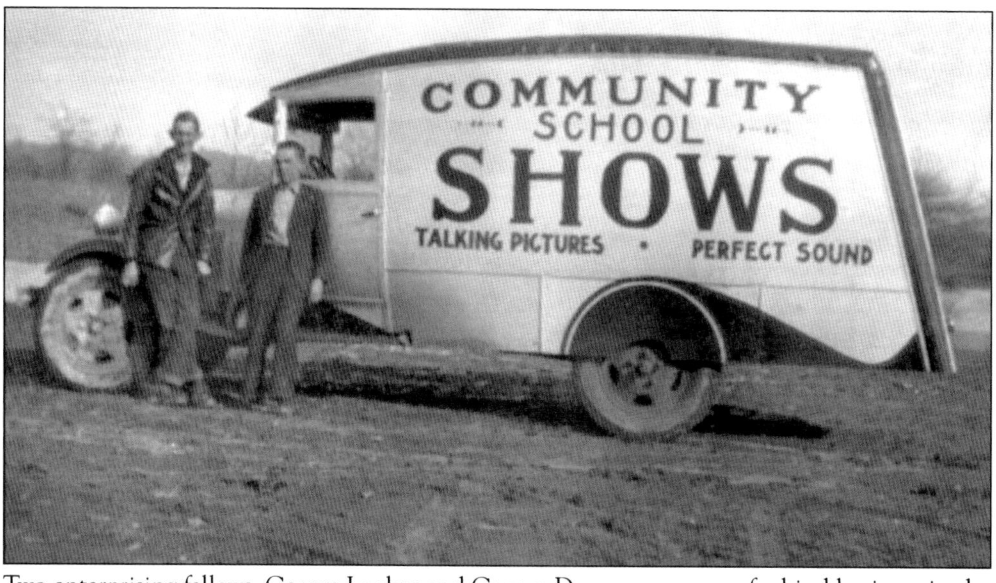

Two enterprising fellows, George Locker and George Dunn, ran a one-of-a-kind business in the 1930s. Using this converted 1928–1930 Model AA truck, Locker and Dunn brought moving pictures to the people of the county. Most often shown at local schools, they also presented their movies at other community gatherings. They carried a small tent where they sometimes presented the moving and talking pictures. (Courtesy of Claude Nimmo.)

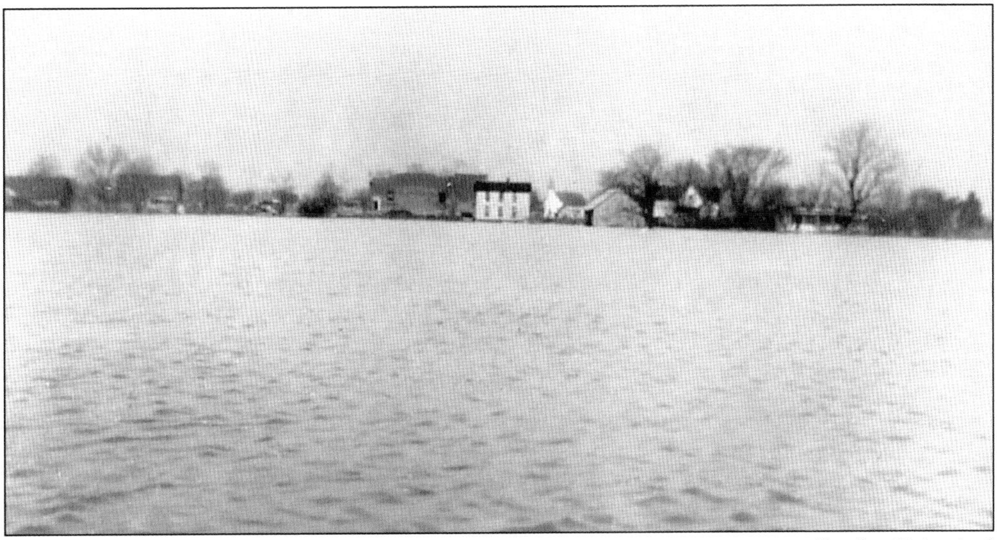

Birmingham sat directly on the bank of the Tennessee River. *Lemon's Handbook of Marshall County* noted that it was above the high watermark. However, several of the first warehouses were built so that goods could be unloaded directly from the steamboats into the lower floors of warehouses. This photograph was taken from a boat crossing the Tennessee River during the early days of the flood of 1937. (Courtesy of Claude Nimmo.)

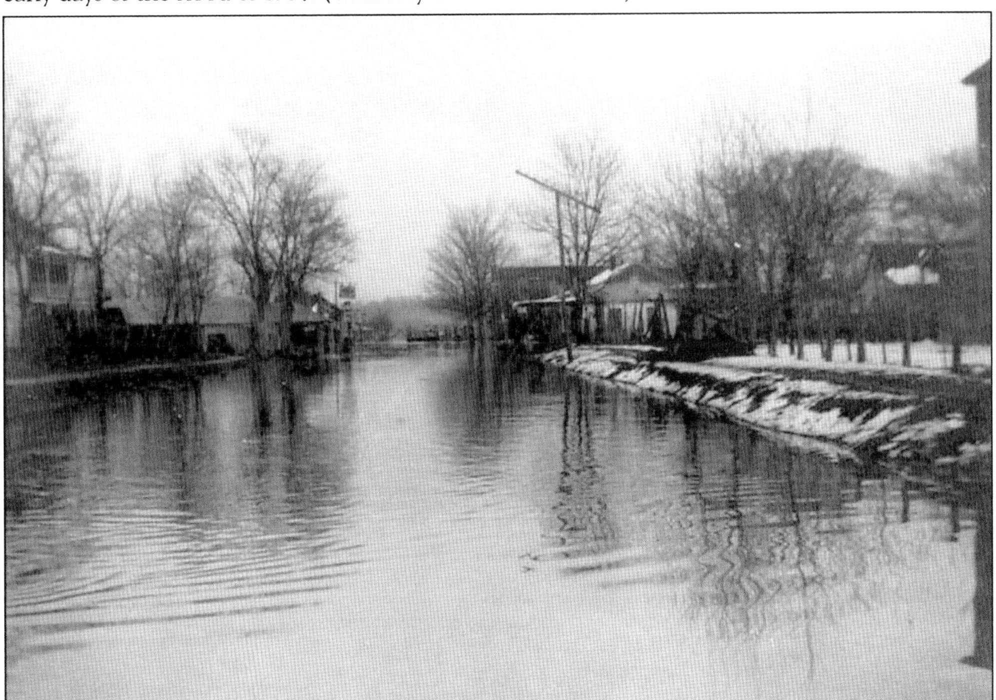

January 24, 1937, became known as Black Sunday. Tennessee and northward experienced at least 27 days of rain in January. Rivers began rising on the 17th in the Cumberland, Tennessee, Ohio, and Mississippi River basins. The water rose in the Ohio and Tennessee Rivers to record levels of over 80 feet above flood level. This view of Birmingham was taken looking down Main Street. (Courtesy of Claude Nimmo.)

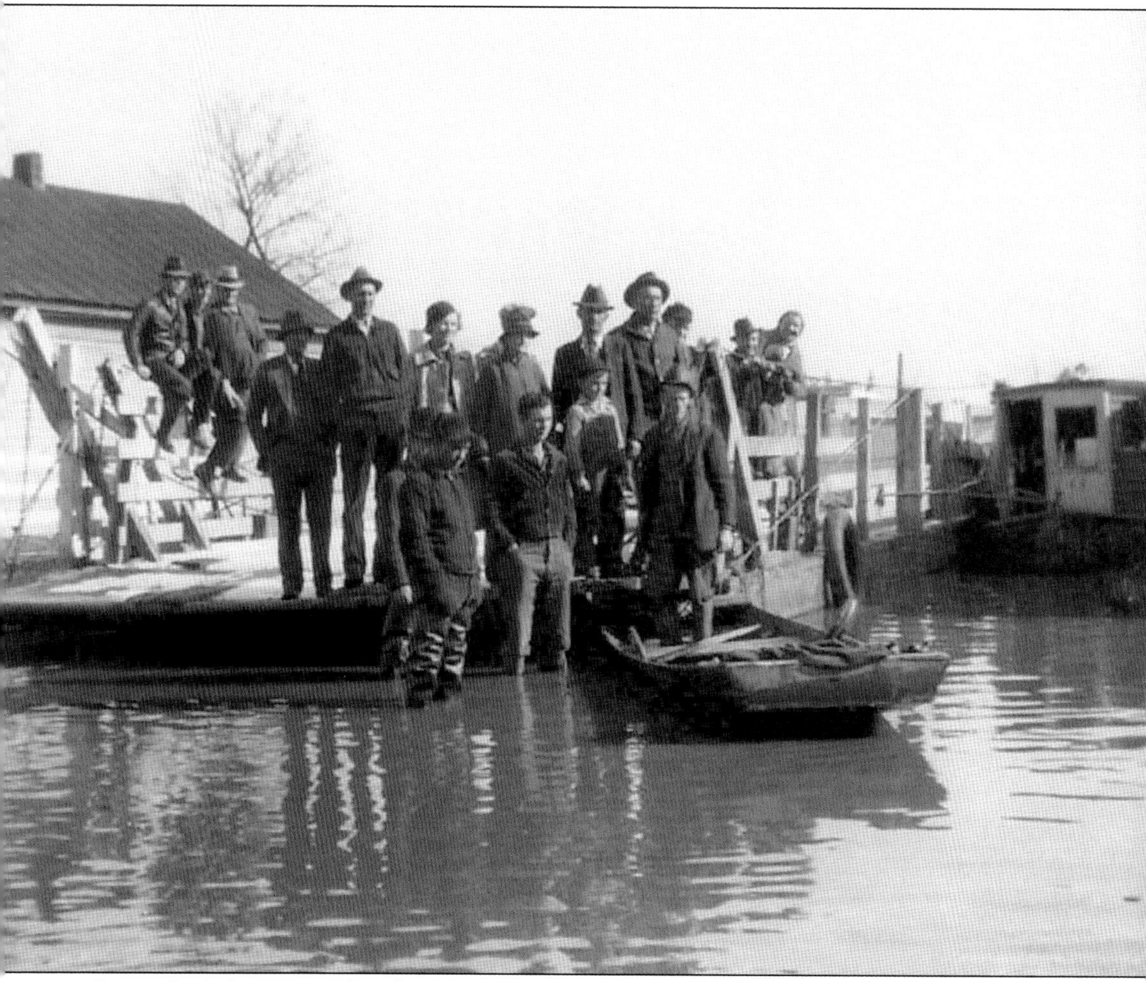

George L. Goheen ran a ferry business in Birmingham that crossed the Tennessee River to Lyon County. The fare was 25¢. During the flood, the ferry was pressed into service rescuing local families and livestock. As the waters rose, dead livestock and other debris could be seen floating downstream. Drinking water became scarce, and many areas could not receive needed supplies of food and medicines. (Courtesy of Claude Nimmo.)

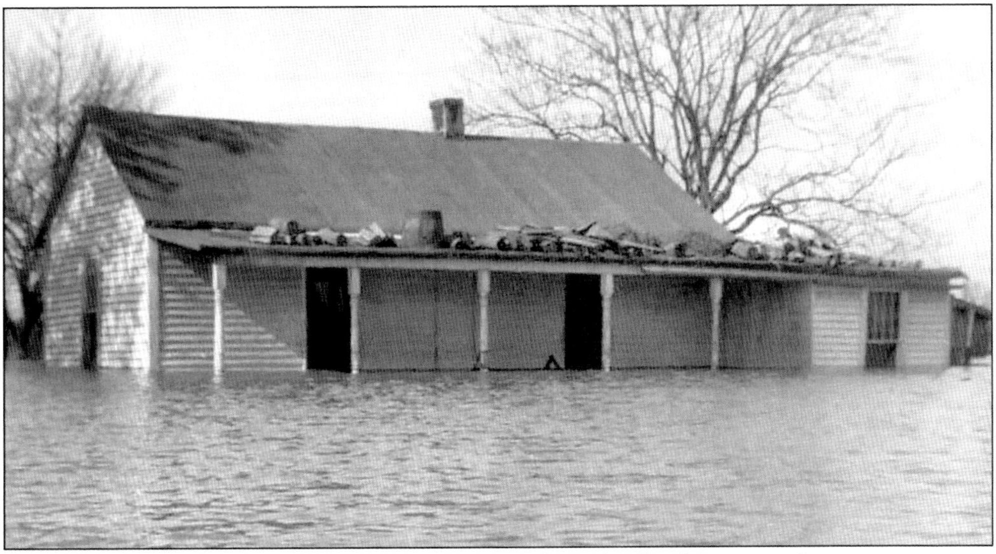

Birmingham suffered some of the worst devastation from the flood. Because the town sat so near the river, almost every home and business flooded. Anyone who had lived along the river for any period of time had seen flooding. As the waters begin to rise, some residents tried to stay in their homes. Nowadays, they tell stories of watching the water rise as much as three to four inches per hour. Many simply removed themselves and their belongings to the second floor or the roof of the home. They suffered throughout the first days and nights as the water rose. They could hear logs and other debris ramming ominously against their houses. There was no way out. This photograph is of Charles Goheen Jr.'s home. (Courtesy of Claude Nimmo.)

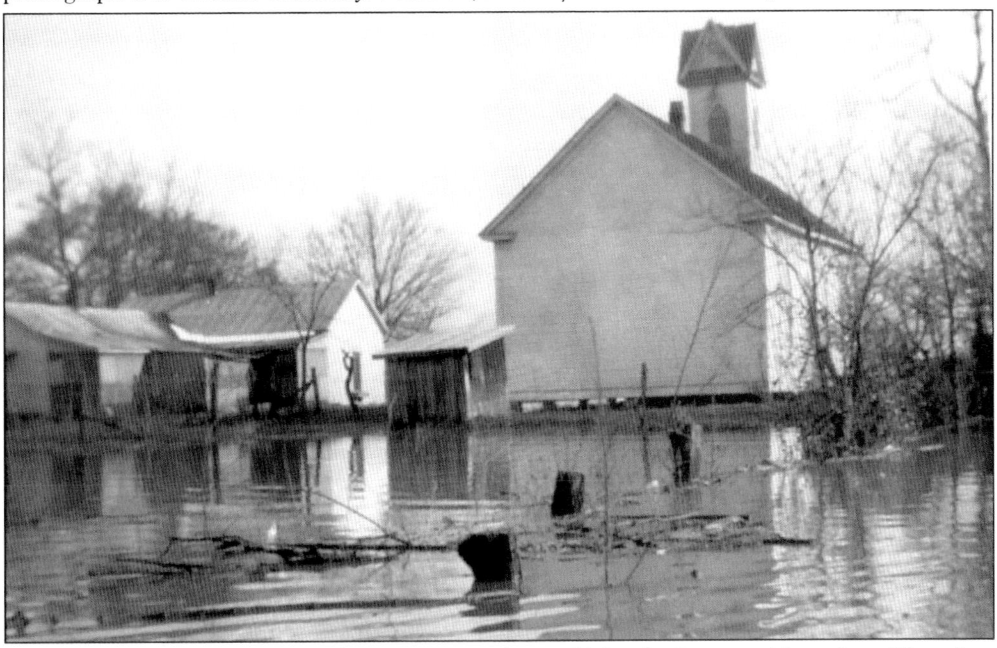

Birmingham's Methodist Church was organized in 1850 by the Reverend Levi Lee. Their first church burned in 1868. In 1893, the congregation tore down their second building to build a new, larger structure. In the 1937 flood, waters rose precariously close to the building and the parsonage next door. (Courtesy of Claude Nimmo.)

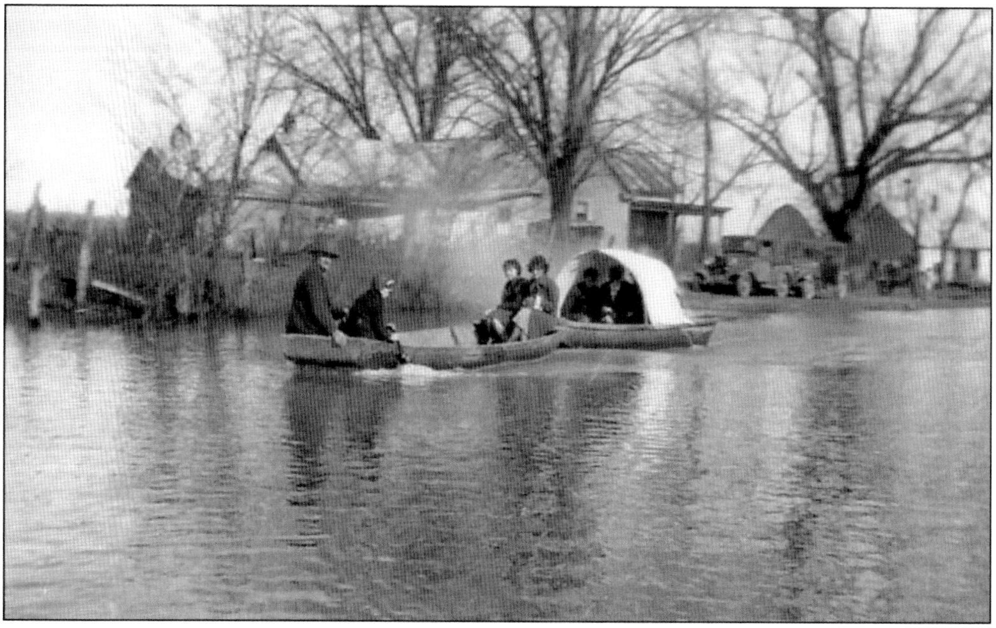

Other residents fled the rising waters in private boats along Highway 58. The J. L. Edwards home is visible in the background with the two automobiles and the tractor parked on high ground. Schools were closed, and in some school buildings, refugees took up residence. More than 270,000 people were left homeless. In many areas, schools stayed closed until the last week of February. (Courtesy of Claude Nimmo.)

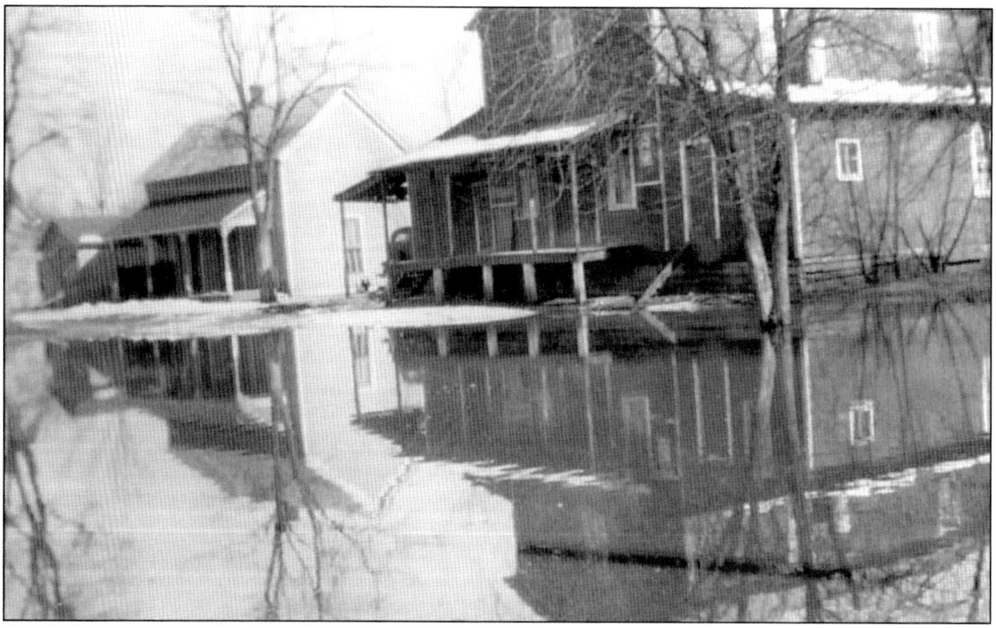

Water rose right up to the Birmingham mill. William Heath owned and operated the mill and feed store. He also ran a huckster wagon that traveled to surrounding farms. His home sat next door to the mill. When the TVA purchased Birmingham, Heath moved his mill to the intersection of Highway 68 and the Briensburg Road. He was adamant that something of Birmingham remain in the county after Birmingham was inundated by Kentucky Lake. (Courtesy of Claude Nimmo.)

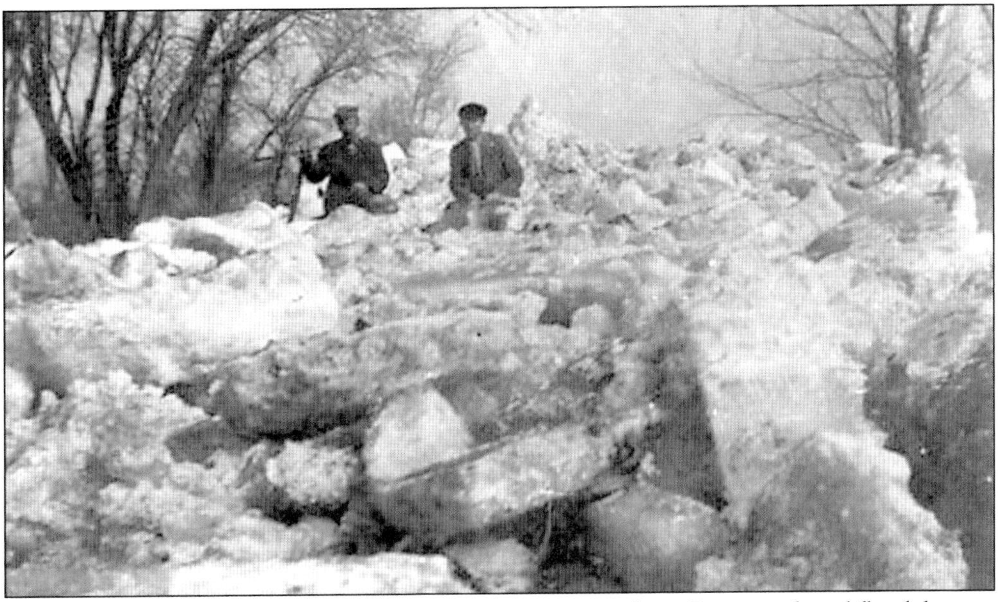

The floodwaters left 20 to 25 feet of ice in areas near Birmingham. Reports of total flood damage by the Weather Bureau for the entire state of Kentucky were $250 million, an incredible sum in 1937. (Courtesy of Claude Nimmo.)

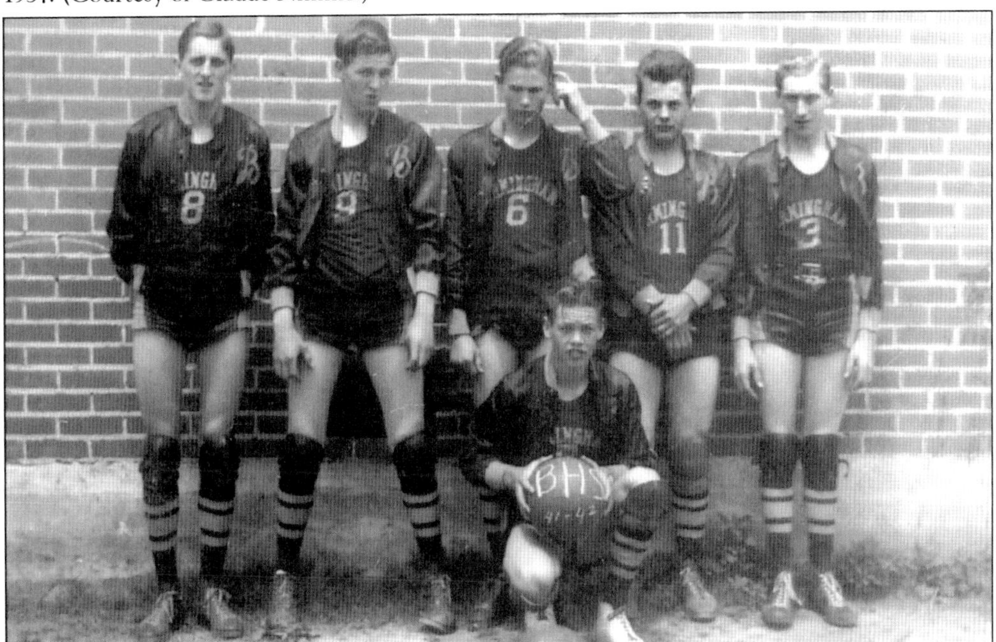

Birmingham recovered from the flood of 1937. Then the arrival of TVA representatives brought a sense of foreboding to the town. Yet Birmingham High School's boys' basketball team hoped to win the state tournament before future-NBA-star player Joseph Franklin "Jumping Joe" Fulks transferred to another county school, another disaster for the small community. The 1942 team consisted of, from left to right, Louis Locker, Max "Red" Bohannon, James Frizzell, Henry Shoemaker, Bob Henson, and Gene Clayton, in front holding the basketball. Gene married cheerleader Elizabeth Winters before dying in World War II. (Courtesy of Madelle Sirls.)

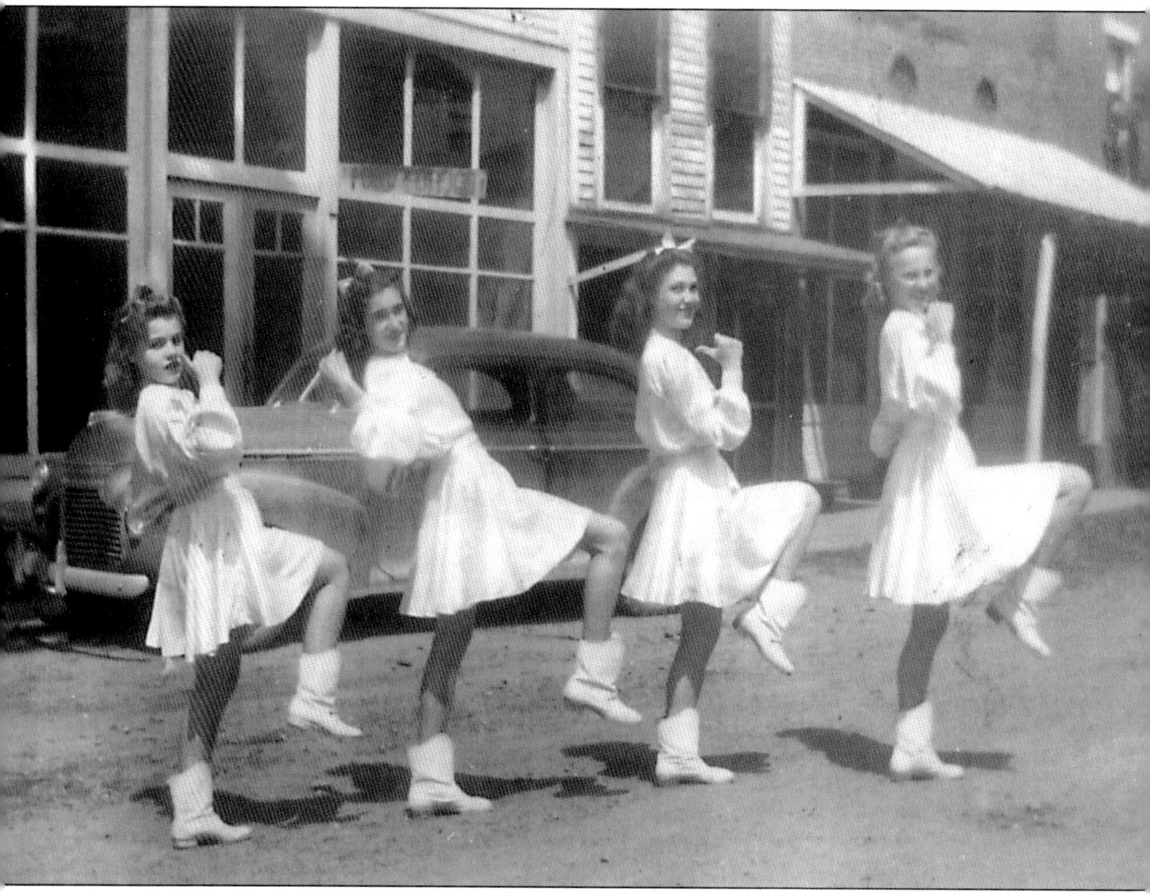

In early 1938, the news arrived: the new dam was to be constructed at Gilbertsville. Birmingham would be inundated. Businesses moved out of town. Farmers sought land in other parts of the county or other counties. Soon it was 1942, and the Birmingham High School cheerleaders—from left to right, Jackie Clayton, Madelle Love, Ruby Allen, and Elizabeth Winters—strutted their stuff on Main Street in front of the Birmingham Post Office. It was the last year for Birmingham High School before the waters of Kentucky Lake rose and covered the small river port. (Courtesy of Madelle Sirls.)

Four

CALVERT CITY

The first pioneers to the area surrounding what would become Calvert City had visions of fine farms in the bottomlands along Big Cypress Creek, the Tennessee River, and Clear Pond. Some early settlers may have arrived in the late 1700s, even before the Chickasaw Indians had moved westward. In 1836, Gideon Haydock and his brother-in-law, Josiah Kuykendall, established ferry service across the Tennessee River from near Calvert City and their trading post at Smithland. The partners had business interests on the western bank of the river as well. Over the years, the spelling of Haydock has been changed to Haddock, thus Haddock Ferry Road.

Calvert City's first store was Haddock and Ferguson; it opened sometime after 1831. However, the city did not boom until about 1864, when Potilla W. Calvert proposed that the Paducah and Elizabethtown Railroad come to area. He allowed a right-of-way across his land, along with a depot, if the station was named Calvert City. After the arrival of the railroad, the small town incorporated on March 18, 1871. John Taylor, a blacksmith, was elected mayor, and Pete Summers was the first town marshal.

The *Kentucky Gazetteer* of 1879 lists the following businesses: M. A. Bryan, shoemaker; W. F. Calvert, cabinetmaker; W. P. Calvert, hotel owner; E. Cox, tobacco merchant; H. Denman, teacher; T. M. Freeman, general store owner; L. L. Hurt, grocer; A. N. James, blacksmith; S. E. Lander, druggist; J. K. Pinner, physician; and F. M. Sellau, wagon maker. By 1894, Calvert City was noted to have a depot; a mill; two churches, Missionary Baptist and the Union Church occupied by the Methodists and Christians; two general stores; one drug store; one blacksmith shop; two physicians; and several mechanics.

In the fall of 1906, Luther Draffen opened a harness repair shop in a small house in the rear of the J. B. Barnes store. The next year, with his brother, Matt, he borrowed $300 from their father and established Draffen Brothers. Luther Draffen proved to be a successful businessman and was influential in many improvements that would come to Calvert City both before and after the construction of Kentucky Dam.

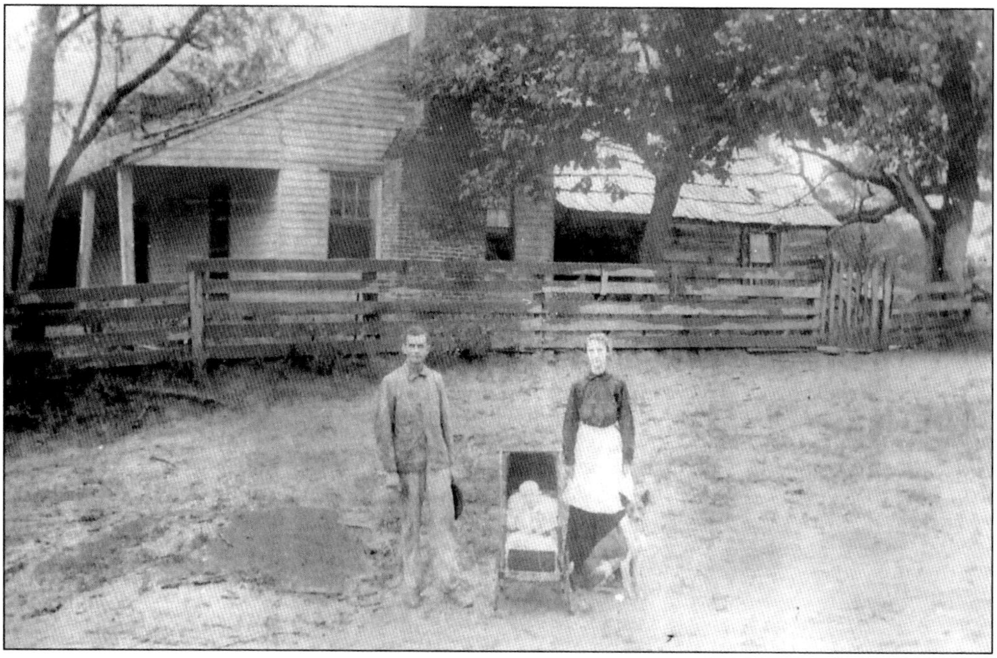

About 1820, Stephen Howard settled in the northern part of what was to become Marshall County and built the log portion of this home. The front part is believed to have been added about the time of the Civil War. Pictured are Stephen Howard's son, John Allie, his wife, Verda Hoover, and their son, Wendell Elihu, with dog, Alec. (Courtesy of Elizabeth Harrell.)

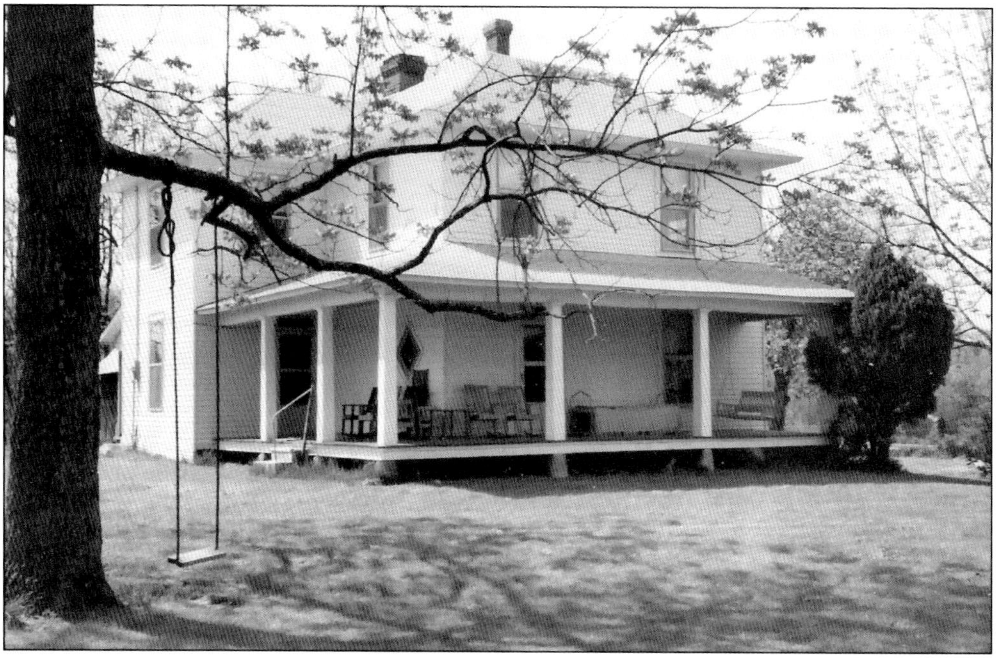

John Allie and Verda Howard built this house in Calvert City in 1917 on the location of Stephen Howard's *c.* 1820 house, shown above. The original home was torn down and much of the material used to build this second family home. This home stands on Patterson Ferry Road. (Courtesy of Elizabeth Harrell.)

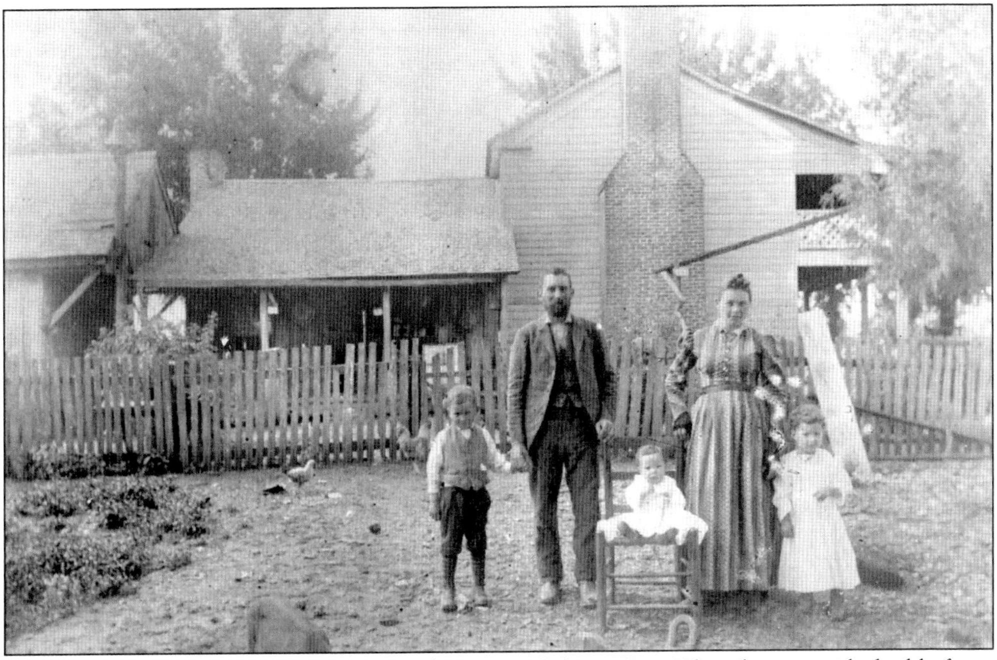

John and Rosa Peck owned a prosperous farm near Calvert City. Their house, with double front porches, was enlarged with extensions to the back. By 1893, John and Rosa had three children, Milburn, Lela, and Willie. The house was located across from the Peck Cemetery on the Lone Valley Road. (Courtesy of Bobbie Foust.)

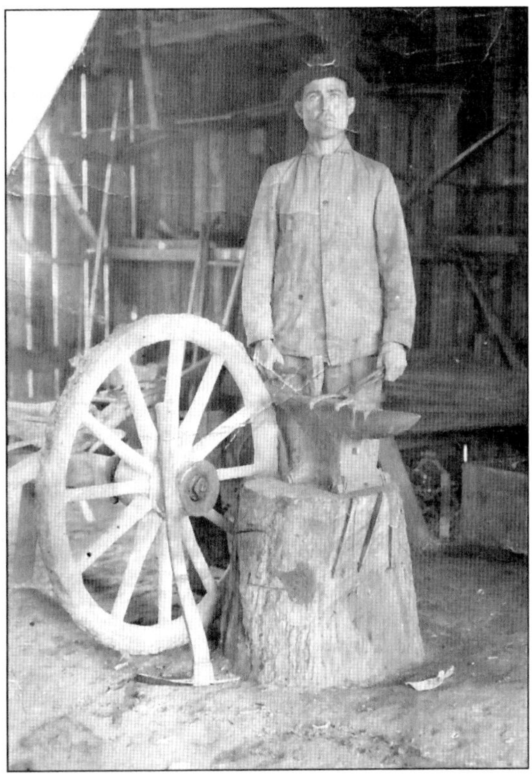

John Davis owned a blacksmith shop in Calvert City. He was known as an excellent blacksmith. His home and shop were located on A Avenue next to the home of Sallie Calvert. John and his wife, Mayme Head, had more than 10 children. (Courtesy of Natalie Fowler Johnston.)

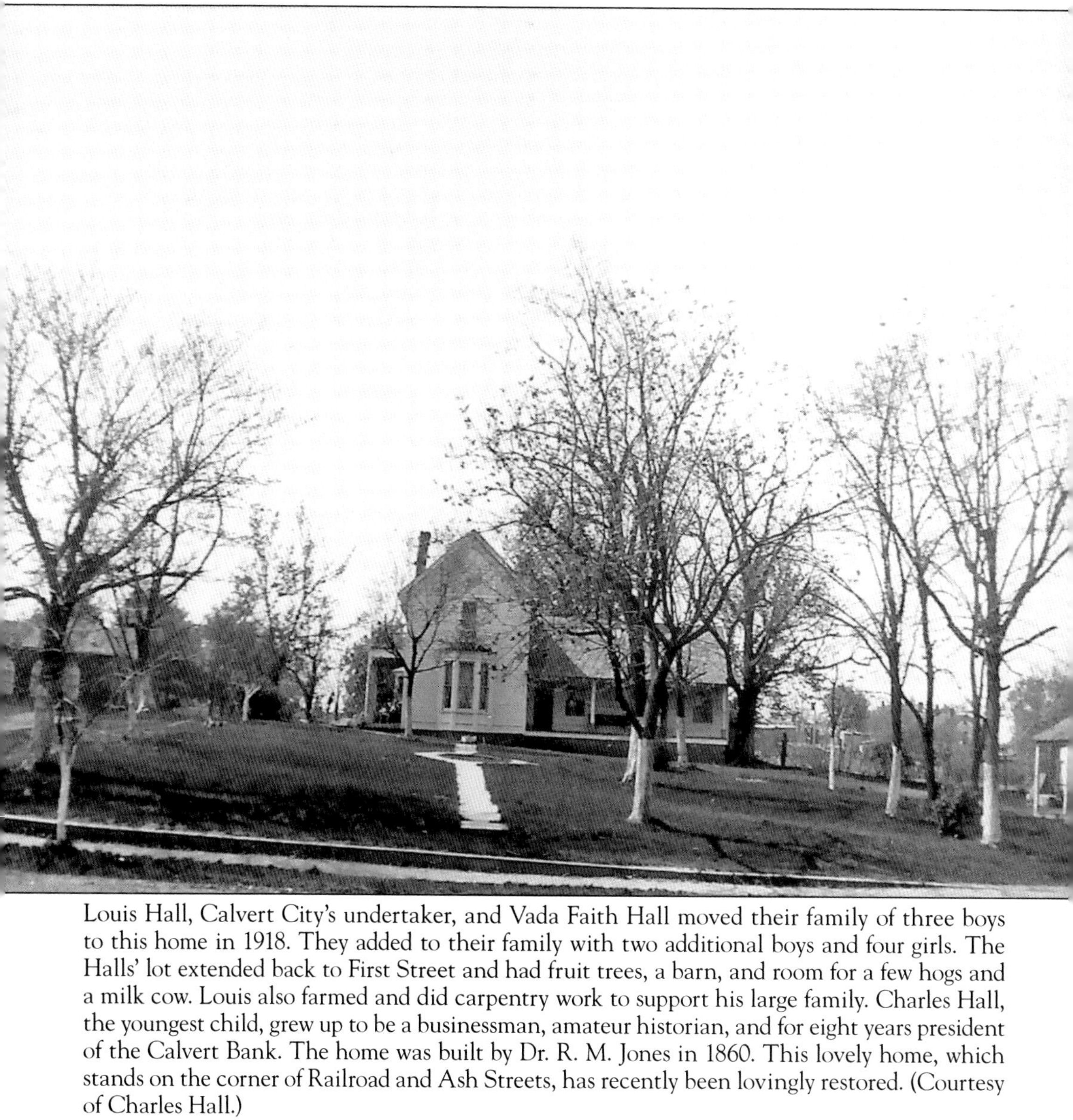

Louis Hall, Calvert City's undertaker, and Vada Faith Hall moved their family of three boys to this home in 1918. They added to their family with two additional boys and four girls. The Halls' lot extended back to First Street and had fruit trees, a barn, and room for a few hogs and a milk cow. Louis also farmed and did carpentry work to support his large family. Charles Hall, the youngest child, grew up to be a businessman, amateur historian, and for eight years president of the Calvert Bank. The home was built by Dr. R. M. Jones in 1860. This lovely home, which stands on the corner of Railroad and Ash Streets, has recently been lovingly restored. (Courtesy of Charles Hall.)

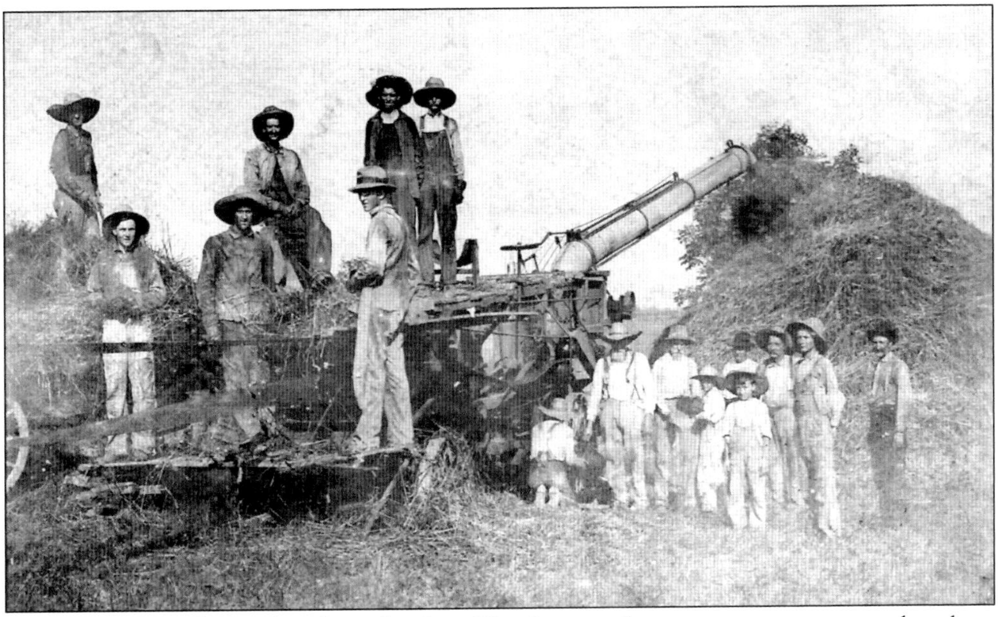

John Allie Howard owned a wheat thresher. Threshers used steam power to separate the wheat from the straw and chaff. Farmers who owned mechanized equipment often traveled from farm to farm, helping with the harvest for a portion of the crop proceeds. At each farm, neighbors helped out with the work in return for the help of their neighbors as crops were harvested. (Courtesy of Elizabeth Harrell.)

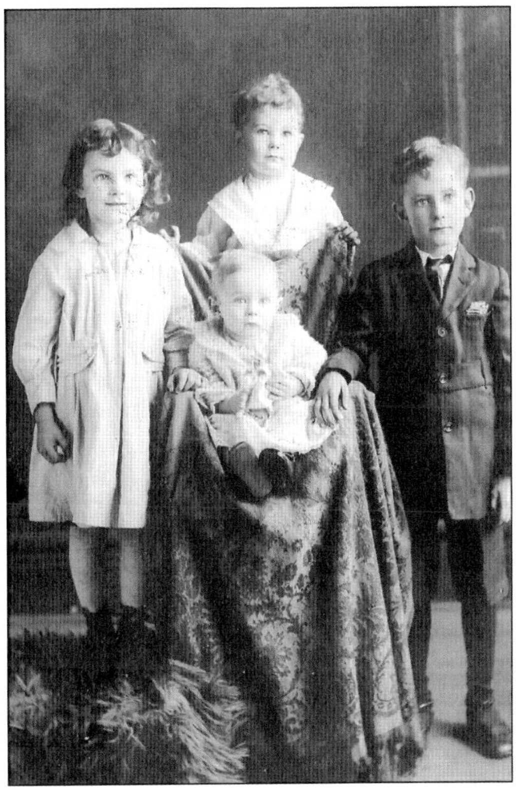

Prosperous farmer J. A. Howard and his wife, Verda, had four children. Clockwise from left are Elizabeth, Hoover, Wendell, and John. This photograph was made in the autumn of 1918. In 1904, J. A. Howard ran for county sheriff on the Democratic ticket. He lost by three votes. Close political races seem to be a tradition in Kentucky's counties. (Courtesy of Elizabeth Harrell.)

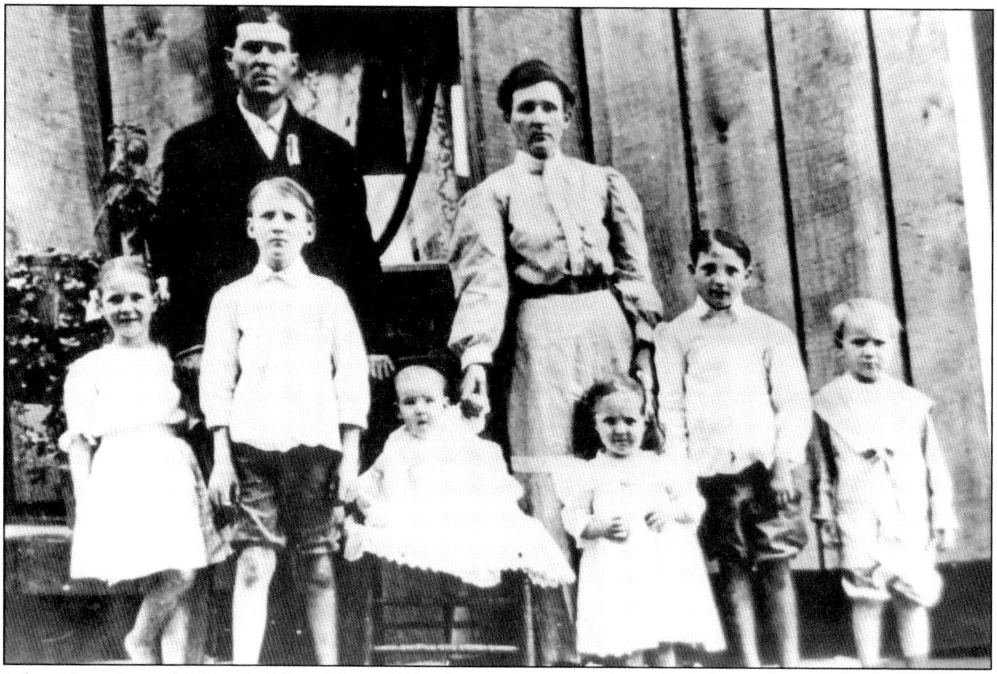

John Francis and Maggie Mae (Davis) Fowler were married on October 2, 1900, at Morganfield in Union County, Kentucky. They lived in Calvert City, and by 1910, when this photograph was taken, they had six children. From oldest to youngest are the twins, Luther and Lyman (Sambo), Verlie, Richard, Lorene, and Rose Mae. (Courtesy of Brian Davis.)

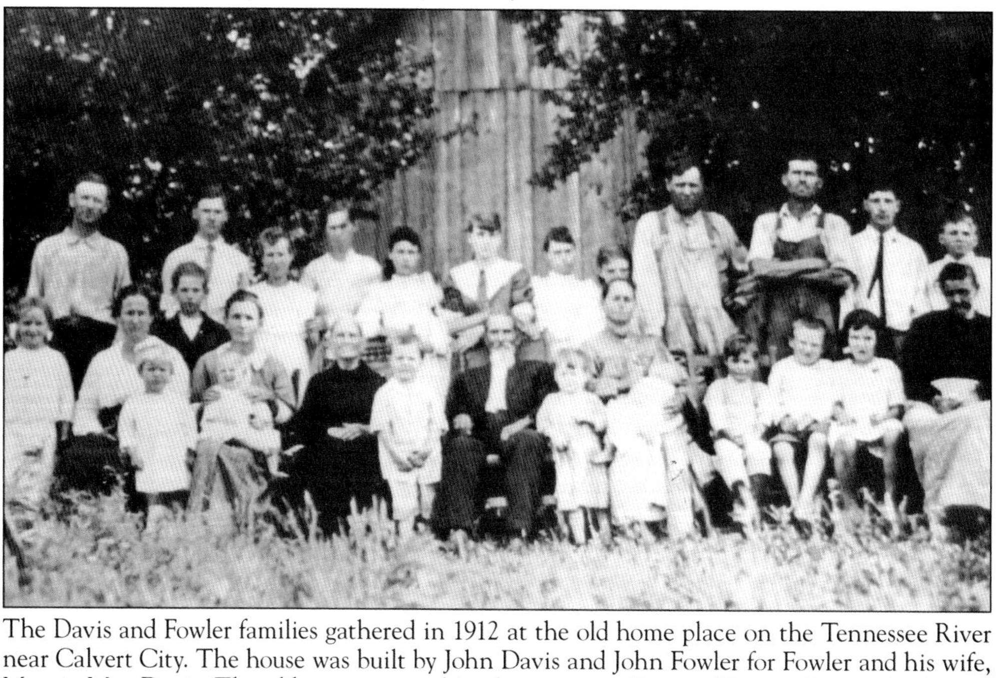

The Davis and Fowler families gathered in 1912 at the old home place on the Tennessee River near Calvert City. The house was built by John Davis and John Fowler for Fowler and his wife, Maggie Mae Davis. The older man seated in the center is Dewitt Clinton Davis, the first of his family to move to Calvert City from Alabama. His wife, Martha Jane Smith, sits to his left. (Courtesy of Brian Davis.)

After their wedding in Central City, Kentucky, Roy and Amie Fredonia (Harrell) Coursey returned to Calvert City. Roy was a signalman for the Illinois Central Railway. They lived in the Coursey community on the Haddock's Ferry Road. Their third child, son Harrell, shown here, was born in 1918. They had seven children; five lived to maturity—Jewell, Kenneth, Harrell, Donald, and Albadean. (Courtesy of Johnny Harrell.)

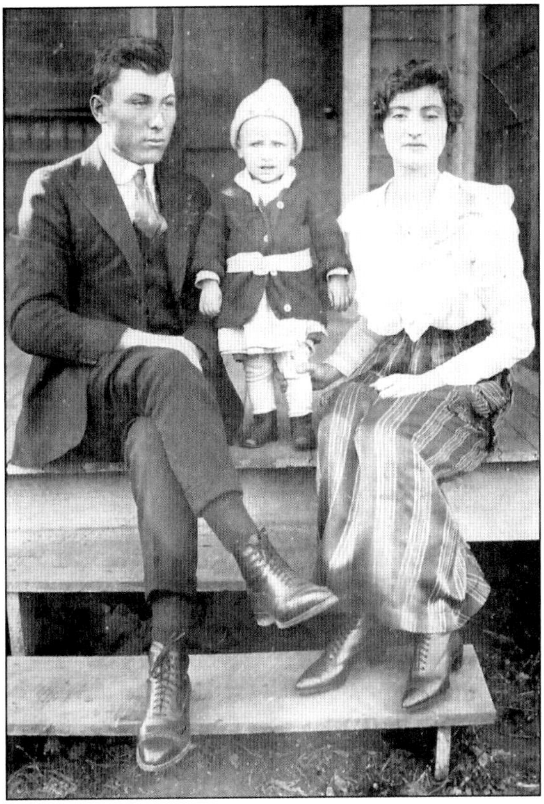

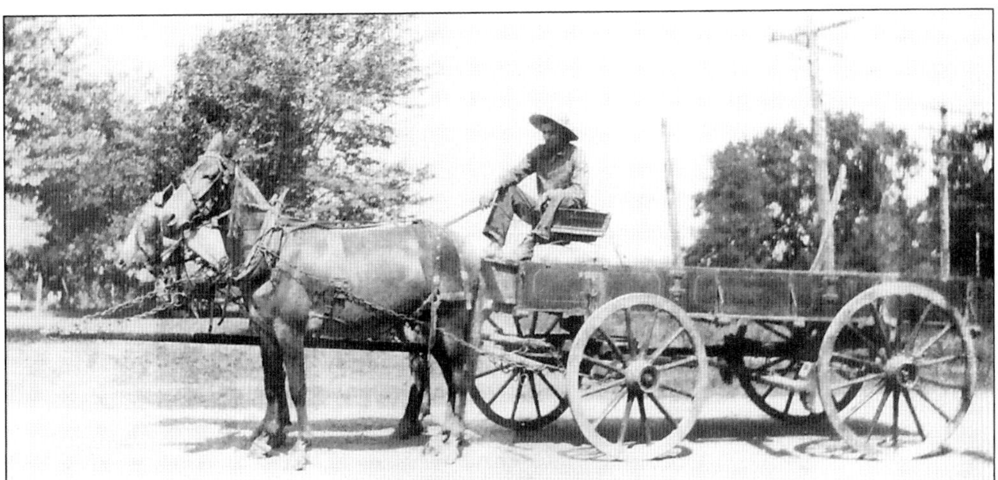

Even after the introduction of electricity to parts of the county, horses, mules, and wagons continued to be common forms of transportation for farm goods as well as people. A Lone Valley area farmer, Roy Pugh, is shown with his two-mule hitch and wagon. (Courtesy of Bobbie Foust.)

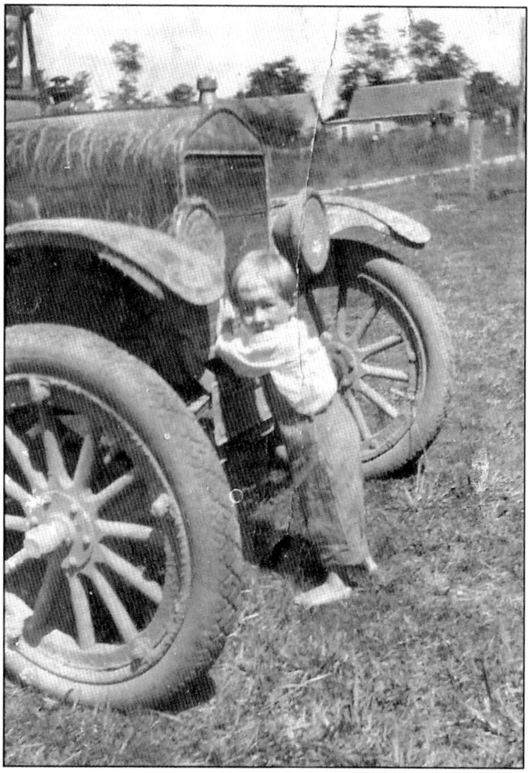

A barefoot James Draffen tried to crank his father's automobile, c. 1920. His father, Luther Draffen, first established a harness repair shop before partnering with his brother, Mert, in 1906, to build their first general merchandise shop. The family continues to own several businesses in Calvert City. James married Sue Morris, "a dam girl," so called for her family's arrival for employment during Kentucky Dam's construction. (Courtesy of James L. Draffen.)

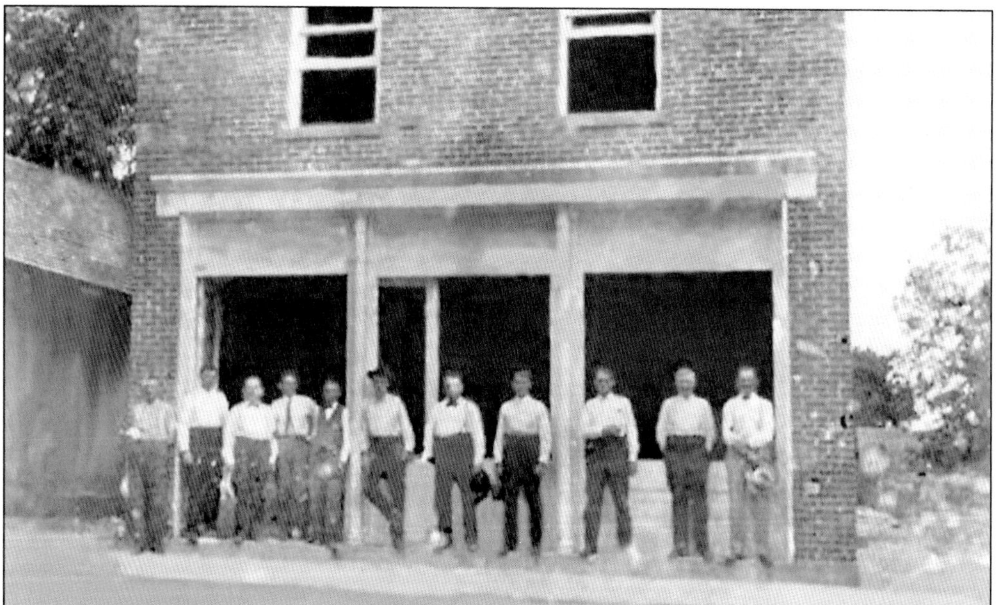

The Bank of Calvert City opened on January 1, 1908, and was incorporated on September 18 of that same year. On two occasions in the early 1930s, attempted robberies of the bank were foiled, the first by Dr. Little, who gave the alarm, and the second by the sturdy inner doors of the safe. On the second occasion, the thieves escaped with about $100 in nickels and pennies. (Courtesy of Johnny Harrell.)

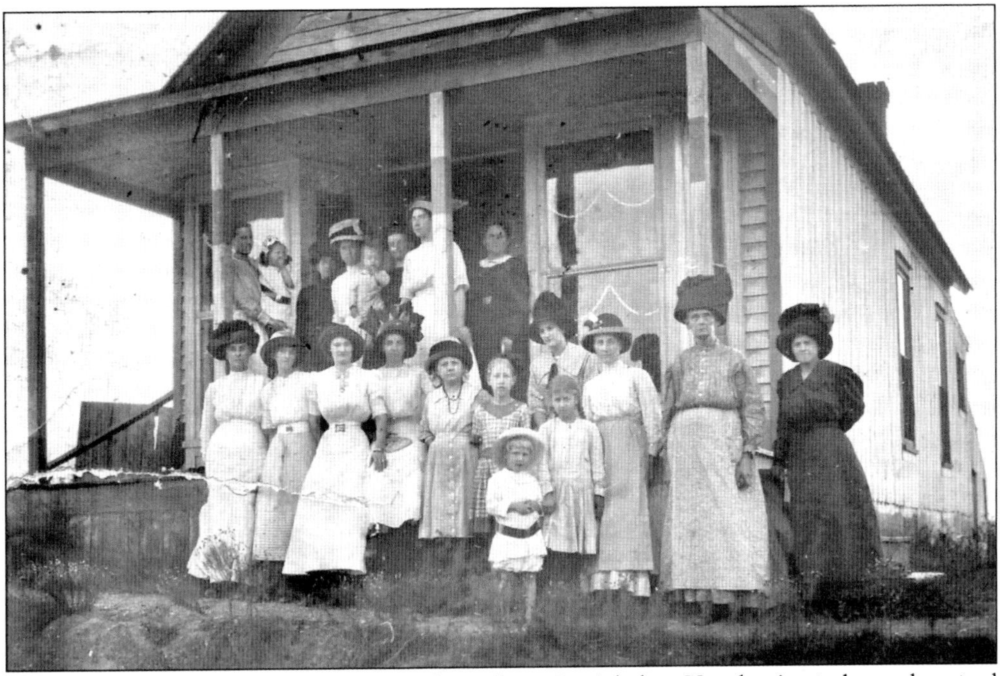

Elnora Attebury's Millinery created hats for Calvert City's ladies. Her shop's windows advertised and displayed her handmade creations. Several of her clients showed off her hats as well as their children in this 1911 photograph. (Courtesy of Virginia Tucker.)

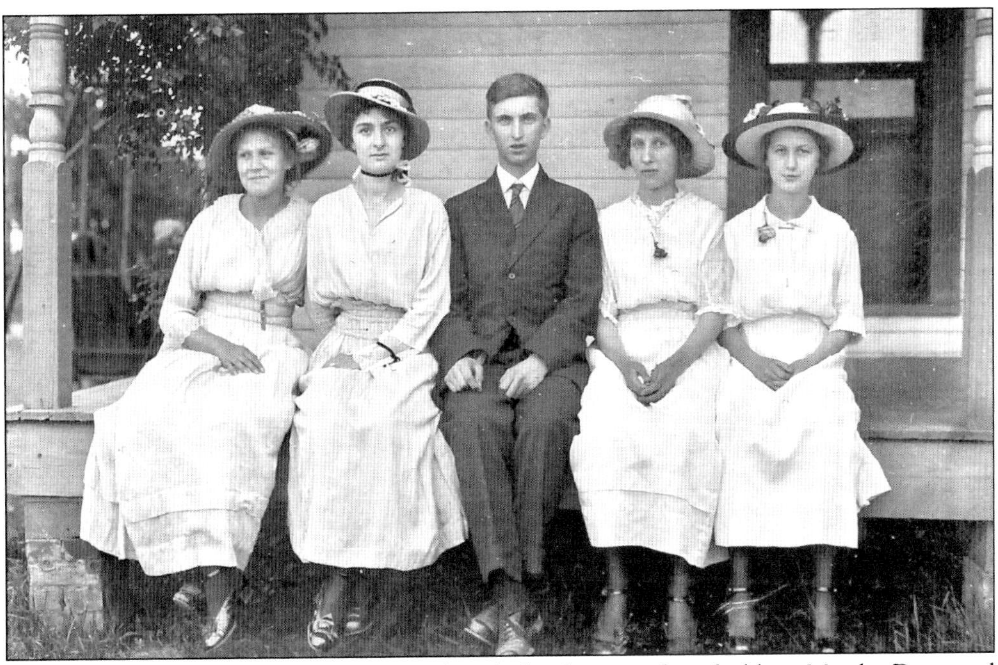

From left to right, Estelle Sowell, an unidentified girl, an unidentified boy, Martha Dees, and Helen Green dressed in their finest for a photograph at the Green home. The house was then the last house on the left on Aspen Street in Calvert City and sat directly behind the old Draffen store. (Courtesy of Johnny Harrell.)

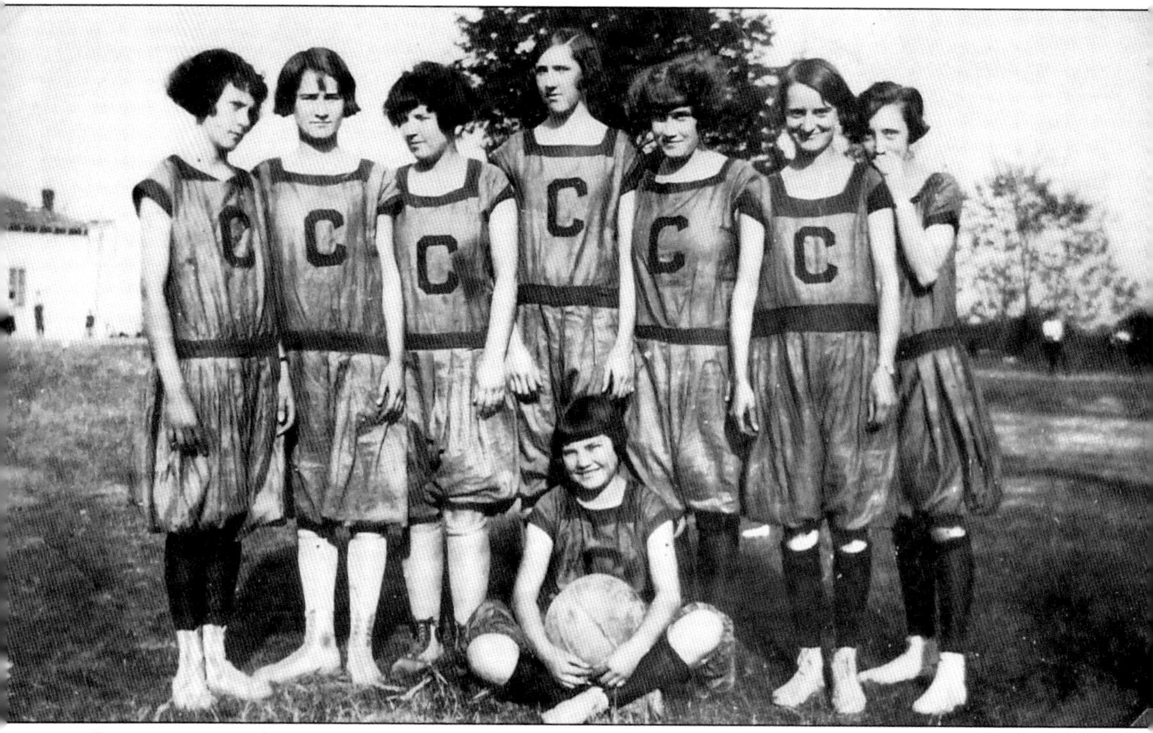

Even in 1924 and 1925, basketball played a large role in the Marshall County athletic scene. The Calvert City High School girls' team consisted of girls from many of the surrounding small towns that did not have their own high schools. Team members were, from left to right, (standing) Ellen Cloud, Henryetta Holland, Francis Humphrey, Mable Solomon, Roberta Holland, Marion Owen, and Lucille Jolly; (seated) Pet Fox. Marion Owen lived between Calvert City and Gilbertsville. She rode the train to school, as her father worked for the Illinois Central, and she received a pass. To catch the train, she walked a mile east to Gilbertsville and rode past her house, going west, on the way to Calvert City. She reversed the trip each afternoon. (Courtesy of the Wade family.)

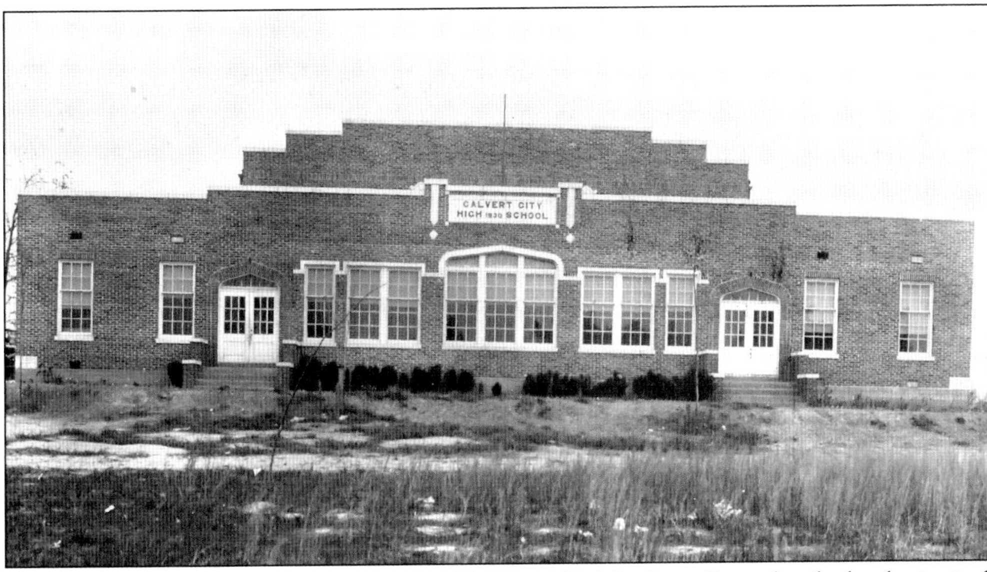

Calvert City High School moved to this building in 1930. Miss Lucy Foust, local school principal, began the drive to build a high school. Her proposal asked residents to pay for 50 percent of the cost with the remainder to be paid by the county. The drive met with enthusiastic approval. The city's first two-year high-school program opened in 1919, with a four-year program by 1922. (Courtesy of the Marshall County Genealogical and Historical Society.)

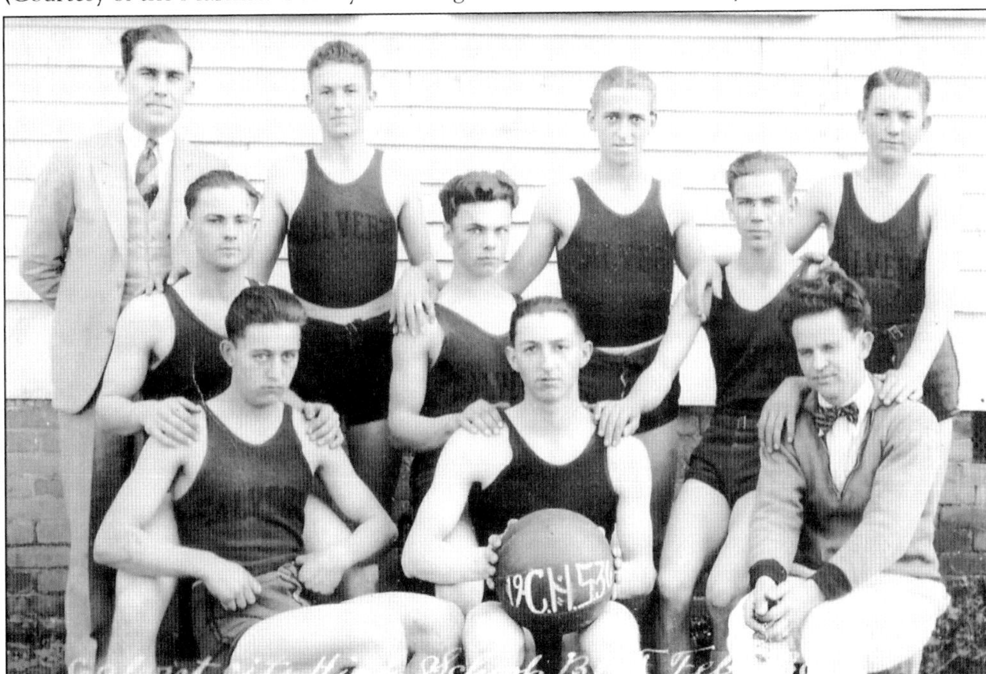

Loy Kennedy coached the boys' basketball team at Calvert City. From left to right are (first row) Cleatus Kingcade, William Chumbler, and Coach Kennedy; (second row) Albert Harrell, Edward Freeman, and Theodore Fox; (third row) Buel Moore, Eric Hurst, Wesley Story, and Clem Dismore. Within a few years, Loy Kennedy left teaching and opened a funeral home in Calvert City. (Courtesy of Elizabeth Harrell.)

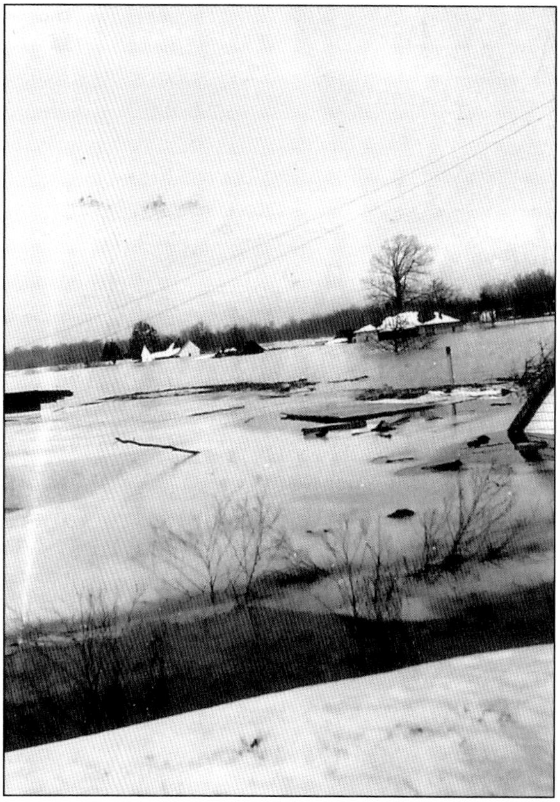

Although Calvert City lies a bit farther from the Tennessee River than Gilbertsville and Birmingham, the effects of the flood of 1937 were still devastating to the community. Almost the city's entire main residential and business district flooded. The ice formed by freezing temperatures in the days following the high water created harsh conditions that were not soon forgotten. (Courtesy of Elizabeth Harrell.)

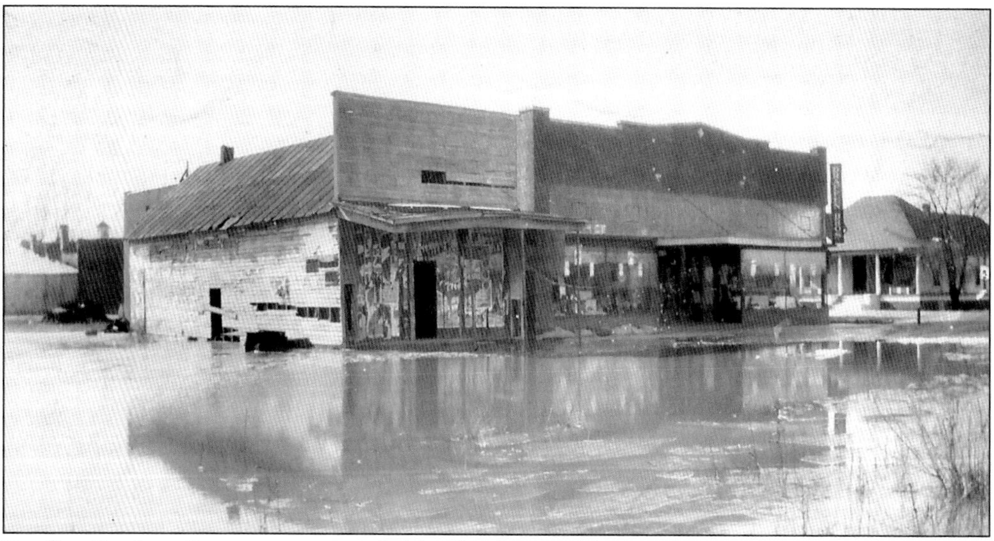

Draffen Brothers Store was surrounded by floodwaters like many of Calvert City's main street businesses. At another location owned by Luther Draffen was stored some 10,000 feet of cypress lumber and 10 barrels of coal tar. Carpenters volunteered, and his garage became a boatyard. Quickly constructed boats were used in the rescue of more than 2,000 people and were instrumental in the delivery of foodstuffs from Paducah. No lives were lost during the rescue operations. (Courtesy of James L. Draffen.)

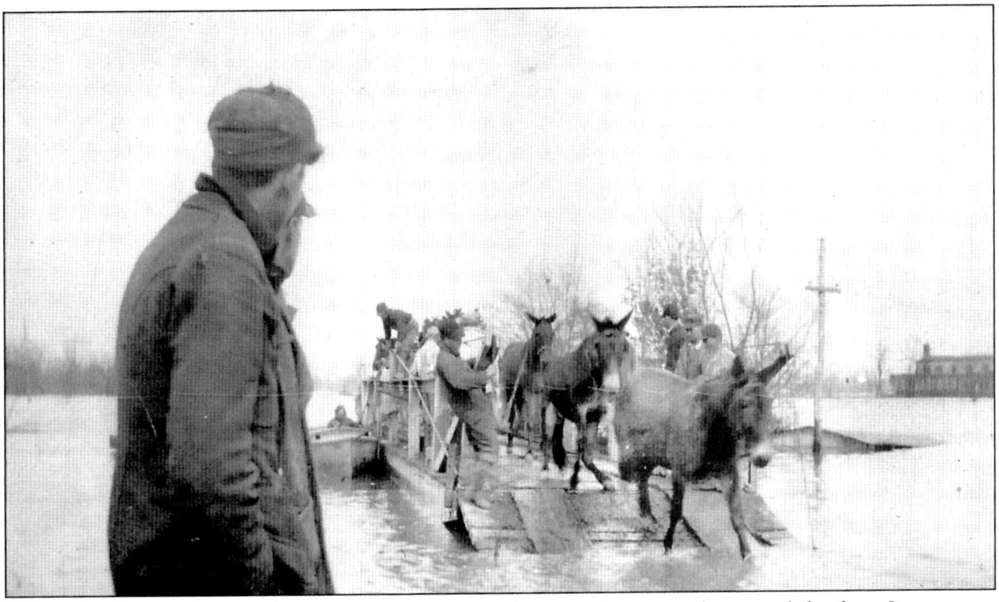

During the 1937 flood, Haddock's Ferry transported mules, horses, and automobiles from Livingston County, where flooding had quickly stranded families and livestock. The boat usually used to pull the ferry was swept away in the quickly rising floodwaters. Local businessman Luther Draffen volunteered a Chrysler boat modified with a Ford V-8 engine. It was used to pull the ferry during rescue efforts. Estimates of rescued livestock were reported at more than 10,000. (Courtesy of James L. Draffen.)

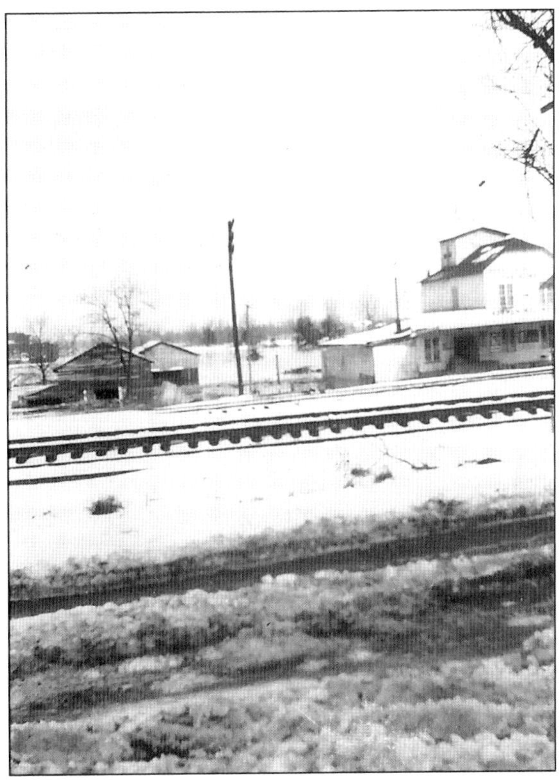

The Norman Milling Company, a feed store and flour mill, sits amid the water and ice left by the flood of 1937. Electric generating equipment, added in 1932, furnished power to Calvert City. The milling company burned during the latter part of the flood. The Norman family rebuilt the electric generating portion of their business and continued to power the community for many years. (Courtesy of Elizabeth Harrell.)

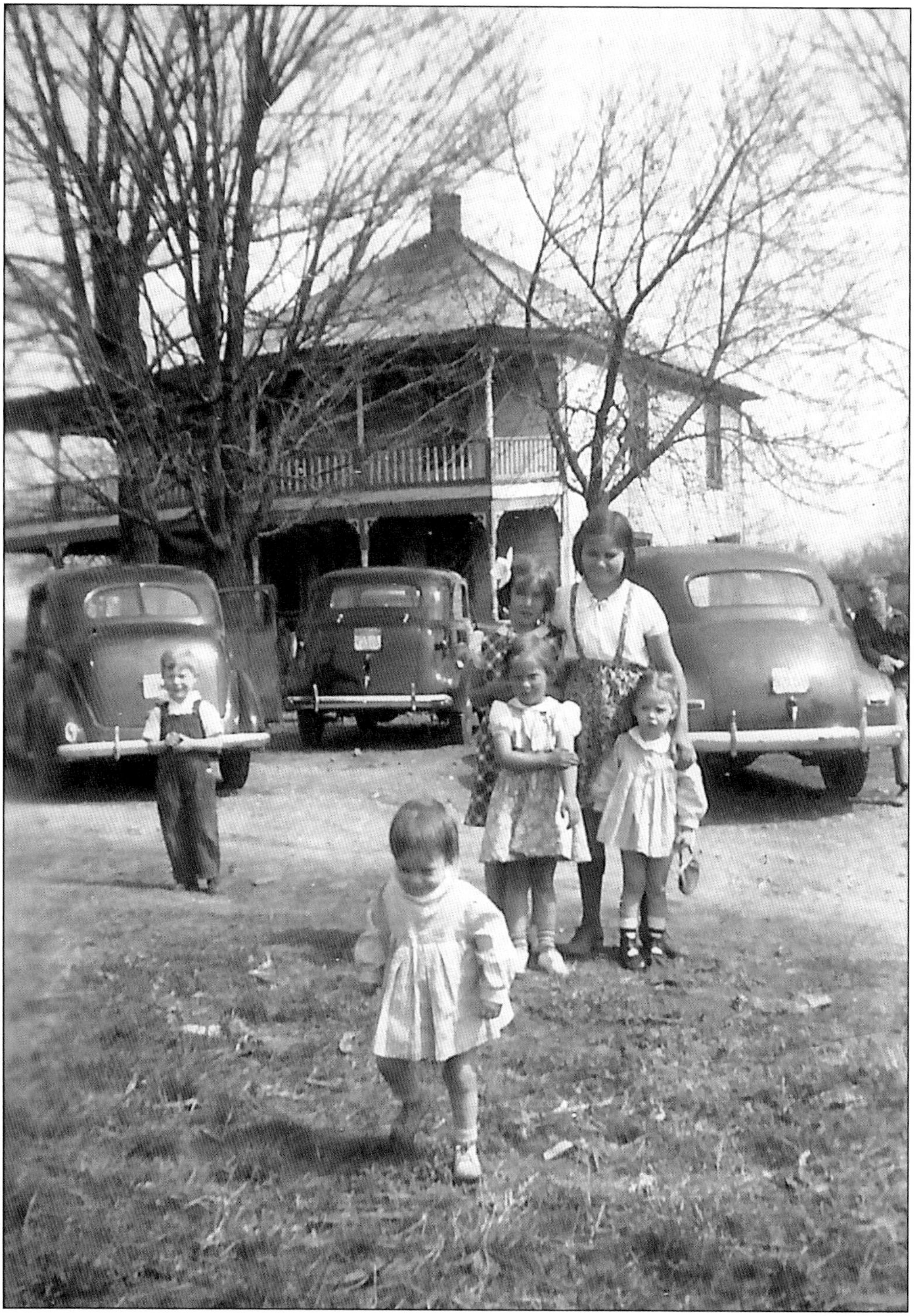

A family gathering, perhaps after Sunday's morning church service, brought Fowler family descendants to the old homestead at Calvert City. This house stood where the Goodrich and Westlake plants are now located. John Francis and his wife, Maggie, owned about 114 acres. (Courtesy of Natalie Johnston Fowler.)

Five

GILBERTSVILLE

The building of a rail bridge brought men of vision to the Tennessee River's western bank where the Chesapeake, Ohio, and Southwestern Railroad would soon bring settlers needing supplies and farming equipment. Arriving by riverboat, Race Jones built a small residence and unloaded a shipment of merchandise. Thomas S. Marshall, formerly of Ohio County, traded for land south of the new rail stop and took up farming. Others quickly followed; the river bottoms were wide both above and below the new settlement, and the soil was extremely productive.

In 1871, city leaders applied for a post office and chose the name Clear Pond for a mile-long lake just north of town. Race Jones served as the first postmaster. Beginning in 1872, the rail line brought business, passengers, and more settlers. Soon the small town boasted of two stores, several residences, and even a saloon before Clear Pond's residents voted it dry. Col. T. B. Waller and Martin Chestnut opened stores. Chestnut also served as the railroad station master.

In 1874, to honor Jesse Gilbert, Clear Pond became Gilbertsville upon its incorporation. Gilbert served in Kentucky's legislature from 1861 to 1863, when he was expelled for consorting with the Confederacy. He served as a Kentucky senator from 1871 to 1875. The town reincorporated in 1902. New businesses arrived, a jail was built, and the one-room school was replaced with a two-story frame building. The Bank of Gilbertsville opened in 1907. By 1912, the town claimed four stores, four filling stations, and rural route delivery of the mail. Despite the town's decision to remain dry, several men, including resident Race Marshall, decided to open a saloon. After about six weeks, the courts ruled in favor of the residents, upholding Gilbertsville's dry status. Race Marshall was fined $1 on each of 162 indictments; his partners had fled.

By 1930, Gilbertsville had a population of about 300. The town's school offered grades 1 through 12, and their mascot was the yellow jacket. Late January 1937 brought extensive flooding and was the beginning of the end for old Gilbertsville.

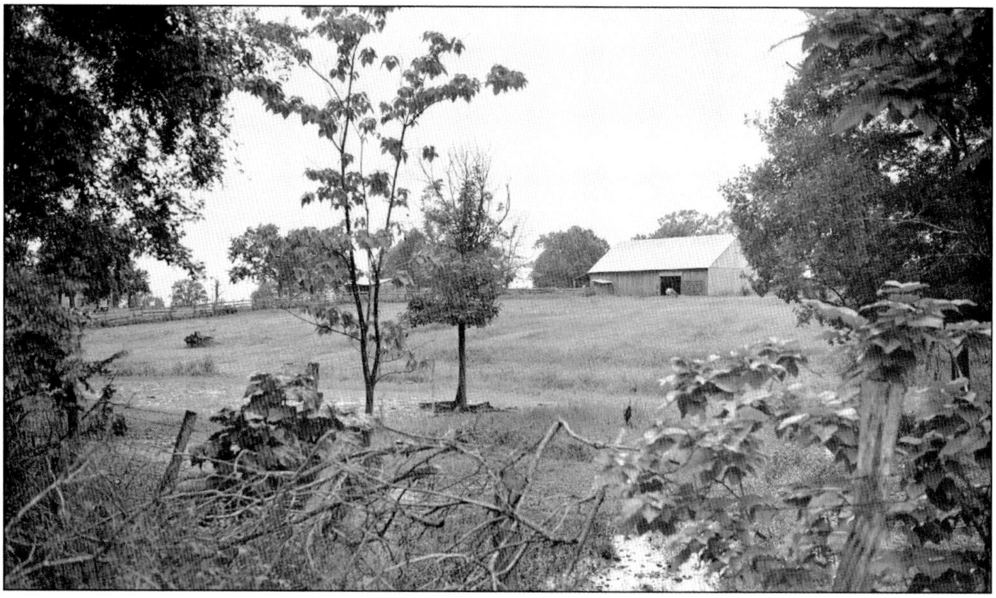

Lemon's Handbook of Marshall County, Kentucky, written in 1894, states emphatically that Gilbertsville is surrounded by "one of best sections of farming lands in the county and will always be a good trading point." The rich bottomlands along the Tennessee River near Gilbertsville yield fine crops of corn and tobacco for the area's farmers. (Courtesy of the U.S. National Archives and Records Administration and the Tennessee Valley Authority.)

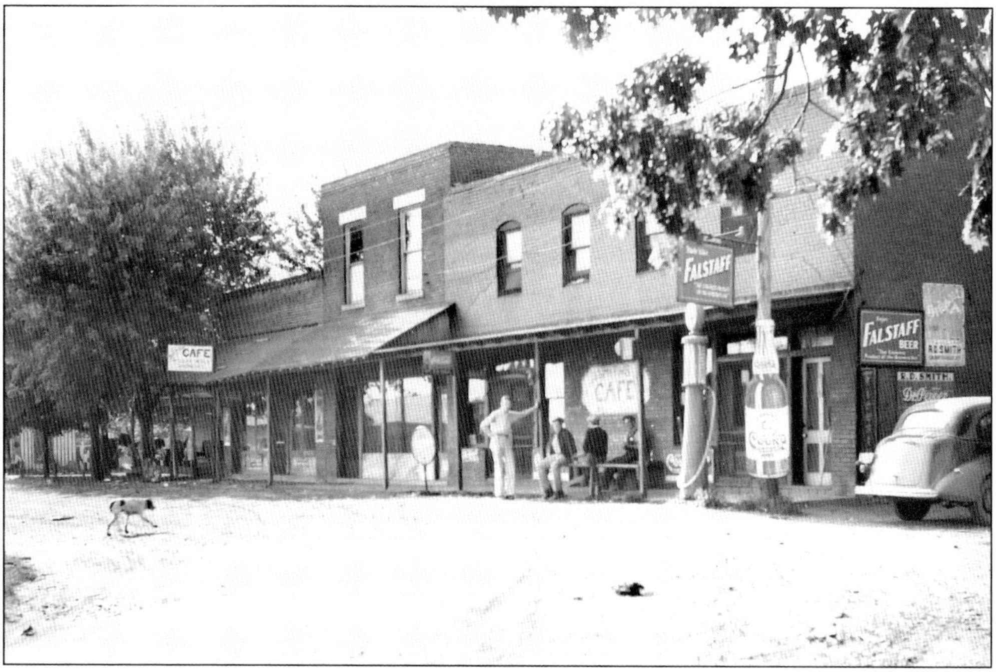

R. D. Smith's Café also sold gasoline to passing motorists. Gilbertsville's main strip featured J. D. Wood's Café and the Bank of Gilbertsville. R. D. Smith was instrumental in establishing West Gilbertsville when the Tennessee Valley Authority forced the closing of the original town. (Courtesy of Bobby Culp and the Tennessee Valley Authority.)

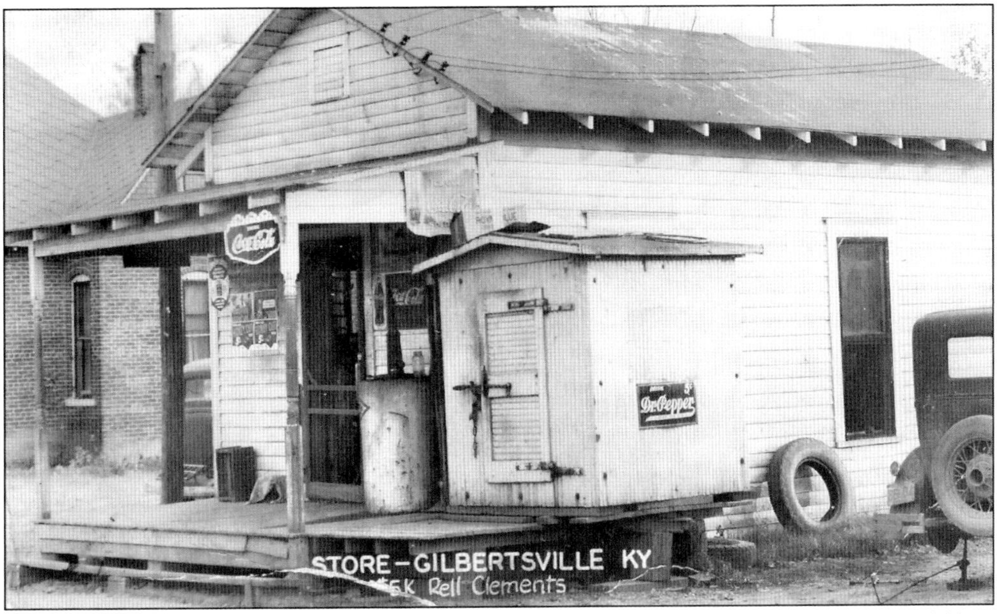

Satterfield's Store sold all types of foodstuffs. From the ice box on the right, customers could buy for 3¢ enough ice for their tea at lunch. Double-dip ice cream cones sold for 5¢. (Courtesy of Viola Satterfield Collins and the Tennessee Valley Authority.)

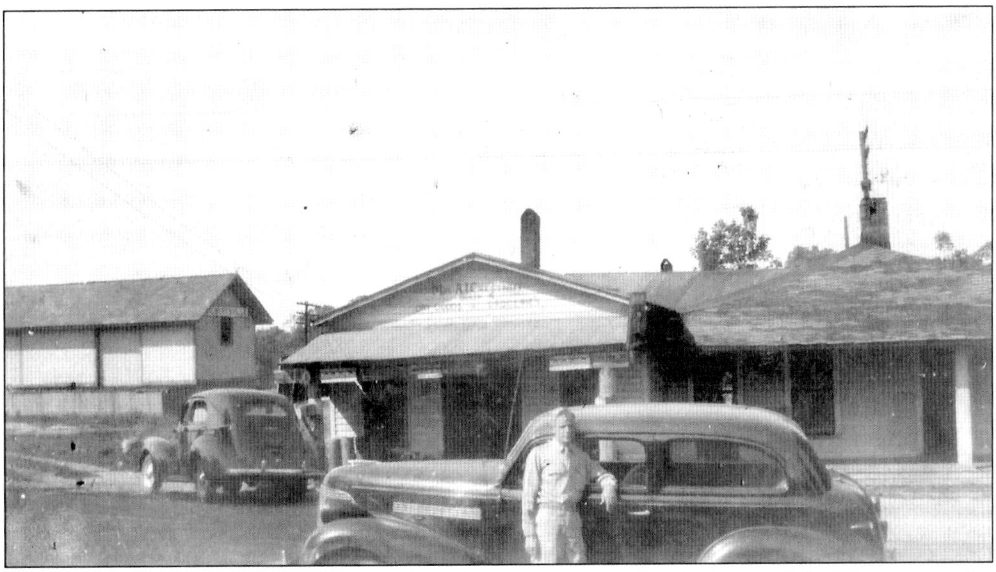

Mrs. A. I. Chestnut, dealer in dry goods and groceries, was also Gilbertsville's ticket master for many years. Her store sat next to the train depot, and she lived in the right-hand side. The noise of passing trains provided cover on Halloween as a group of local boys would dismantle a farm wagon and place it atop Mrs. Addie's store. The next day, the same boys would appear and offer to remove the wagon for the widow—for a small fee, of course. This photograph was made in September 1942, when James Moore (shown here) was home on leave. (Courtesy of Mayme Ruth "Tootsie" Moore Brooks.)

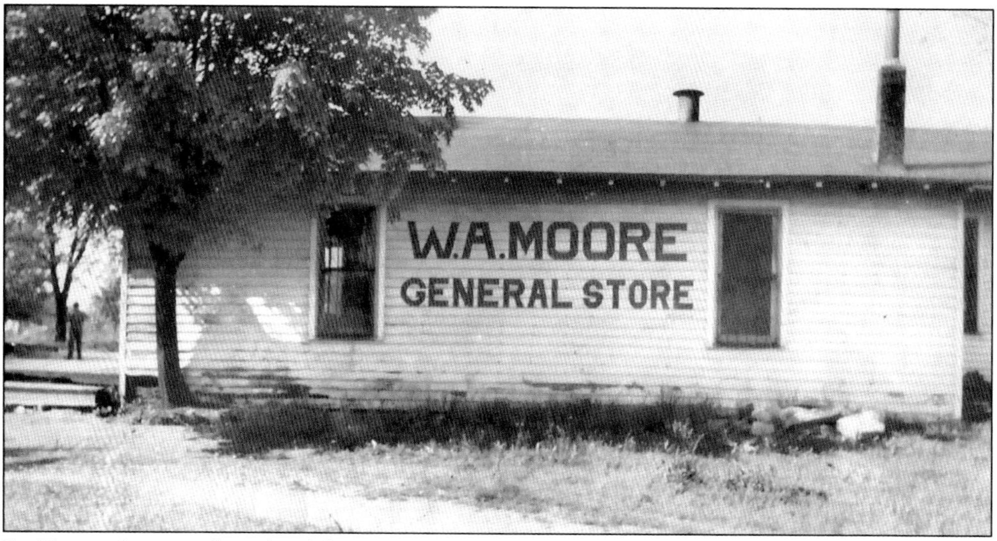

Emblazoned across the side of the store, W. A. Moore General Store was known to all in town. William Moore first went into the store business with his uncle, Race Marshall, whom he later bought out. An excellent businessman, William had only a bit of formal schooling, so he attended the local Moonlight School in order to improve his spelling and writing. One night, he took along his youngest child, Tootsie, who proceeded to help him with the evening's assignment. Her insistence that "been" was spelled "ben" was his only mistake in that night's work. That was the only time she was allowed to attend school with him. (Courtesy of Mayme Ruth "Tootsie" Moore Brooks.)

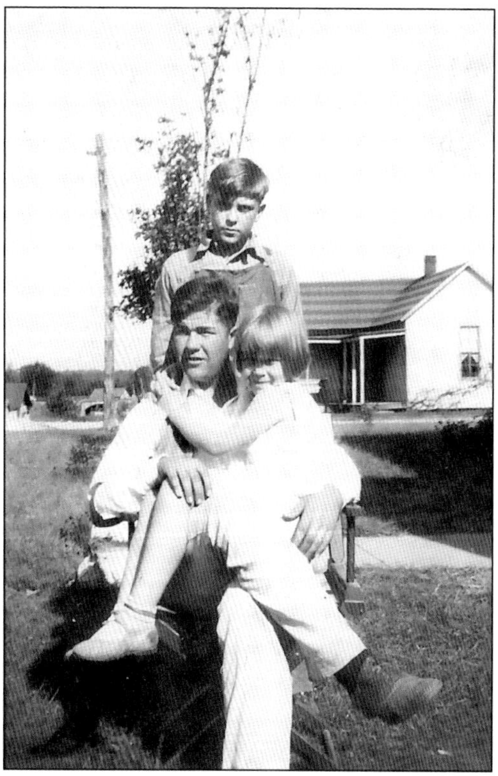

Siblings James, Harold (seated), and Mayme Ruth Moore were photographed in their front yard. The Biggs family home can be seen in the background. A few years later, Harold worked on the construction of Kentucky Dam. (Courtesy of Mayme Ruth "Tootsie" Moore Brooks.)

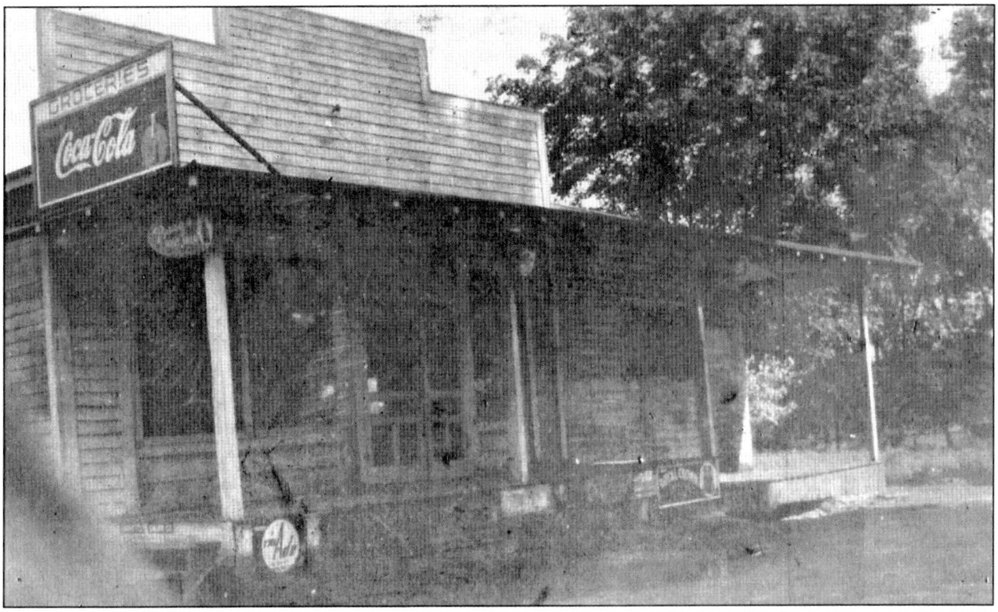

William Moore's store sold a great variety of goods, from horse collars to foods. Moore would only sell Armour brand meat, traded in chickens and eggs, and provided entertainment as well. The store had a radio where the local men would gather each evening to hear Walter Winchell, whose broadcast of the *Jergens Journal* mixed entertainment news with matters of national importance. One of the smaller listeners was Moore's youngest daughter, Mayme Ruth, known as "Tootsie." Even though she was only a young child, Tootsie enjoyed the discussions of politics and events that followed each broadcast. (Courtesy of Mayme Ruth "Tootsie" Moore Brooks.)

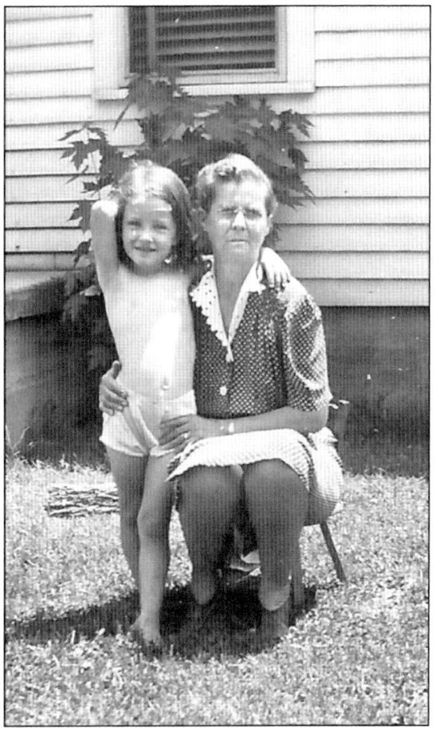

Stella Moore and daughter Faustine were photographed in the dog days of summer in 1942. Faustine, like many young children, played in very little clothing. Marshall County summers were often hot and humid. (Courtesy of Mayme Ruth "Tootsie" Moore Brooks.)

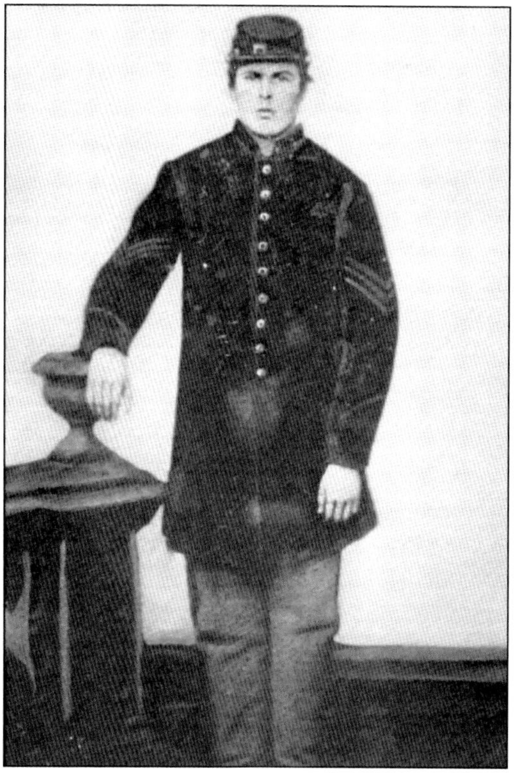

Thomas Fieldson was born in England in 1843 and immigrated to the United States as a child. He entered the Union army at age 17, where he served gallantly, losing a leg during the Battle of Gettysburg. After the Civil War, Fieldson married Ella and lived near Gilbertsville, where he served as postmaster until his death in 1910. Ella and Thomas bore eight children; three of which—Arlene, Lorenz, and Charles—lived to maturity. (Courtesy of Harvey Culp.)

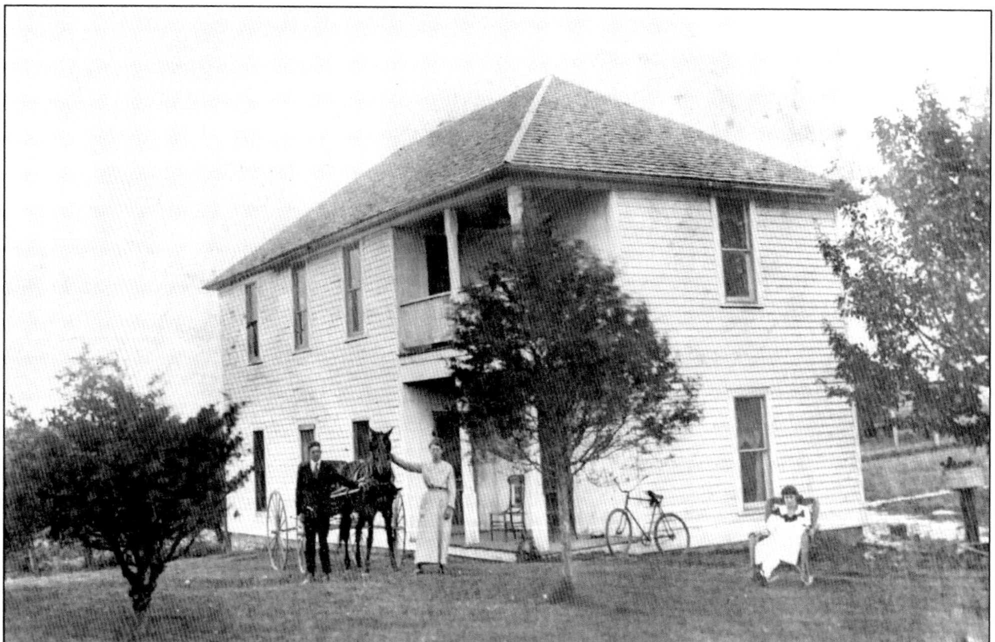

Postmaster Thomas Fieldson and his wife, Ella, enjoyed this home, which was located south of Gilbertsville toward Birmingham. In this *c.* 1920 photograph, Ella; Lorenz, her son; and her daughter, Arlene, are shown. By the early 1930s, Ella, now a widow, had moved to Gilbertsville and her now-married daughter, Arlene, shared this home with her family. (Courtesy of Harvey Culp.)

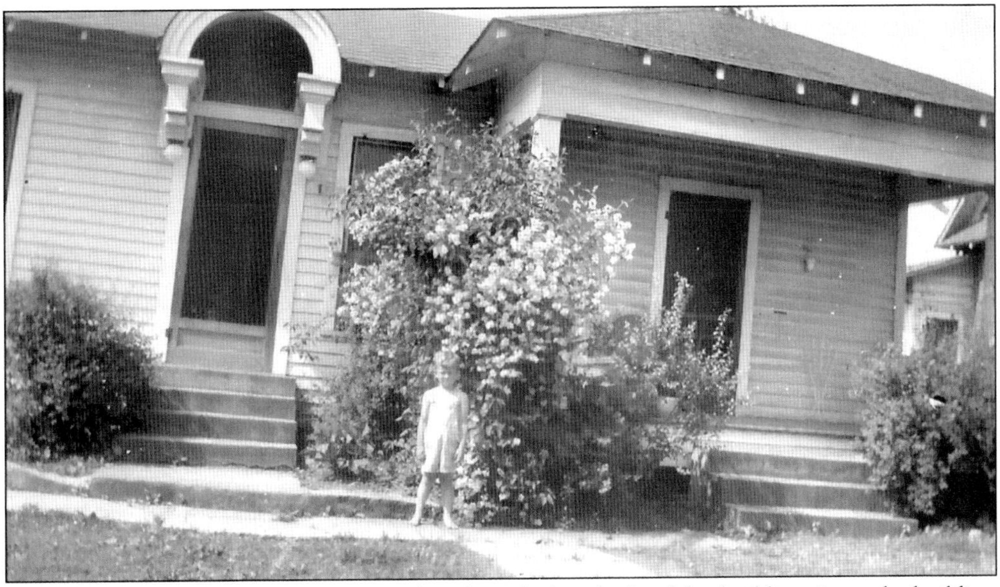

Gilbertsville's first post office was located in the right-hand side of this building. Later the building was enlarged and became the local funeral home. The Moore family moved to this home after the TVA began making plans for the new dam and purchased the Moore home for housing and offices. Harold Keith Moore stands in front of the home; he was William and Stella Moore's grandson, son of Harold "Chub" Moore. (Courtesy of Mayme Ruth "Tootsie" Moore Brooks.)

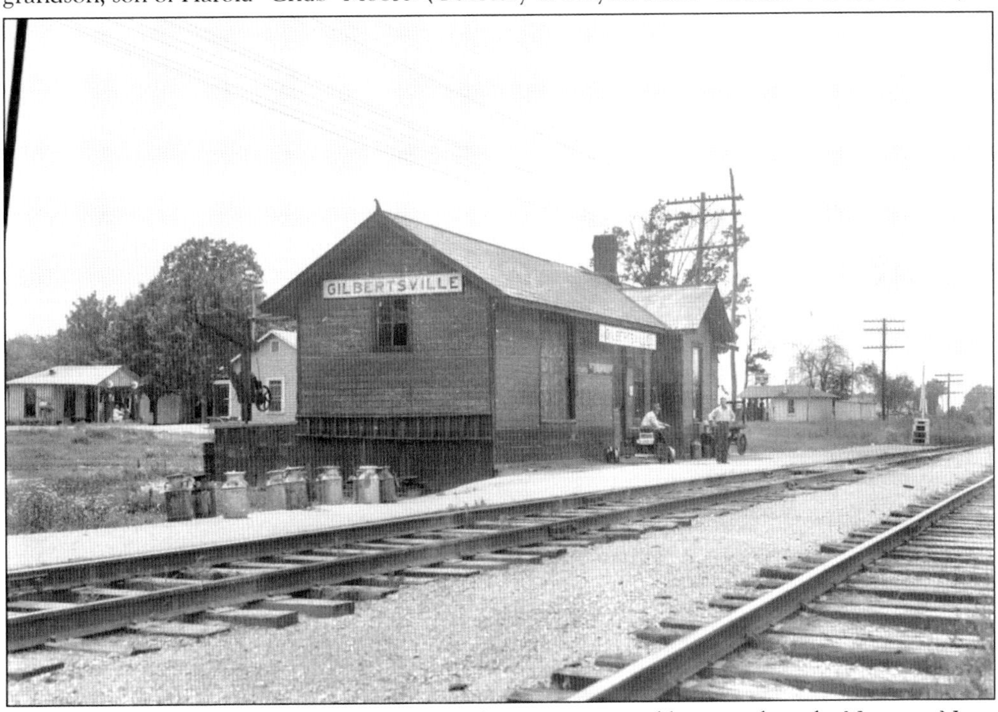

Milk cans sit alongside the Gilbertsville train depot. Various rail lines, such as the Newport News and Mississippi Valley and the Chesapeake, Ohio, and Southwestern, served the community beginning in the early 1870s. The Illinois Central took over the route in 1896. (Courtesy of the U.S. National Archives and Records Administration and the Tennessee Valley Authority.)

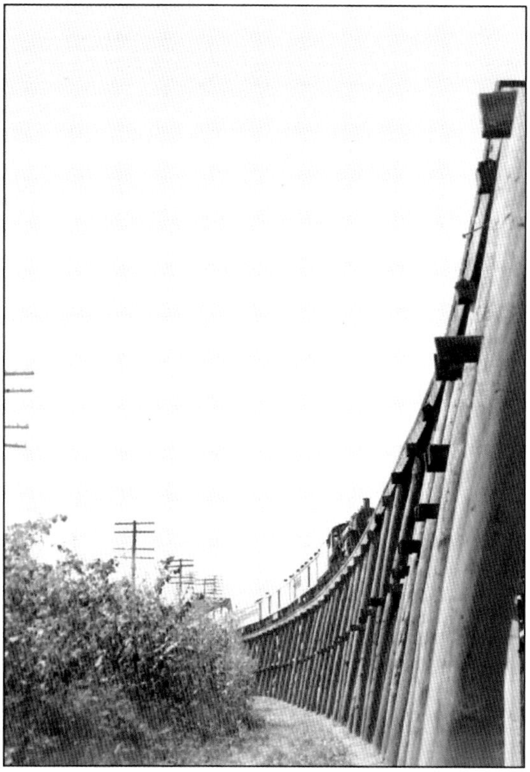

A new bridge brought the Illinois Central Railway to Gilbertsville in 1905 after the old wood and iron drawbridge was condemned. (Courtesy of Bobby Culp and the Tennessee Valley Authority.)

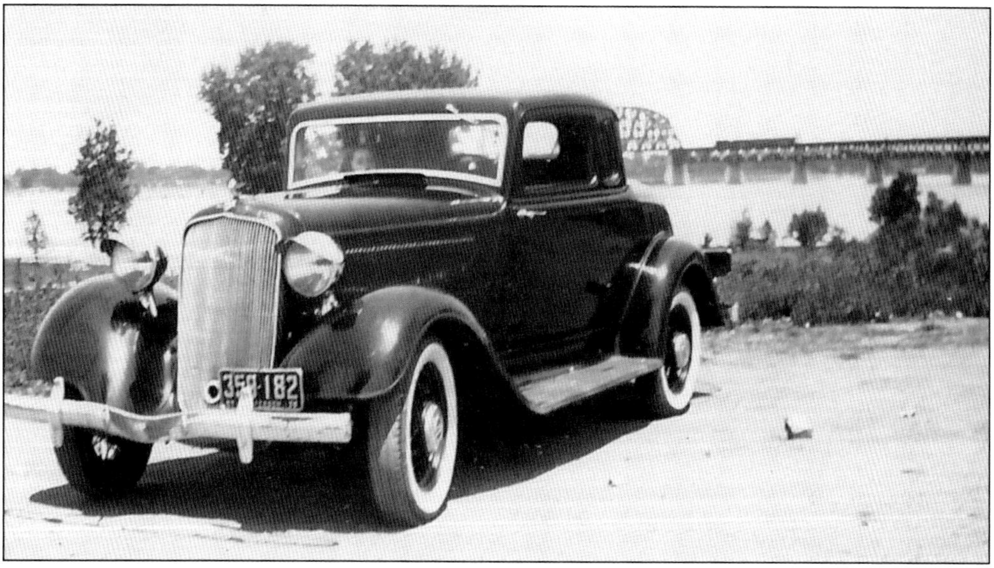

Behind the 1933 Plymouth coupe, one can see the Illinois Central Railroad bridge over the Tennessee River at Gilbertsville in this 1938 photograph. The railroad bridge had a swing span to allow for river traffic. The bridge was removed after completion of new tracks across Kentucky Dam, a joint venture of the Tennessee Valley Authority and Illinois Central Railroad. When the old bridge was demolished, the swing span was moved to Trotter's Landing in Tennessee to make a new bridge for the Nashville, Chattanooga, and St. Louis Railway. During times of low water, the piers from this bridge can still be seen below the dam. (Courtesy of Natalie Fowler Johnston.)

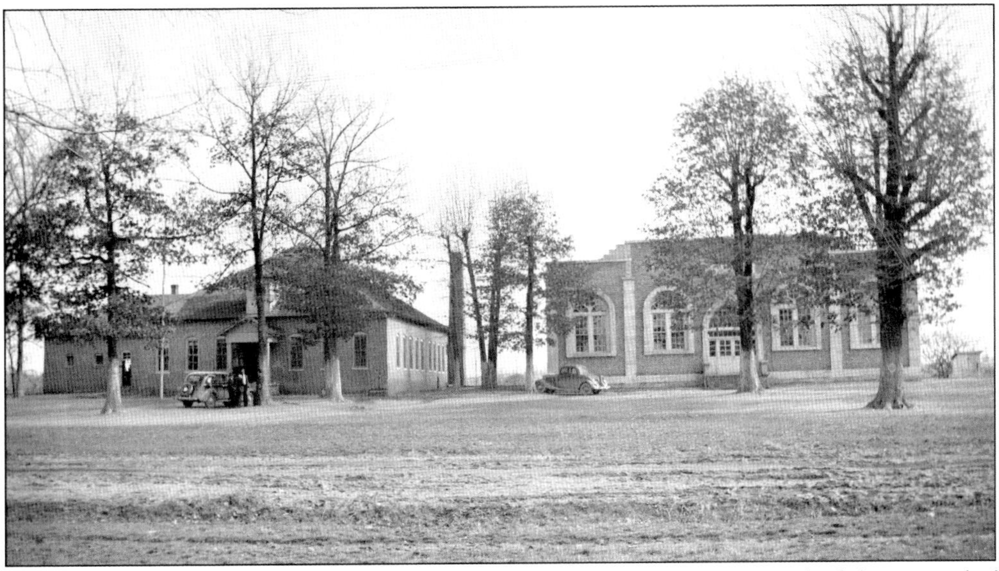

By the late 1920s, Gilbertsville's graded school, high school, and gymnasium (right) consisted of two modern brick buildings. Until 1886, Pinnacle School, two miles south of town, served the local children. That year, Gilbertsville's enterprising citizens rented a room and hired Annie Harrison to teach their children. In 1888, a one-room frame building was built to house the school. In 1902, the one-room school was replaced by a two-story frame building. (Courtesy of the U.S. National Archives and Records Administration and the Tennessee Valley Authority.)

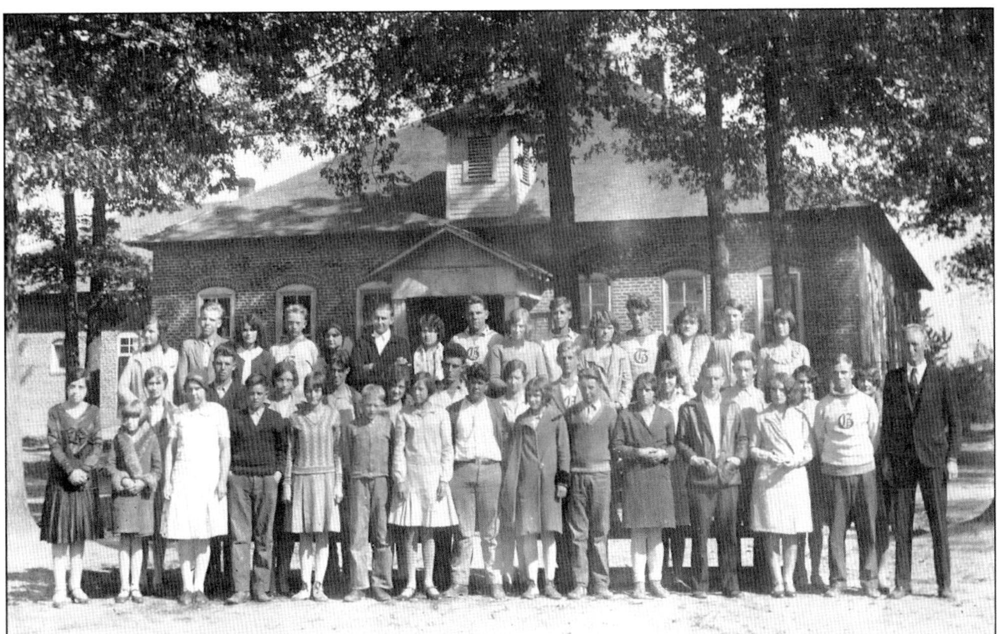

About 1923, the Gilbertsville School's upper grades posed for this photograph in front of their classroom building. Gilbertsville did not have a high school at this time, and students wishing to further their education had to travel to Calvert City, Benton, or Birmingham. Gilbertsville added a high school in 1929. It closed in 1939. (Courtesy of Mayme Ruth "Tootsie" Moore Brooks.)

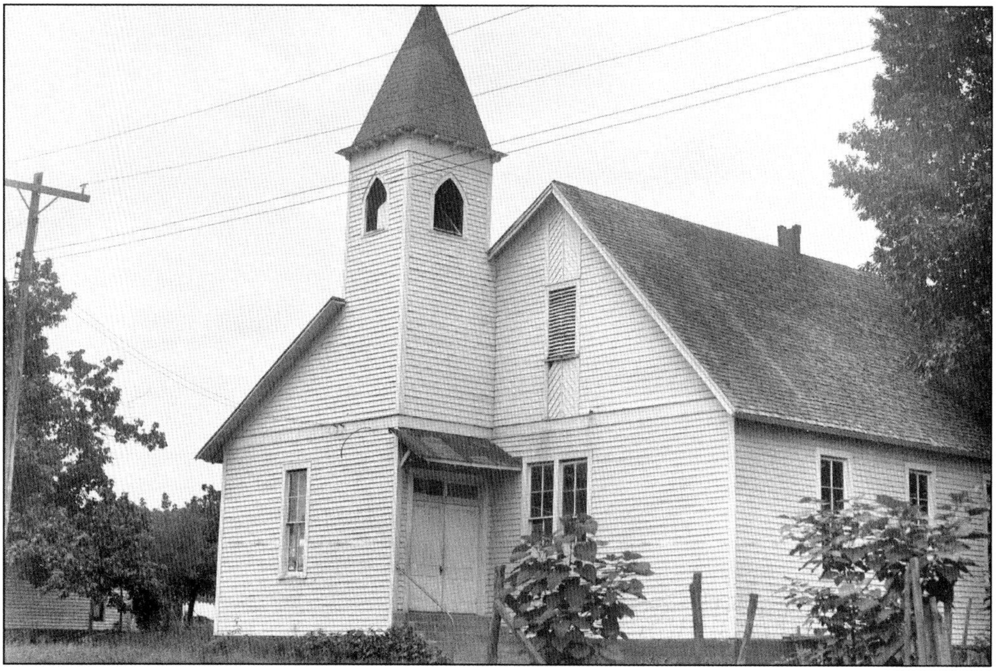

Organized under a brush arbor on August 23, 1893, the Gilbertsville Baptist Church was built in the late 1870s. During the construction of Kentucky Dam, this building was moved to the new settlement of West Gilbertsville. The front extension and bell tower were removed at that time. (Courtesy of the U.S. National Archives and Records Administration and the Tennessee Valley Authority.)

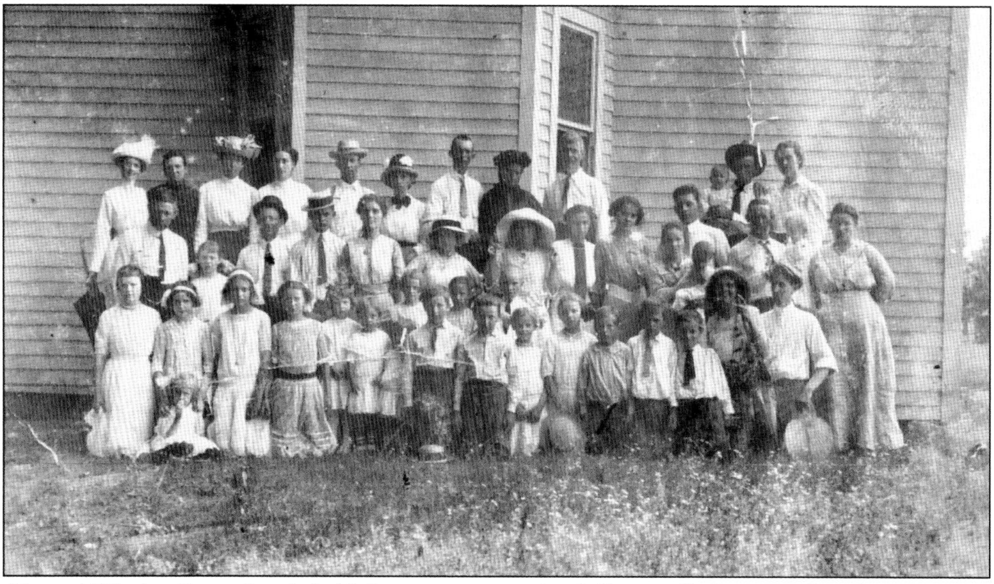

About 1913, the Owen family held their reunion at the Gilbertsville Baptist Church. Dressed in their Sunday finest, they had their photograph made behind the building. On the far right of the second row were Gilbertsville residents Lena Rivers and Leslie Owen holding their son, Paul. In the upper right, the photographer's fingerprint can clearly be seen on this old picture postcard. (Courtesy of the Wade family.)

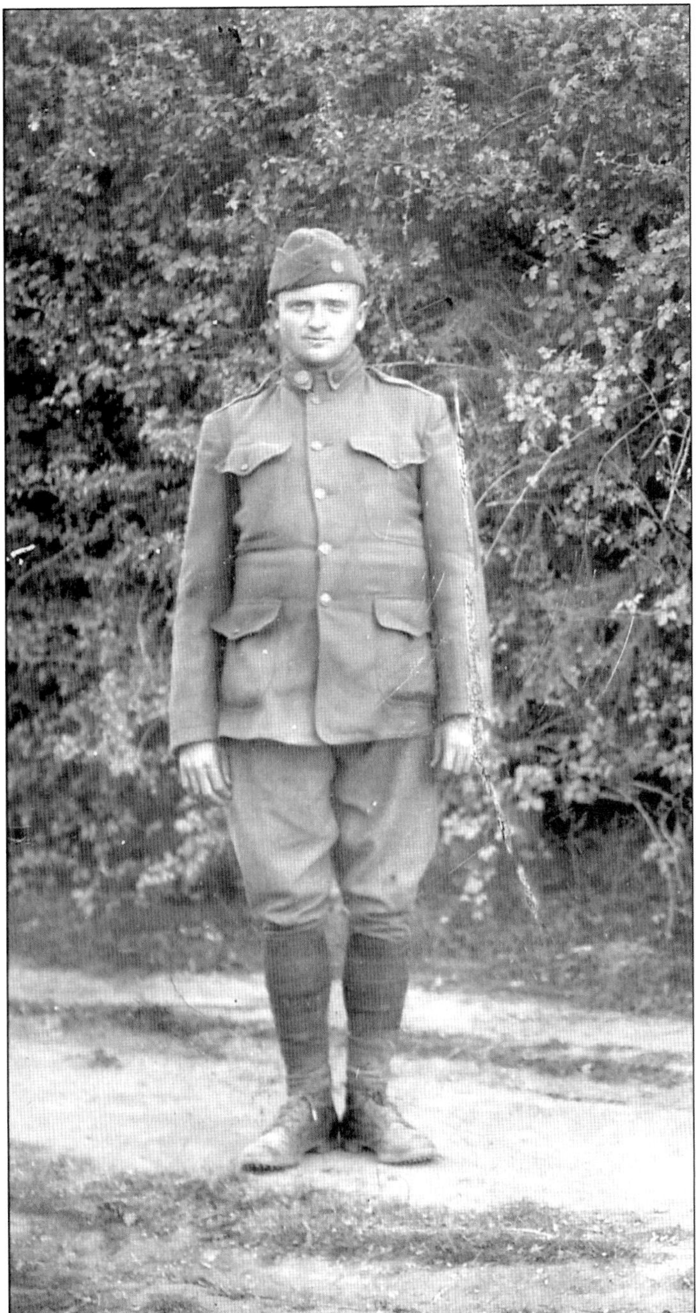

Jessie Anderson Nash sent this photograph to Kathleen Owen of Gilbertsville while he was stationed in France during World War I. He wrote on the back of the card, "The best in France is the present time of course I think so if you don't . . . somewhere in France." Jessie was born in 1895 to Lige and Mattie Nash, who lived near Gilbertsville. Jessie served in Headquarters Company, 323rd Field Artillery and was overseas from June 10, 1918, to May 13, 1919. As the Armistice was signed on November 11, 1918, Jessie most likely wrote this note to Kathleen after that time. (Courtesy of the Donohoo and Capps families.)

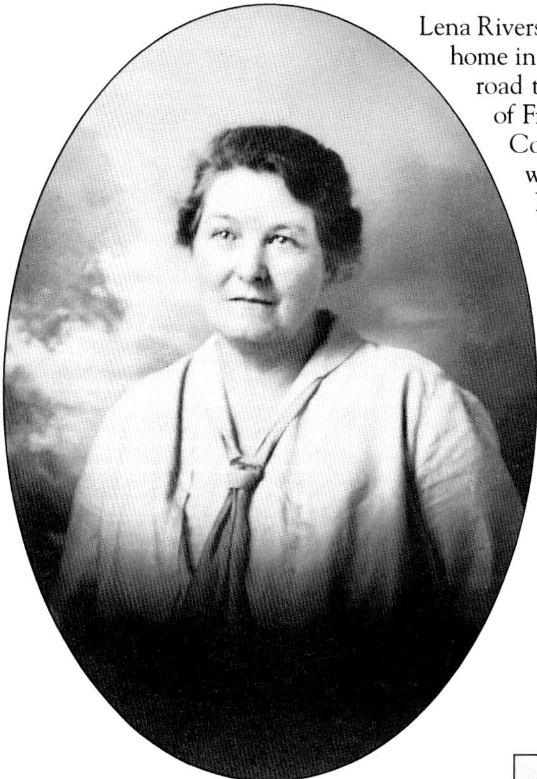

Lena Rivers "Munnie" Scillian Owen stands beside her home in Gilbertsville. The home was located on the road to Calvert City. Munnie was the daughter of Francis Marion Scillian, one of the county's Confederate Civil War veterans. Scillian was assigned to Company A, 3rd Infantry Regiment, Kentucky Volunteers. He fought at Shiloh and Vicksburg and then served under Gen. Nathan Bedford Forrest. Under Forrest's command, his unit returned to Kentucky and fought at Paducah and across the Jackson Purchase. Scillian returned to Gilbertsville after the war, married twice, had nine children, and ran a shanty boat on the Tennessee River. (Courtesy of the Wade family.)

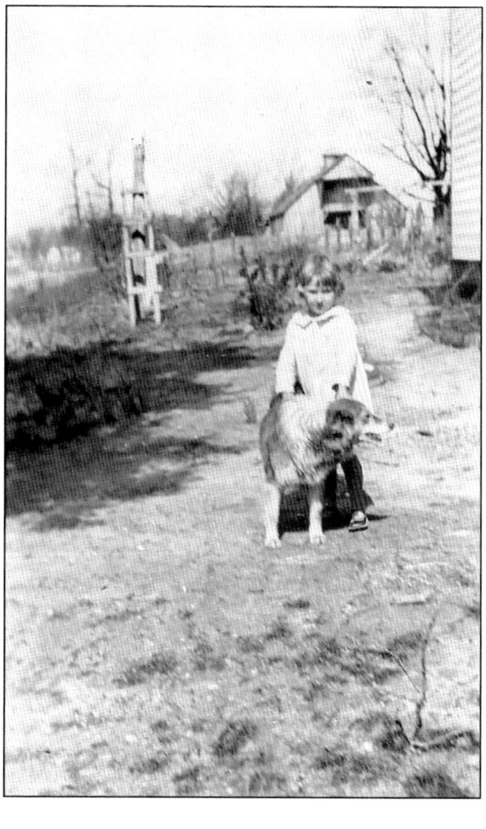

Alma Rivers Donohoo plays in the yard of her Grandmother Owen's house at Gilbertsville with Ol' Shep. In the background can be seen Leslie Owen's distinctive barn with its cupola. This barn is still standing on the edge of TVA property along Kentucky 282. (Courtesy of the Donohoo and Capps families.)

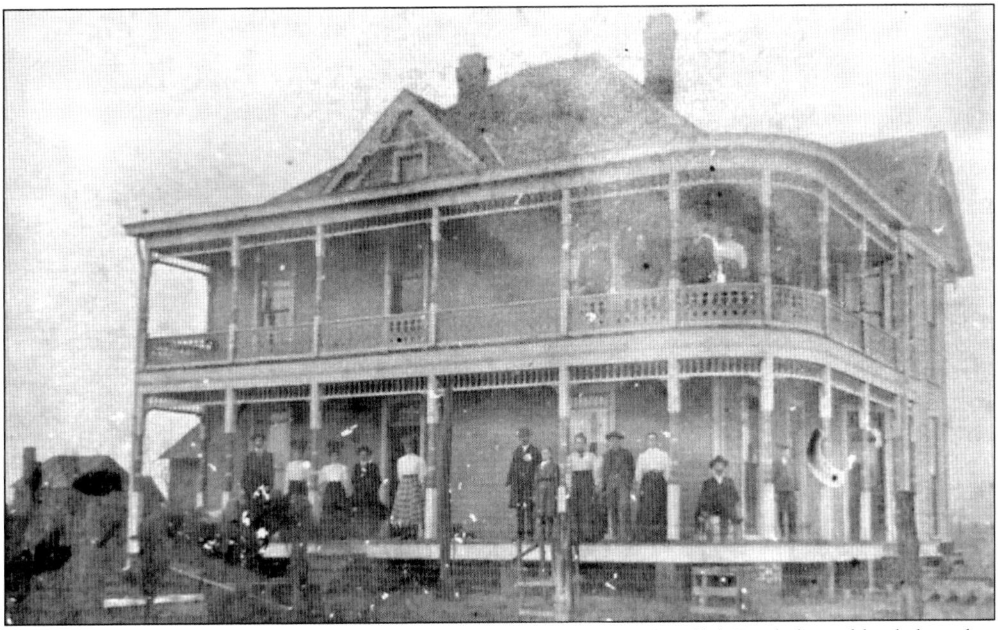

Gilbertsville native Rollie Frank Jenkins married Mary Alice (Molly) English and built her this beautiful home. Rollie and Molly had seven children; three died in infancy. Rollie Frank served as president of the Bank of Gilbertsville, was a merchant and farmer, and attended the Gilbertsville Baptist Church. His son, farmer Rollie Cecil, and his family shared the Jenkins home before it burned. (Courtesy of the Marshall County Genealogical and Historical Society.)

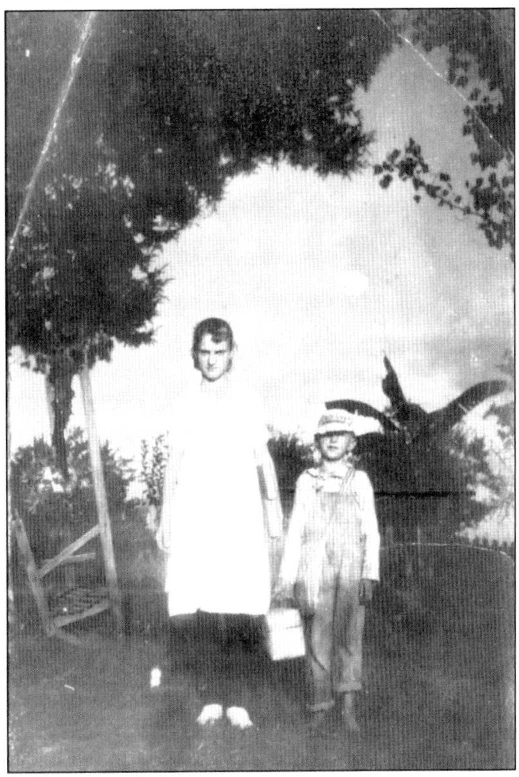

Known as "Teet" and "Mutt," the last of seven children of Gilbertsville residents Lena Rivers and Leslie Owen, they walked to the local, one-room school house carrying their lunch. Teet's nickname was her only slightly older cousin's version of "sweet baby," while Mutt's came from his small stature. The Owen home place was at the west end of the property purchased by the TVA. (Courtesy of the Wade family.)

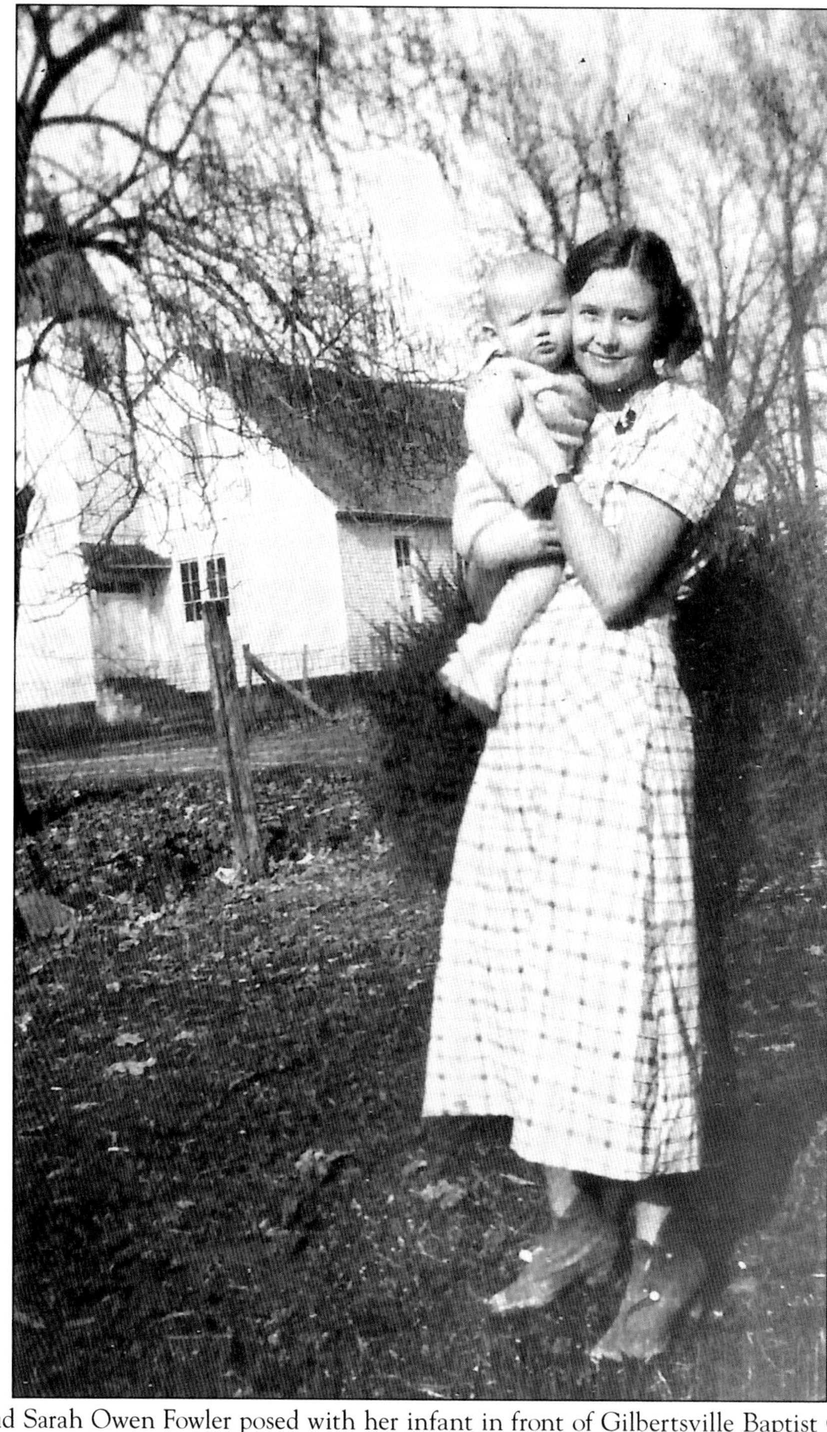

A proud Sarah Owen Fowler posed with her infant in front of Gilbertsville Baptist Church. Sarah's grandfather, John H. Owen of Ohio County, for whom her father was named, was the first of the family to move to Marshall County. John opened a hotel at Gilbertsville about 1879. He died of typhoid in 1882. John left two daughters and five sons. John Jr. was less than a year old when his father died. (Courtesy of Natalie Fowler Johnston.)

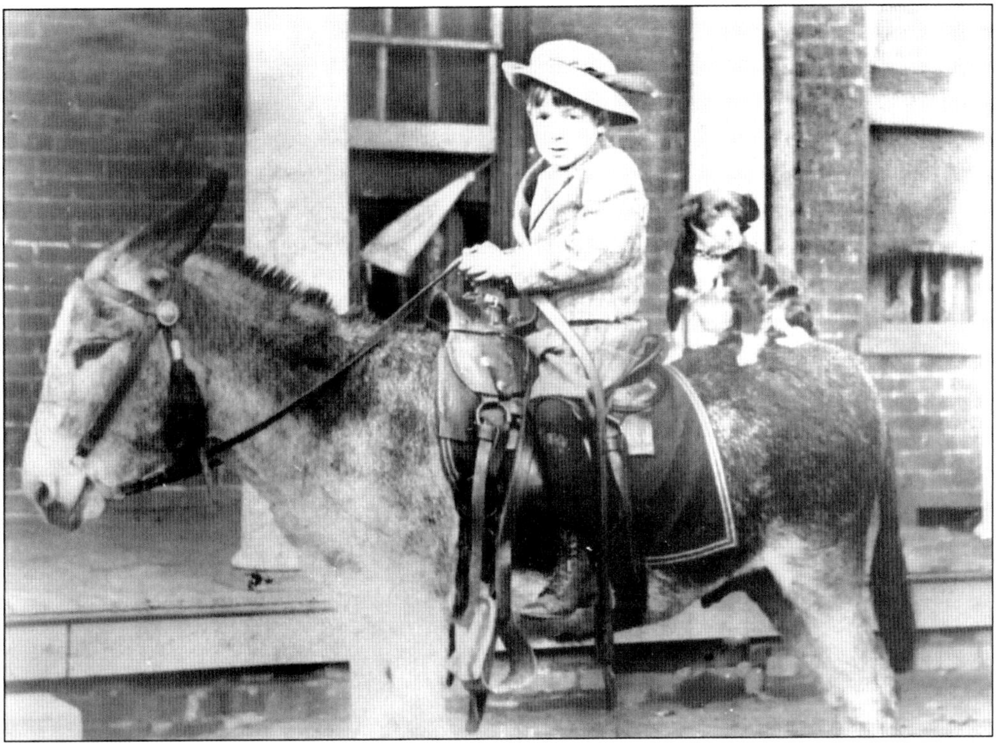

A traveling photographer captured this image of Floyd Berry Wade, age seven. The donkey and dog belonged to the photographer. Floyd's father, James Jessie Wade, worked for the Illinois Central Railroad. Floyd, later known as "Shine," became an ironworker and helped to build several suspension bridges, including the world's longest over Mackinac Straits in Michigan. (Courtesy of the Wade family.)

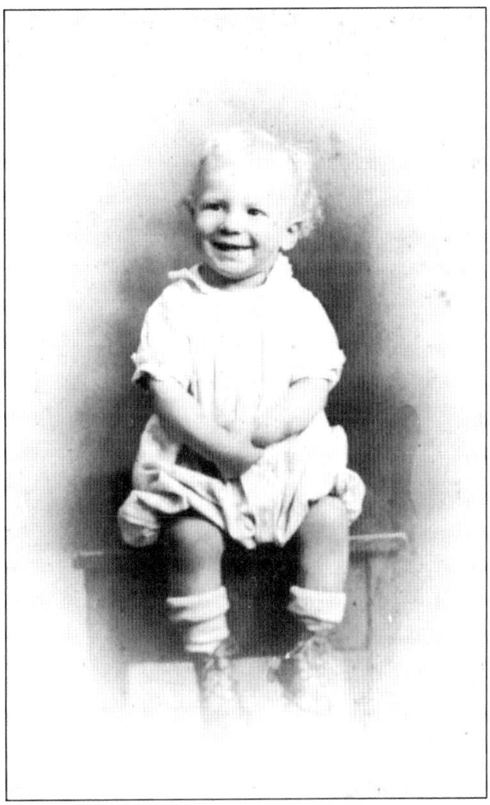

James Leslie, known as J. L., was the child of Floyd and Marion Wade. J. L. remembered a story about his Poppa Owen, who once bought a pair of black mules over in Livingston County and worked them in a good manner. J. L. would take him a drink of water late in the day just so he could ride one of the mules home. One day, as the mule bent to drink, J. L. slipped over the collar and right into the pond. "By jinx," said Poppa, "that's the wrong place to be." (Courtesy of the Wade family.)

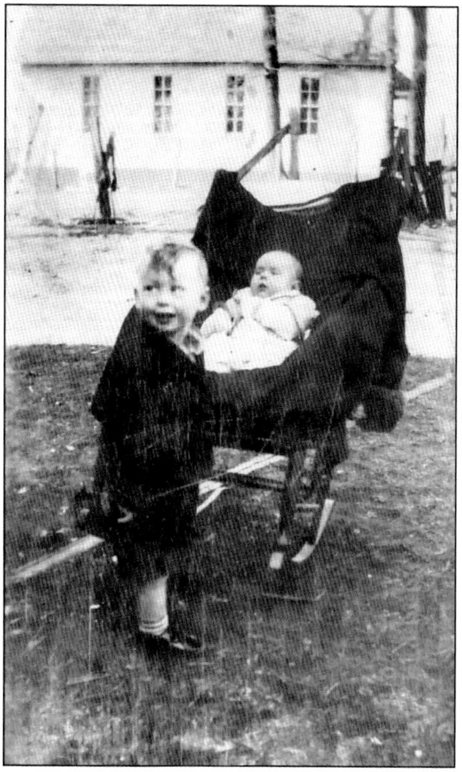

Harvey Culp checked out his baby brother, Bobby, in the side yard of grandmother Ella Fieldson's home next to the Gilbertsville Methodist Church in 1930. (Courtesy of Harvey and Bobby Culp.)

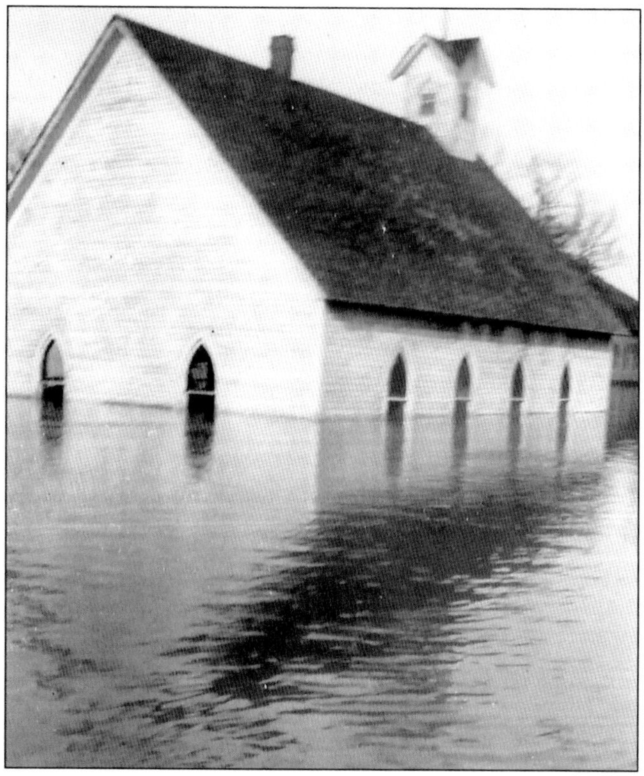

Gilbertsville's Church of Christ sits amid the floodwaters of 1937. Gilbertsville sat on the first and second terraces above the Tennessee River. On the first terrace parallel to the river were its three churches, school, gymnasium, and many of its homes. On the second terrace sat its main street business district, rail depot, and additional homes. In 1937, floodwaters covered the first terrace, causing extensive damage to that part of town. Few businesses and homes on the second terrace received flood damage. (Courtesy of Mayme Ruth "Tootsie" Moore Brooks.)

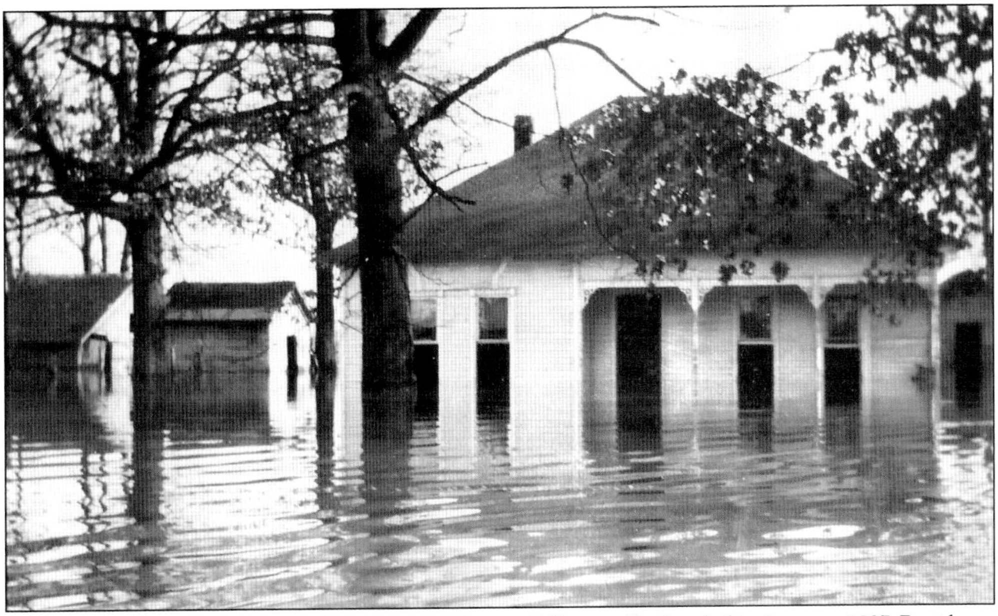

Like every low-lying area along the Tennessee River, Gilbertsville flooded in January 1937. Residents who remember the flood speak of a time of hardship but also of a time of sharing. Families whose homes did not flood took in whole families. Children played and entertained themselves, the women worked tirelessly to cook for those who were homeless, and the men worked unselfishly to salvage personal belongings and livestock. (Courtesy of Harvey Culp.)

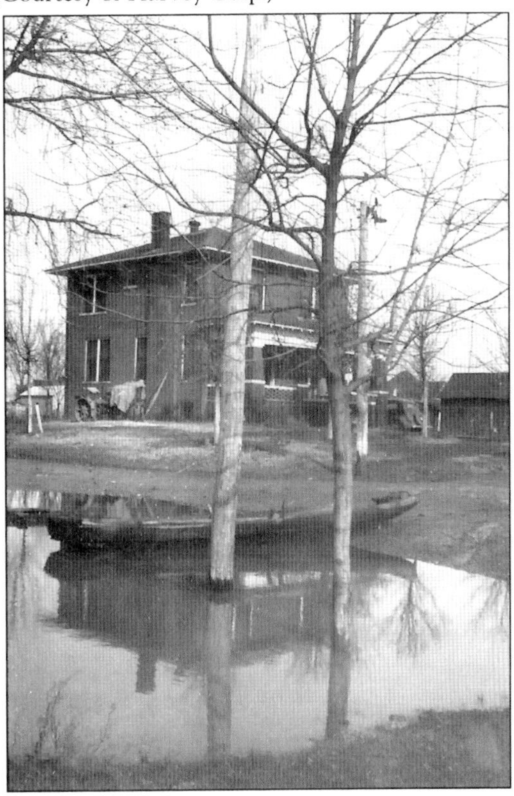

Mr. Shirley Jones's brick house sat on the second terrace from the river. The standing water in the roadway in front of the house is as close as the 1937 floodwaters came. Shirley Jones was a prosperous, respected farmer and owned a tractor, which can be seen parked next to the home. (Courtesy of Mayme Ruth "Tootsie" Moore Brooks.)

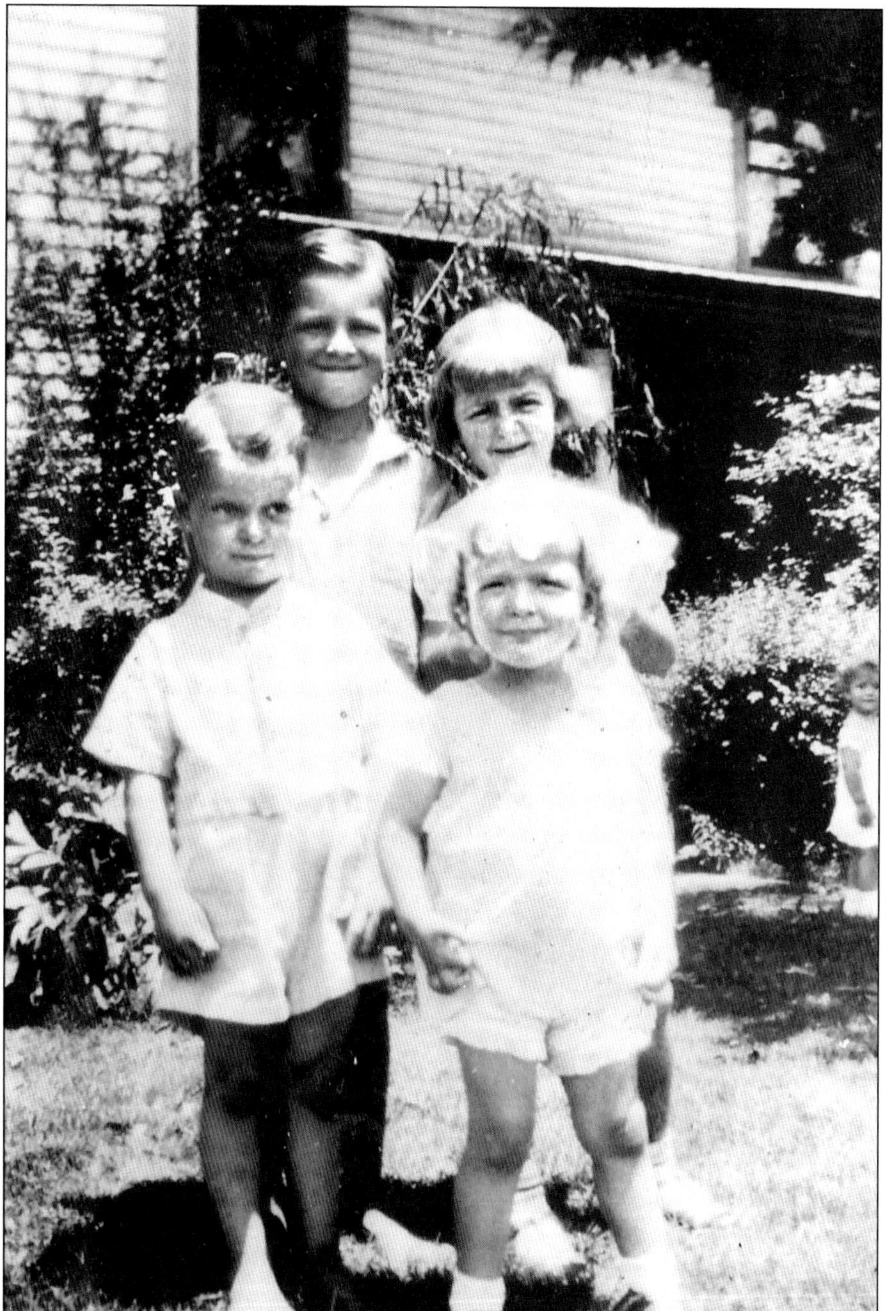

Four Wade siblings and a cousin can be seen in this c. 1935 photograph taken at the Gilbertsville home of their Owen grandparents. The boys are Peter (front left) and James Leslie (J. L.). Katie stands next to J. L., and in front is Lena Carl, known as Sissa. Off to the side is cousin Amelia Donohoo. Descended from some of Gilbertsville first residents, their family included farmers, railroad men, teachers, fishermen, and shanty boat operators. Like many children born in the late 1920s and early 1930s, they saw and remember the changes wrought by the TVA and the building of Kentucky Dam. Their ties to the county remain strong. (Courtesy of the Wade family.)

Six

NORTHEAST

Looking at an early topographical map of Marshall County, one would note that the northeastern portion of the county was dominated by river bottoms, some cypress swamp, and low-lying hills covered with forests. Cypress Creek, which runs into the Tennessee River, has high banks surrounded by rich farming land.

Gilbertsville and Birmingham sat beside the Tennessee River. Briensburg, Tatumsville, and later Draffenville developed as small, inland communities. Small and large farms dominated the landscape. This chapter looks at those communities that developed and then often disappeared to be remembered only as road names.

Briensburg, once incorporated, was laid out in 17 city blocks. Early on, Briensburg residents organized two churches. Before 1860, James Lindsay and others built a log church, which they named Union Church. It was associated with the Christian denomination and later renamed the Briensburg Church. The Briensburg Methodist Church was organized in 1854 and included members from the old Mount Vernon church. The town prospered until the beginning of the 20th century. As the early 1890s brought rail transportation to Benton, Briensburg began its decline. Its post office closed in 1904. Many of those who departed Birmingham with the building of Kentucky Dam settled in the Briensburg area.

Draffenville developed much later as construction began on Kentucky Dam and people traveled along Highway 641 toward Benton. Named for Charlie Draffen, the area was noted for being a "wild place" before the county went dry.

Some remembered early one-room schools include Bailey and Stice (both near Tatumsville). Locust Grove (southwest of Gilbertsville) along with Lone Valley and Wilson Ridge (both between Calvert City and Gilbertsville) served farming families around that small town. Norwell School (just west of Draffenville), Briensburg, Pugh, Union Church (near Forgotten Past Museum on Highway 68), and White Oak (near Briensburg) collected children from farms in the eastern central portion of the county. Both Pinnacle and Point Necessity were located between Gilbertsville and Birmingham.

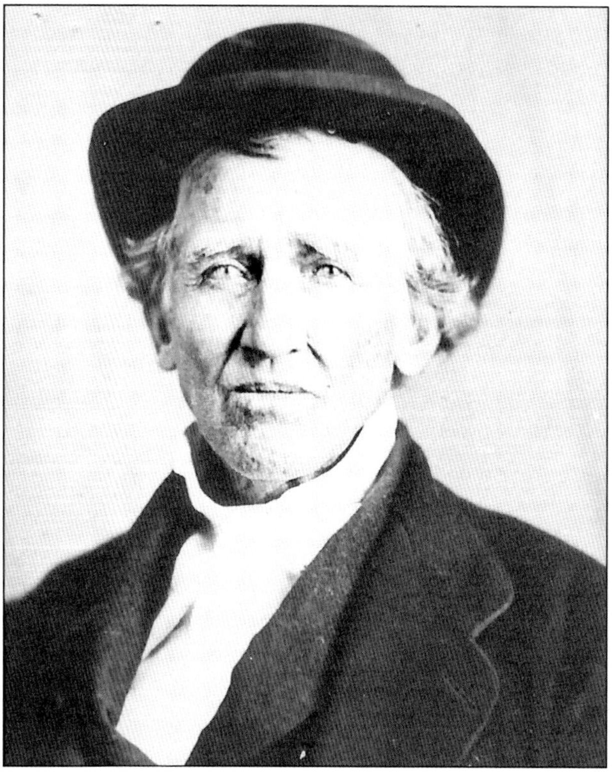

James Boyd Brien, a blacksmith by trade, settled in the area later to be named for him around 1819. James Brien served in the state legislature and was instrumental in the founding of Marshall County. Briensburg incorporated in 1861. By 1894, Briensburg claimed three general stores, one millinery shop, two blacksmiths, two churches (Christian and Methodist), one large school, a Masonic Lodge, a hotel, a tobacco warehouse, and three doctors. (Courtesy of James Boyd "Buck" Brien.)

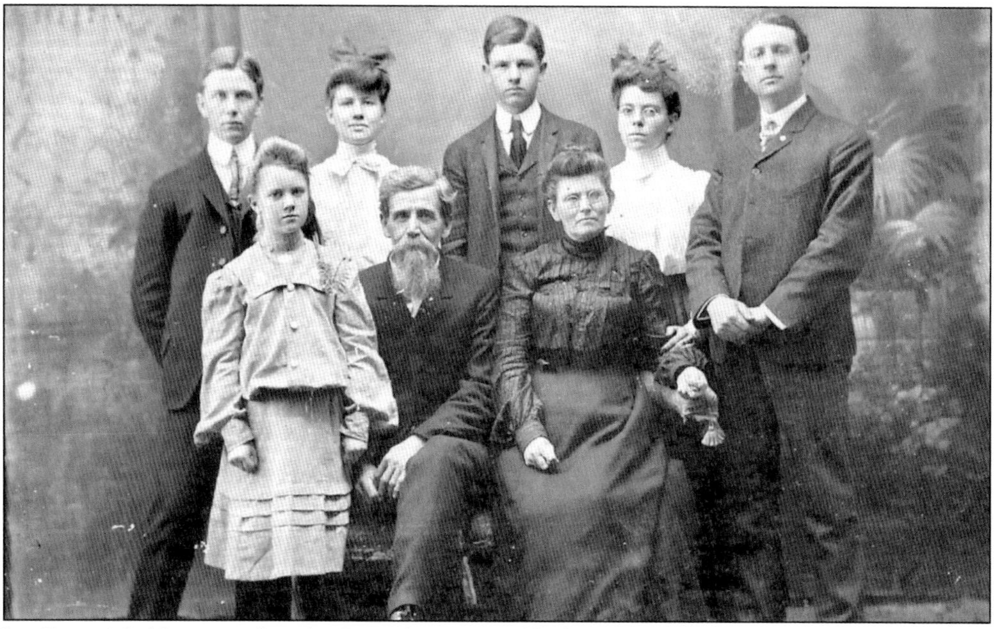

Ira Owen Maddox served as the Briensburg area's blacksmith around the early part of the 20th century. Ira's family included, from left to right, (front row) his daughter, Willa May; Ira; and wife, Mary Sanders Maddox; (second row) his children Harry Davis, Lake (or Linda), Raymond, Sue (or Sadie), and Ernest. Ernest taught at Oak Ridge School in 1894. This photograph was made c. 1902. (Courtesy of the Marshall County Genealogical and Historical Society.)

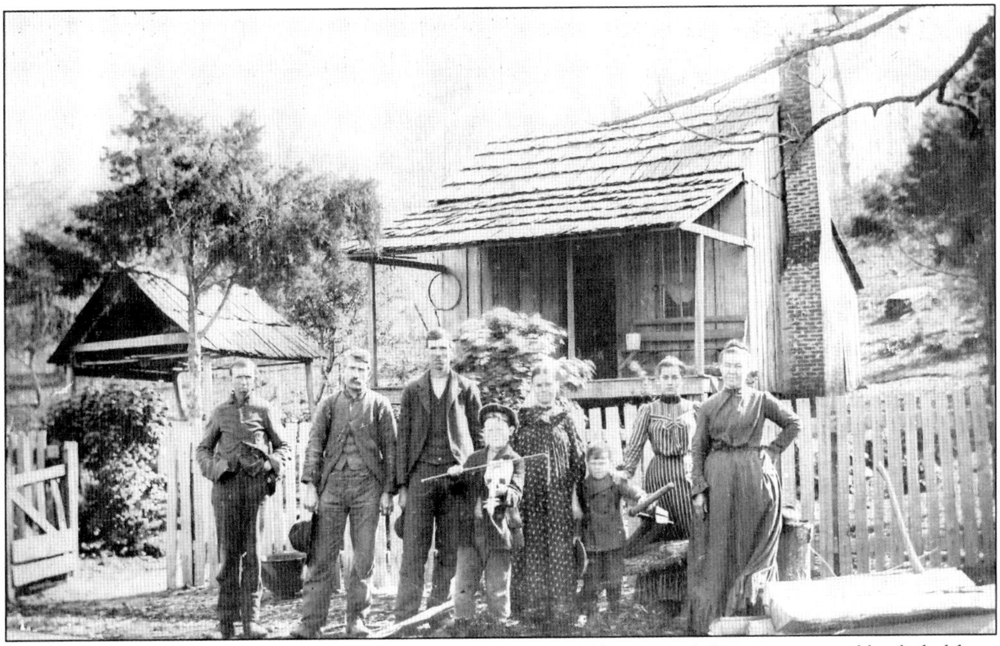

Rhoda Cross Crenshaw Mullinax Hardison (fifth from left) married three times and had children by each husband. Her boys Oscar Mullinax (sixth from left) and Anderson Crenshaw stand beside her about 1910. Her husband J. W. Hardison stands third from left. Also shown are her mother (far right), a sister, and two men who boarded with the family. Rhoda was pregnant with her third son, William Hasting Hardison, when this photograph was taken. Their home was located near the crossroads of Highways 641 and 58. (Courtesy of Billy Hardison.)

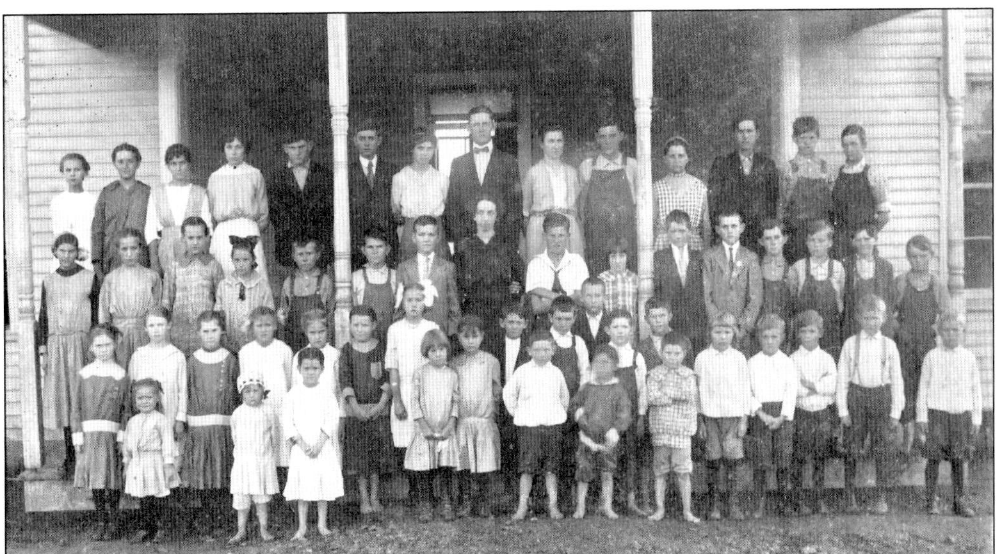

Lizzie Lee taught the younger students at Lone Valley School in 1915. Lone Valley School was built about 1900 just south of Tan Yard Spring. The school may have replaced Sedge Grass School, which was moved nearer to Calvert City. The family of Essie Pearl McGregor (second from the left, second row from top) saved this keepsake. (Courtesy of Billy Hardison.)

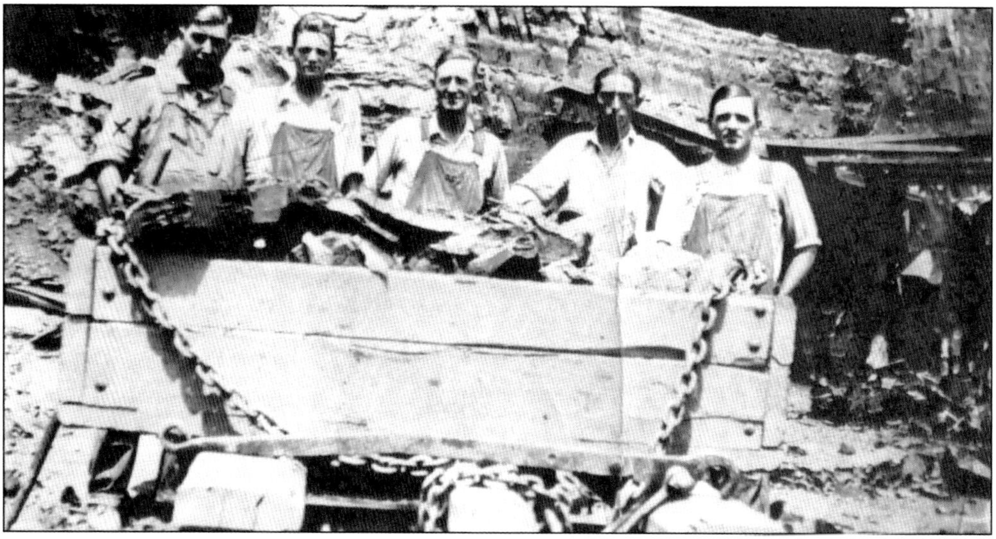

Frank Burradell's farm, north of Briensburg, contained a large supply of kaolin clay. Thousands of tons were shipped to various potteries across the country at a high price before 1928, when the mine closed. Amos Penney, far left, led this crew, *c.* 1920. One of the men is his brother, James Clifford Penney, who was killed during operations at the pit on December 15, 1925. A large mine pit can be seen today off the Old Tatumsville Road. (Courtesy of Claude Nimmo.)

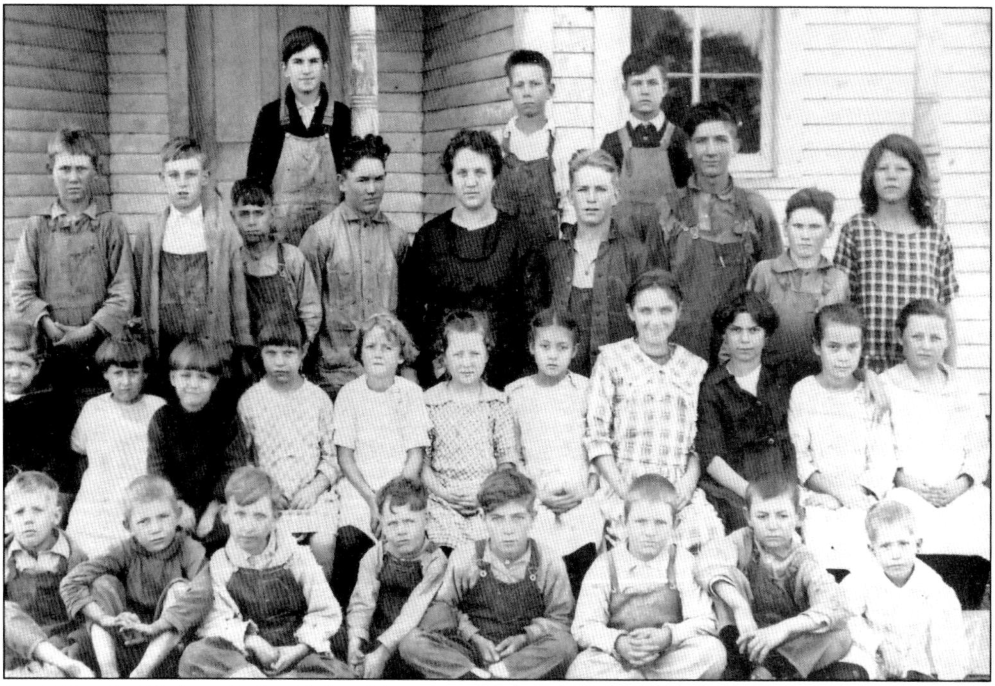

In 1922, the Wilson Ridge School between Calvert and Gilbertsville was taught by Prudy Lawrence. Surnames that year included Driver (four students) and three each of Williams, Swain, Snow, and Egner. Also attending were two named Smith, Fowler, Devine, English, and Margeline. Other names include Sparks, Coursey, Shadwick, Lawrence, and Bean. (Courtesy of Natalie Fowler Johnston.)

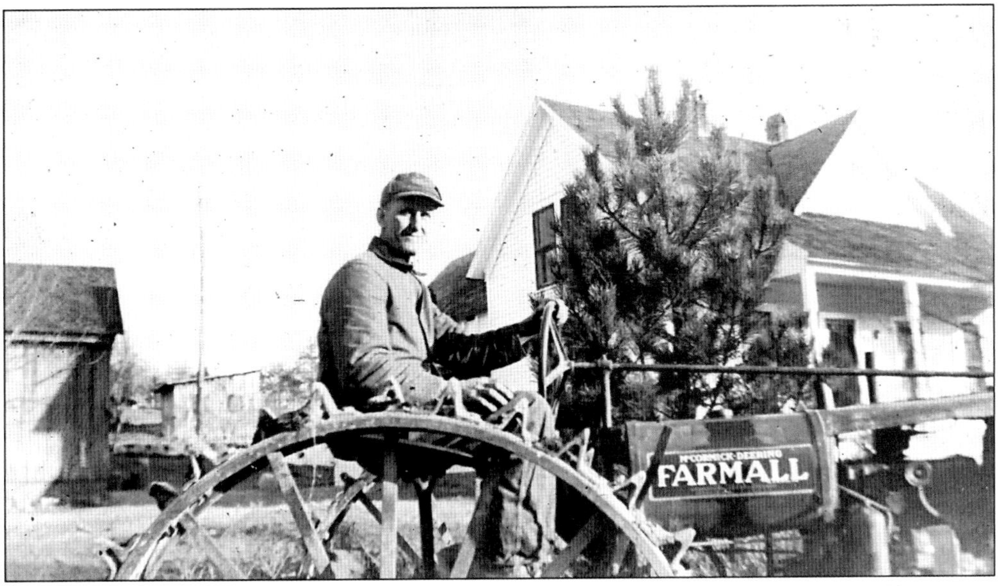

William Fisher Powell was mighty proud of his new McCormick-Deering Farmall Tractor. International Harvester produced their first tractor in 1906 and also produced tractors under the brand names of Farmall, McCormick-Deering, Mogul, and Titan. The Farmall name was introduced in 1924. William also owned a stone burr gristmill that ran from a small engine. Sherman, his son, remembers that when the engine was cranked, it sounded like a shotgun going off and that all of the neighbors knew when William was ready to grind grain. (Courtesy of Sherman Powell.)

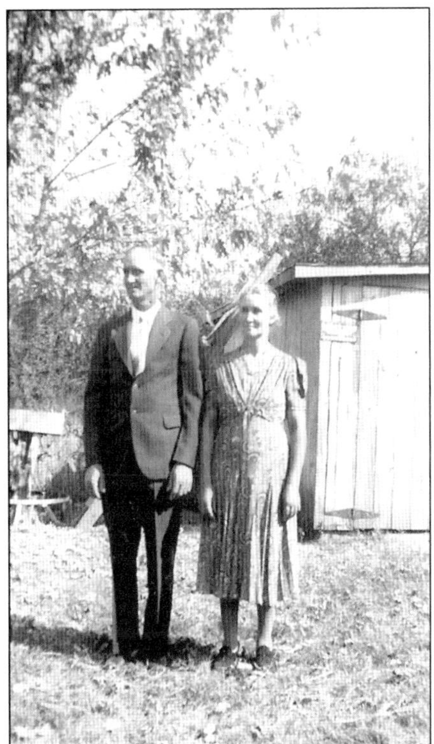

William Fisher Powell and Minnie Pearl stood in their yard for this informal snapshot. The Powell family owned a large farm off the Tatumsville Road. (Courtesy of Sherman Powell.)

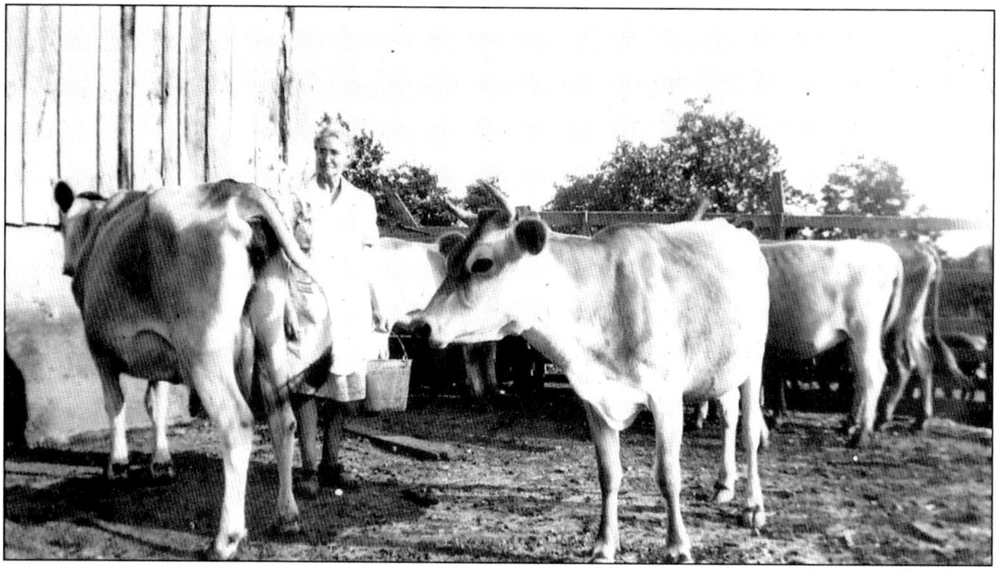

Minnie Pearl Powell was preparing to milk her cows when this *c.* 1935 photograph was taken. Most families owned at least one dairy cow to provide the family's milk and butter. Large farms often owned several dairy cows, and the excess milk and butter were traded or sold to the local store. The Powell family needed a lot of milk with four boys and four girls. (Courtesy of Sherman Powell.)

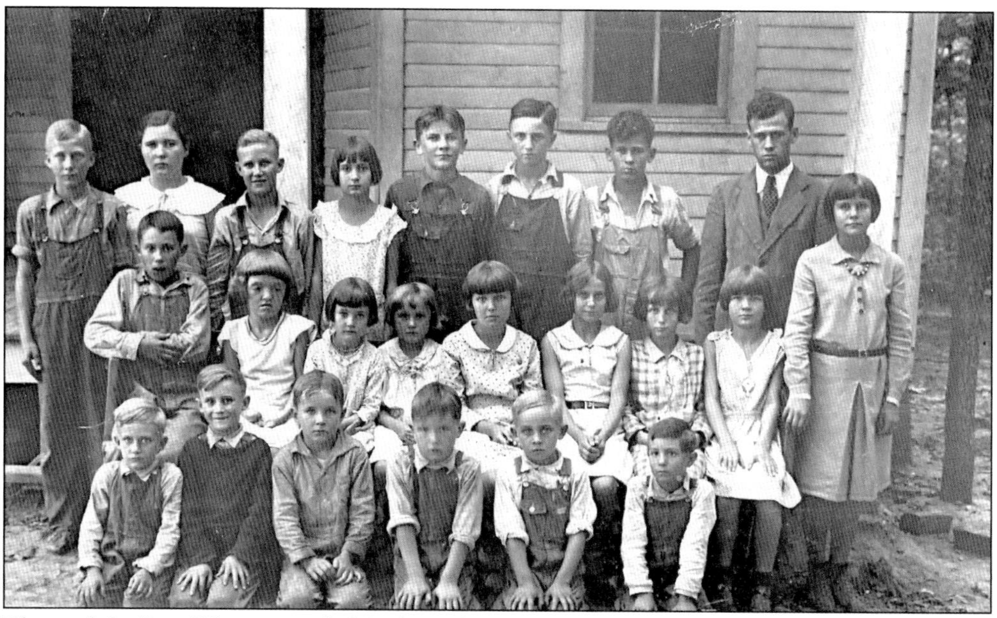

Three of the Powell boys attended Bailey School at Tatumsville during the 1930 to 1931 school year. Kneeling far left is Sherman Powell beside his brother, Thomas Marshall. On the third row, third from the left, is brother Owsley. Hubert Jaco of Gilbertsville was the teacher. Sherman and Thomas both served in World War II. Thomas was killed during fighting for the Philippine Islands. (Courtesy of Sherman Powell.)

Seven

SOUTHEAST

Hardin, Aurora, Egner's Ferry, Olive, Hamlet, Maple Springs, Booker Holler, Fair Dealing, Jonestown, and Walnut Grove are names that bring back memories to Marshall County residents familiar with the southeastern portion of the county. Forgotten schools include Cap Spring and Clark, which were near Fair Dealing. Heights, Liberty, Johnson, Joppa, and Salem were all near Olive. Unity was east of Jonathan Creek near Aurora, as was Alford School. Collie was located near the mouth of Jonathan Creek.

On the banks of the Tennessee River near the Calloway County line sat Egner's Ferry, so named for the ferry service and the small store located there. Nearby Aurora had a post office, a grocery, and a school named for John Alford, an early settler.

Just north along Highway 68 was Fair Dealing, first settled sometime after 1800 by John and Martha Faughn. Their son, Enos, built a store at the crossroads of Highway 68 and the Olive-Birmingham Road and called the store Fair Dealing.

Hardin, once a booming town, was named for landowner Hardin Irvan, who owned the land on which the rail depot was constructed. Laid out in 1891, Hardin was a stop on the Paducah, Tennessee, and Alabama Railway. The first resident in the area was most likely a man named Shemwell who lived in a covered wagon while building his one-room home and photography studio.

The old settlement of Olive may have been started by J. H. Chandler and his wife, who gave land for a church and cemetery about 1856. By 1884, the community had a post office, two general stores, a grocery store, a gristmill, and a blacksmith shop.

The Hamlet, Maple Springs, and Walnut Grove communities grew up around churches, schools, and small stores. Despite their lack of size or amenities, many county residents boasted of being from one of these small entities.

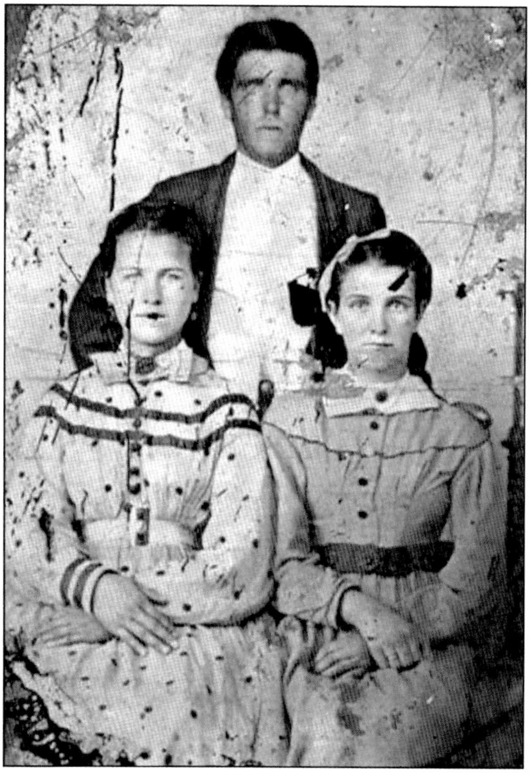

An old tintype shows Lyman Harvey Eggner and his bride, Nannie Alice Berkley, of Trigg County. The girl on the left is believed to be Lyman's sister. Lyman's father purchased the ferry at Aurora about 1848. In 1878, Lyman took over the business. He married Nannie the next year. Lyman died in 1885. Nannie then married Stephen Anthony Whale from Pennsylvania. They operated the ferry until about 1932 before they sold out and moved to Oklahoma. (Courtesy of Claude Nimmo.)

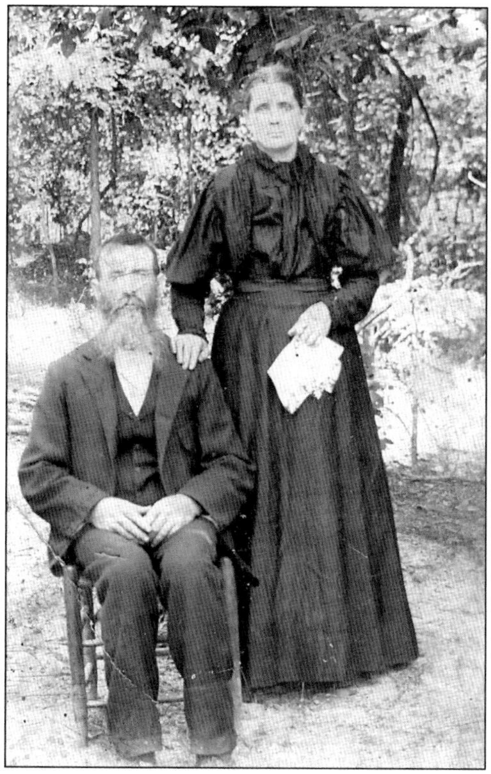

By 1870, Henderson and Nancy Henson lived southeast of Benton on a 300-acre farm. Henry divided the farm between their three daughters, Mary, George Anna, and Rosella, in his will. Today Wyatt family descendants, through Rosella, own the original 300 acres and still live in the farmhouse. (Courtesy of Louise Norton Wyatt.)

The first Methodist church organized in the Jackson Purchase was located in Marshall County. Organized in 1869, by Parson Ogden at the home of Farrar Dunn, it was called Dunn Church for three years before the name Mount Vernon was adopted. Mount Carmel Methodist Church, built in 1881, is a direct descendant of this early church. They built their current brick structure in 1958. (Courtesy of the Marshall County Genealogical and Historical Society.)

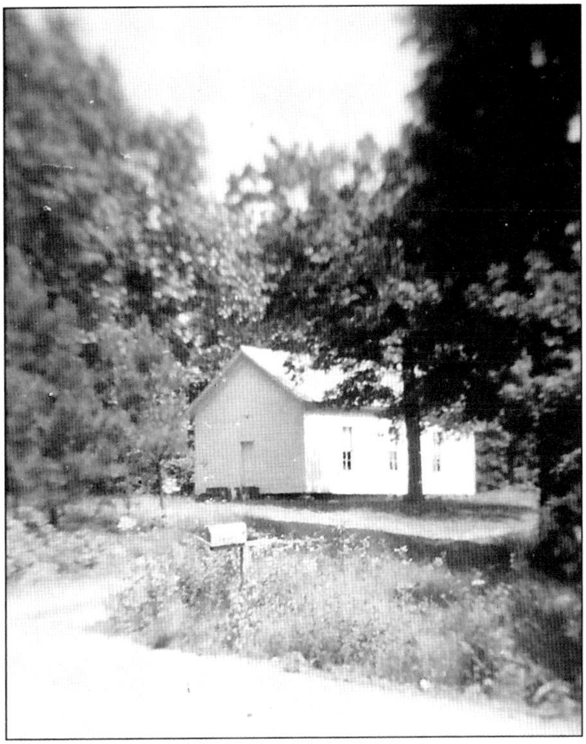

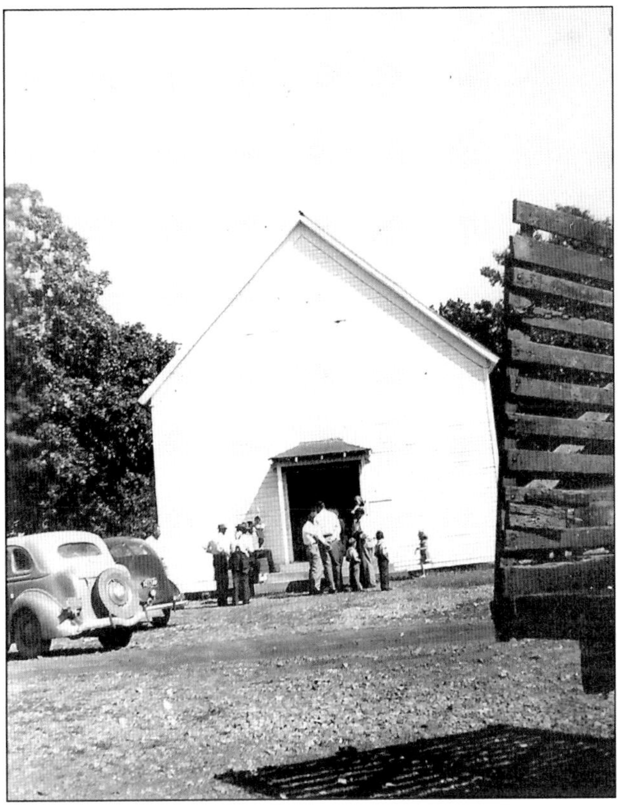

Union Ridge Baptist Church of Christ of Mount Carmel was founded in 1881. Ten years later, it became the Union Ridge Baptist Church. In 1981, the congregation celebrated their 100th anniversary by arriving at church dressed in period clothing and riding in wagons and buggies and on horseback. Their church bell joyously rang 100 times for each year of their historic existence. (Courtesy of the Marshall County Genealogical and Historical Society.)

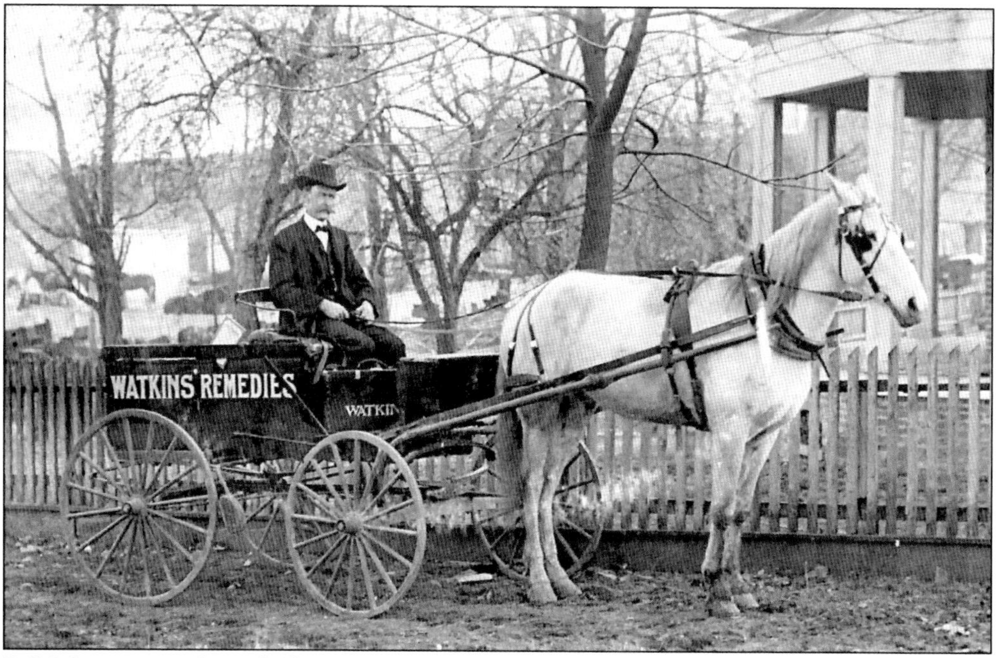

B. F. Johnson served Marshall County as the Watkins Remedies agent for a number of years around 1900. From his wagon, he peddled Watkins products guaranteed to cure most minor ailments. Although doctors were widely available in Marshall County, many residents relied on popular cures and patent medicines. (Courtesy of Claude Nimmo.)

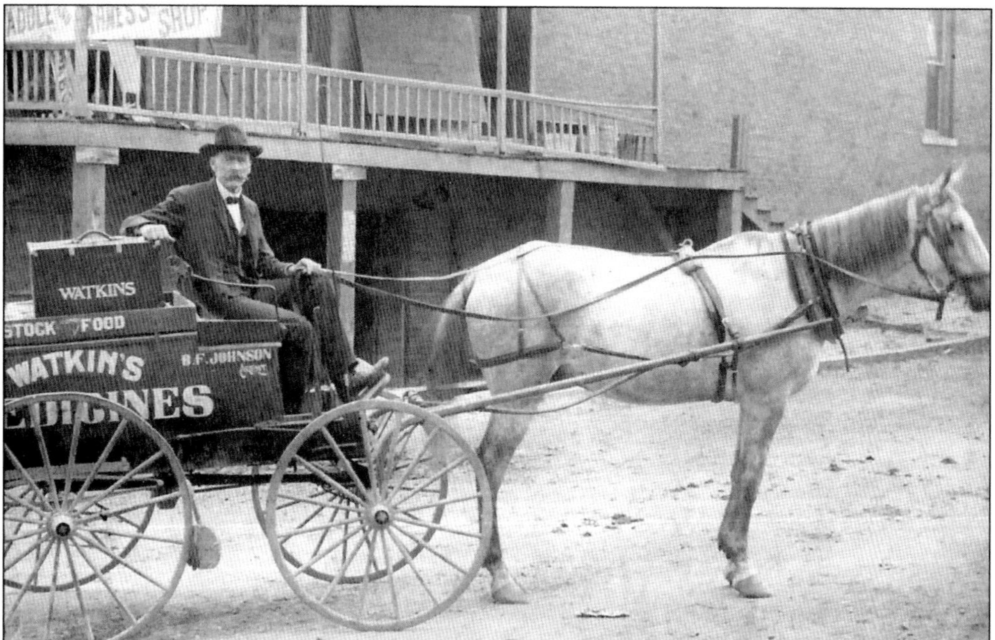

This later photograph of B. F. Johnson was most likely taken in Birmingham or Benton, not his home of Fair Dealing. A saddle and harness shop sign can be seen in the background. The wagon now advertises Watkin's medicines, stock, and food. Watkins is still in business today, selling gourmet food items along with Watkin's first product, Red Liniment. (Courtesy of Claude Nimmo.)

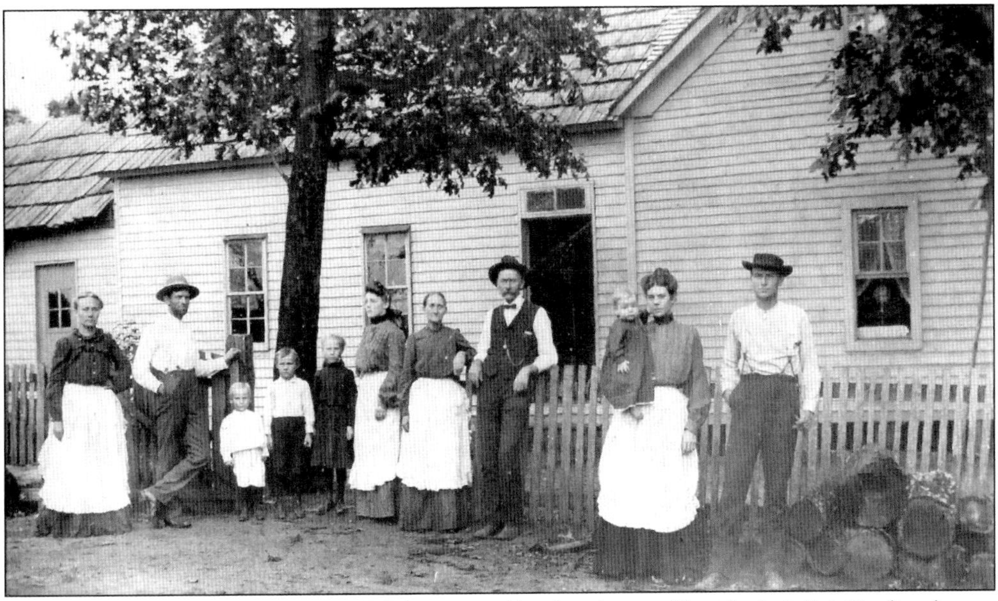

Watkins Remedies agent Benjamin F. Johnson and his family posed beside their Fair Dealing home, c. 1900. Benjamin and his wife, Caroline (McLeod), raised two children, William and Augusta. Their extended family is believed to have also occupied this home. B. F. Johnson, besides being the Watkins dealer, was also a farmer. (Courtesy of Claude Nimmo.)

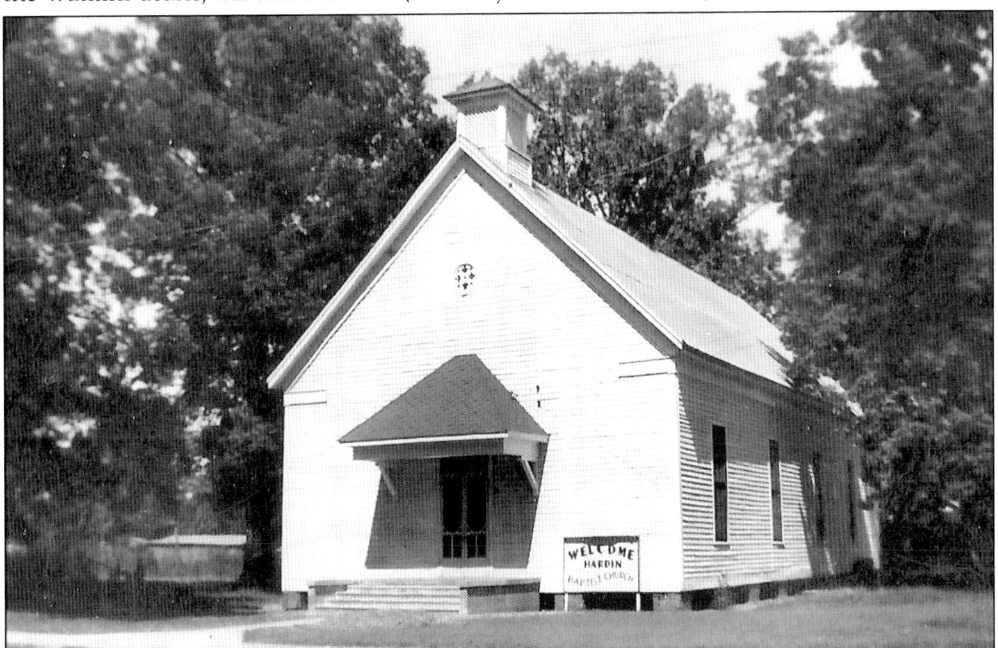

In 1894, Hardin was a booming place with 294 residents, Missionary Baptist and Methodist churches, a school, five general stores, four groceries, a hardware store, a hotel, a boarding house, a blacksmith, and a livery stable. A person could visit two doctors, a photography studio, a barber shop, a shoe store, a tobacco warehouse, and two sawmills. Early family surnames included Shemwell, Lents, Ross, Mathis, and Cole. Hardin's Missionary Baptist Church was organized in 1893. (Courtesy of the Marshall County Genealogical and Historical Society.)

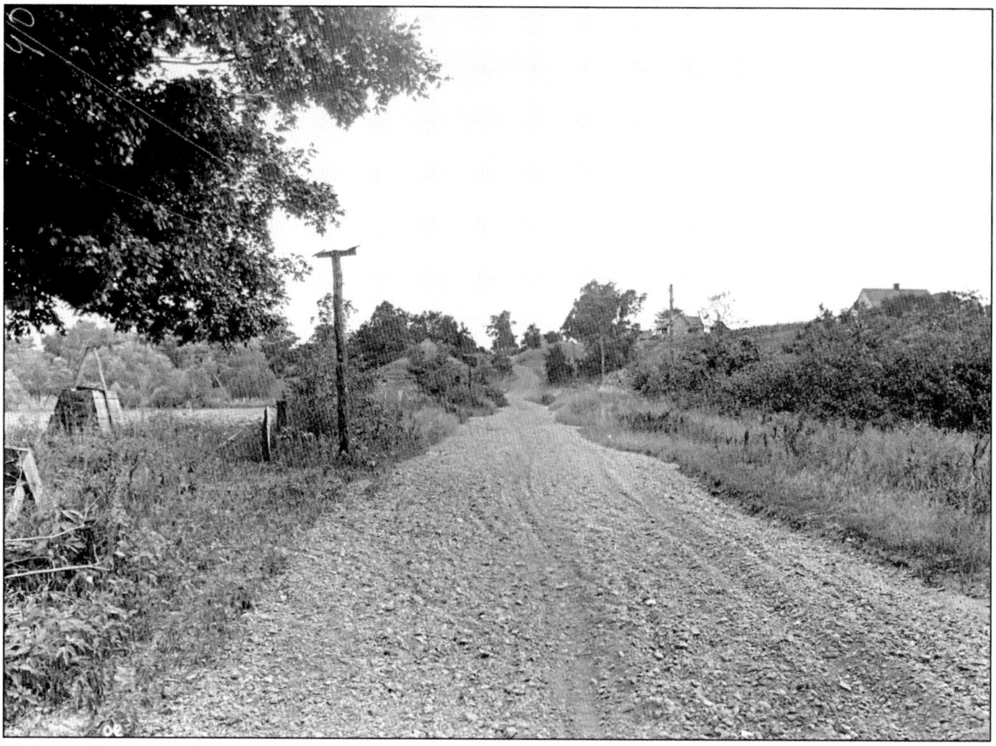

U.S. Highway 641 between Benton and Murray served the southern part of the county leading to neighboring Calloway County through Church Grove, Gladstone, and Hardin. In 1920, the road was dirt and gravel. (Courtesy of the Kentucky Historical Society.)

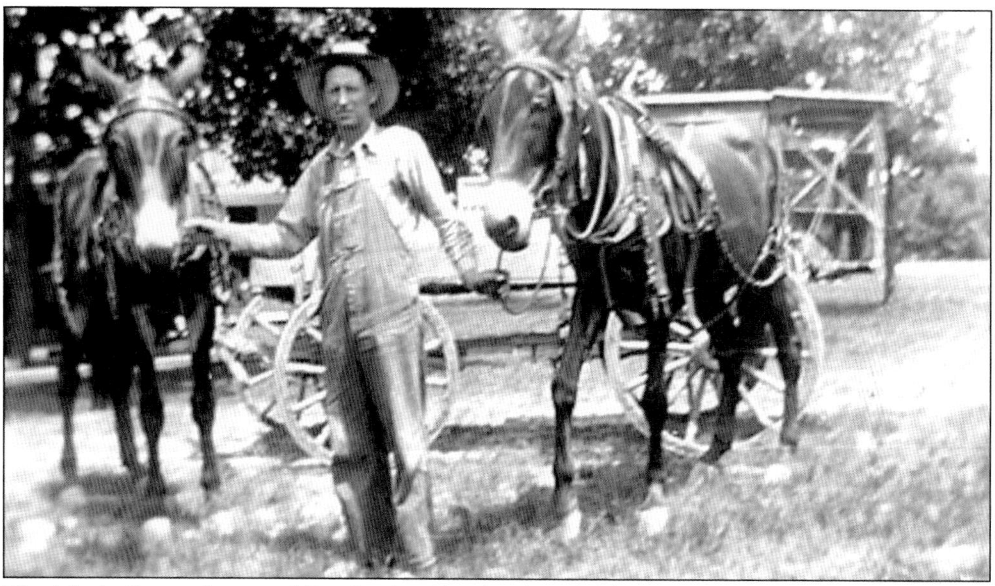

The Maple Spring Store peddler, Jeptha Cleveland Rudolph, traveled the southeastern portion of the county selling his wares. The enterprising Clevie had a chicken coop attached to the back of his wagon so he could sell chickens and eggs to his customers. Clevie, age 44, showed off his mules in this July 1929 photograph. (Courtesy of Claude Nimmo.)

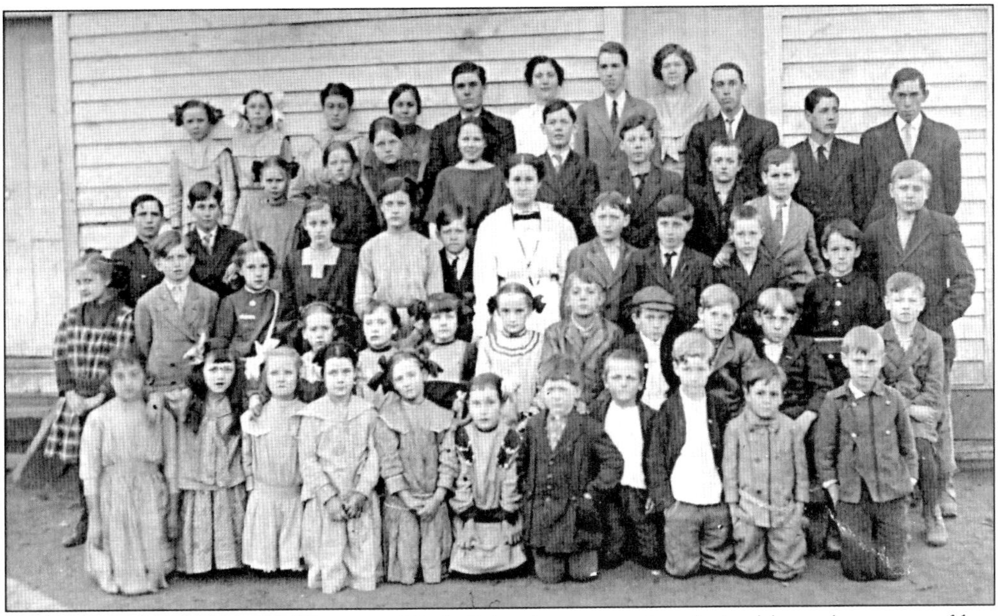

In 1912, teacher Ethel Washburn at Clark School was greatly admired by at least one of her students. After his first day of school, when asked by his mother what he had learned, the boy replied "to love my teacher." Ethel, an Olive native, and the student, Sam Henson, later married. Sam became the Briensburg doctor and is remembered fondly by many older residents of the county. (Courtesy of Louise Norton Wyatt.)

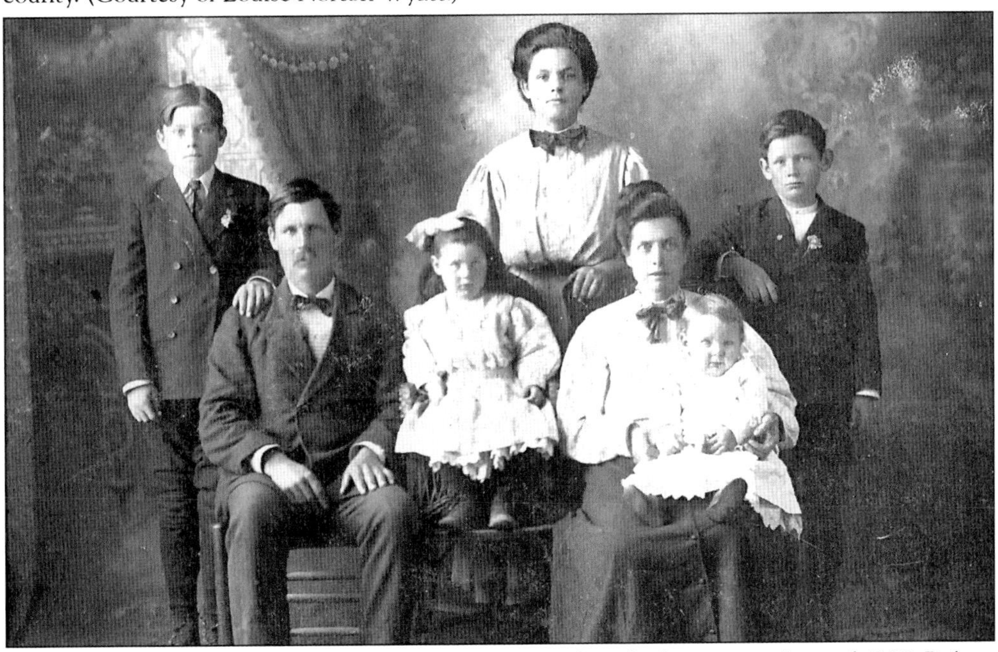

In the early 20th century, family photographs became cherished treasures. Around 1908, Robert and Rosella Kelley dressed their children in their finest clothing. Rollie is on the left. Martha stood behind the group, and Ula is on the right. Little Edward sat on his mother's lap with sister Era Van on the chair. The family lived about two miles from Benton on the old Egners Ferry Road. (Courtesy of Louise Norton Wyatt.)

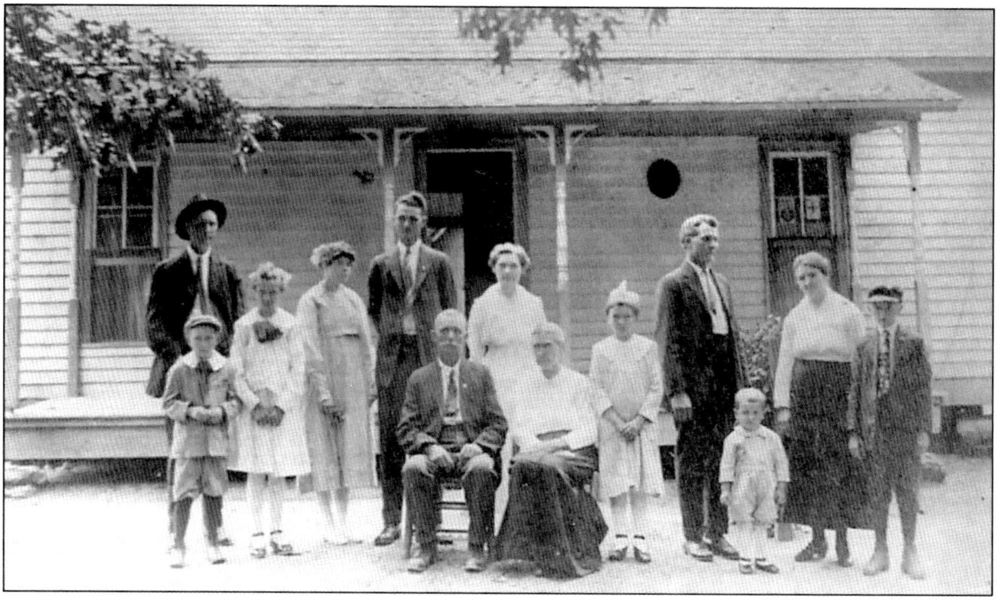

Frank and Laura Anderson married on March 26, 1879, and raised five children—Orah, Floyd, Auston, Emit, and Lillie. Orah operated the telephone switch in Height, between Aurora and Union Ridge, until her death from tuberculosis in 1920. Laura took over the telephone switch until the late 1930s. Telephone operations in many small communities were private businesses and often connected to only one or two other communities, if any at all. (Courtesy of the Marshall County Genealogical and Historical Society.)

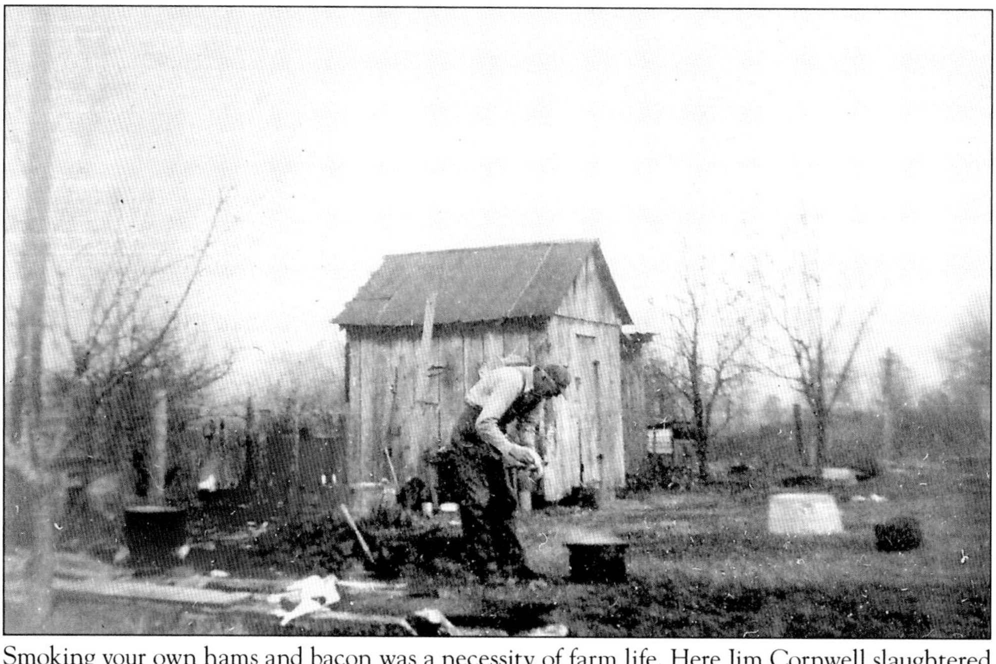

Smoking your own hams and bacon was a necessity of farm life. Here Jim Cornwell slaughtered hogs at the Norton farm off Highway 408. Many families raised and slaughtered their own beef and pork, then smoked the meat themselves. While this old smokehouse is gone, the original Norton farmhouse is still occupied by descendants of the family. (Courtesy of Louise Norton Wyatt.)

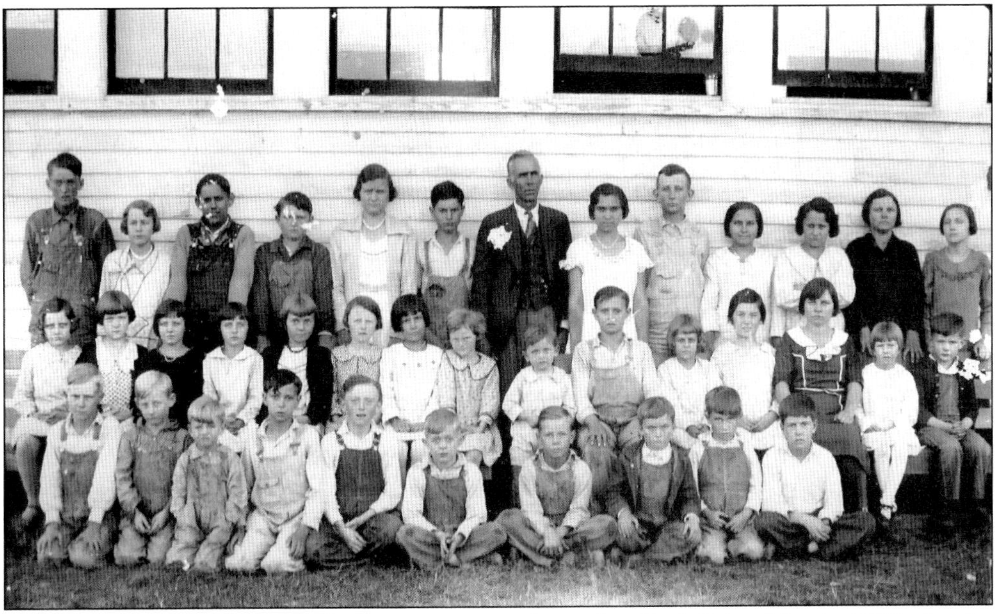

Brother White, a Church of Christ minister, taught at the Clark School in the 1930s. Louise Norton (second row, fourth from right) tells that his favorite punishment was to have students hold down the floor by standing bent over with straight legs, keeping one finger on the floor. This punishment made Brother White very unpopular with his students. (Courtesy of Louise Norton Wyatt.)

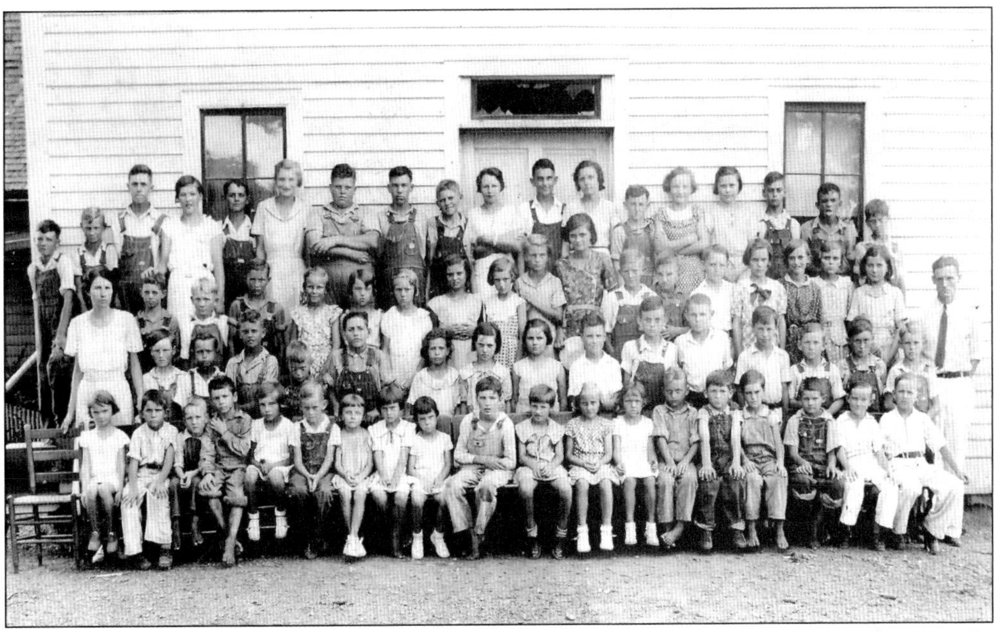

Sixty-nine students and two teachers occupied Olive School in 1935. Hattie Watkins taught the lower grades, and David Inman taught the upper grades. Olive is a very small community northeast of Wadesboro and southwest of Fair Dealing. This photograph was taken at the first school, located near the center of the community on Tom York's land. Norma Norwood is fifth from left in the first row. (Courtesy of Norma Norwood Powell.)

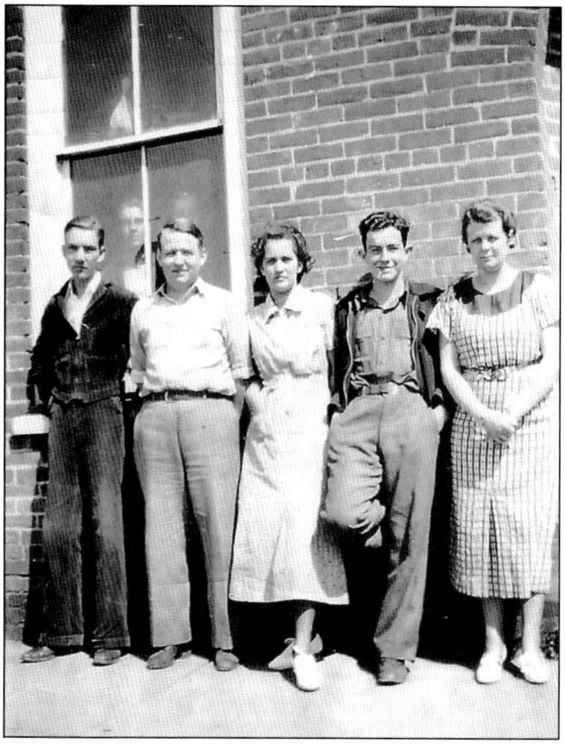

Hardin High School's debate team in 1935 included, from left to right, Julian Stark, Edward Kellow, Mabel Brown, Marvin Prince, and Coach Gladys Jones. Marvin Prince used his debate training well. He became a general practice attorney, serving the county's citizens from 1957 to 1972. (Courtesy of Charles Brown.)

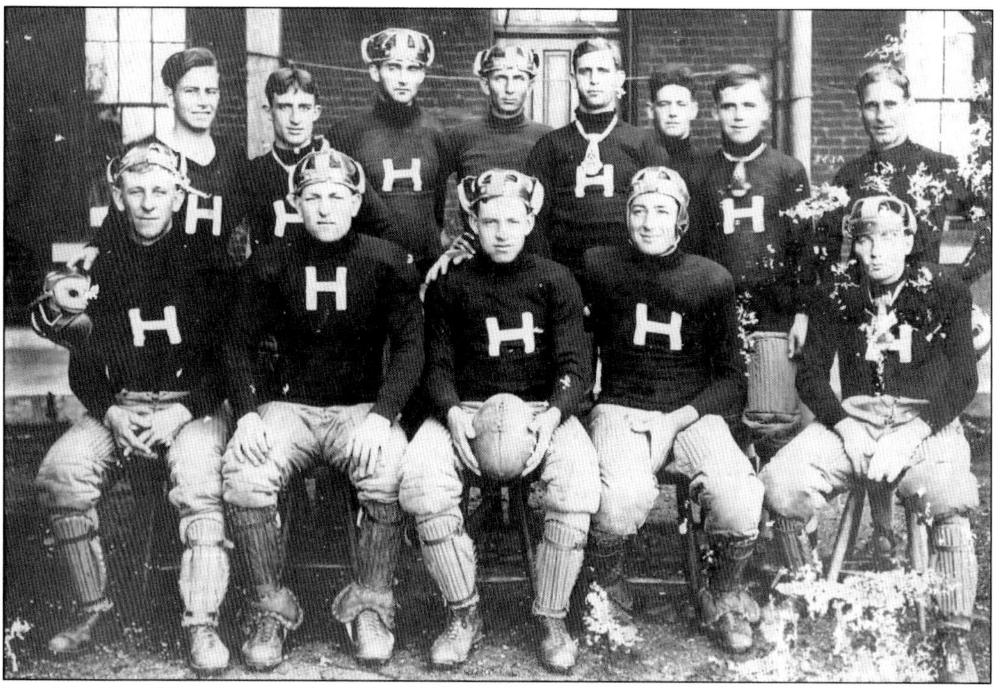

Frank Cooper Watson (second row, fourth from left) played on the Hardin football team c. 1903. Frank later worked for J. A. Howard in Calvert City before being drafted and serving in World War I. Although Frank was born in nearby Union County, he spent most of his life in Marshall County. (Courtesy of Charles Brown.)

Eight

SOUTHWEST

Drive northwest out of Benton toward Symsonia and you pass just north of Harmony, Breezeel, and Oak Level. At one time, driving due west of Benton would take you to Harvey, and if you turned slightly southwest from there, you could go to Vanzora or Melrose or Pleasant Grove. Travel a bit farther, and you might end up at Brewer's Mill. However, a southerly direction from Benton would take you through Church Grove toward where it all began, Wadesboro.

Wadesboro, actually in Calloway County, is where Marshall County began. Possibly named for Bannister Wade, the area was settled about 1818 or 1819 and was the first county seat of Calloway County. When Marshall County split from Calloway County, Calloway County also named a new county seat, and over the years, Wadesboro disappeared.

Brewers was once Brewer's Mill because Peter Brewer built a mill on the west fork of Clarks River. Another water mill was opened nearby, along with a few stores and a post office. Harvey developed around the James Harvey Ivey general store. Oak Level, another store-based community, had a log schoolhouse for many years. After the Civil War, Oak Level gained another store, a tobacco warehouse, a saloon, and a blacksmith shop. Two Oak Level store owners, Hill and Reeves, also ran the area's huckster wagon.

School names that are remembered include Breezeel, Constitution and New Constitution, Pleasant Valley and Pleasant Grove, and of course, Brewers. *Lemon's Handbook of Marshall County*, dated 1894, listed several churches serving the southwestern portion of the county. Mount Moriah Primitive Baptist met near Oak Level after being organized in 1870. Middle Fork Primitive Baptist, located three miles west of Benton, was organized in 1842. Soldier Creek Primitive Baptist, organized in 1820, was the first church constituted west of the Tennessee River. Methodist churches included ones at Oak Level, Church Grove, and Pleasant Grove. Oak Level also had a Christian church. New Zion, near Magness, was Missionary Baptist, along with New Bethel and New Harmony.

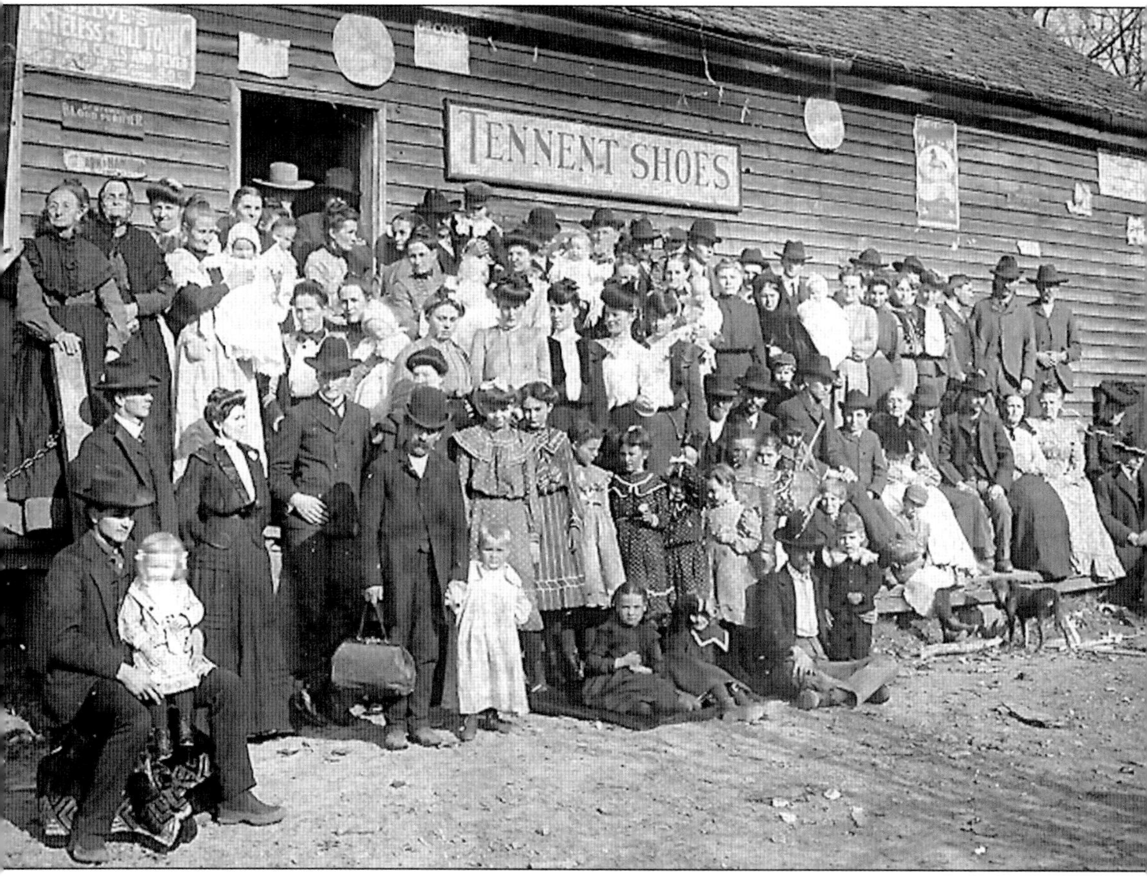

The Smith Store was located off Highway 80 between the road to Vanzora and the Wadesboro Road. This c. 1890 photograph, taken outside the store, illustrates the variety of goods carried by general mercantile stores. Tennent Shoes was a St. Louis, Missouri, company. Grove's Tasteless Chill Tonic was developed by Dr. Edwin Wiley Grove of Paris, Tennessee, in 1878. To establish a national market for his products, his Paris Medicine Company moved to St. Louis in 1889. Also advertised are two other patent medicines, one by D. B. Cox and a blood purifier. (Courtesy of Coy Arnett and Ann King.)

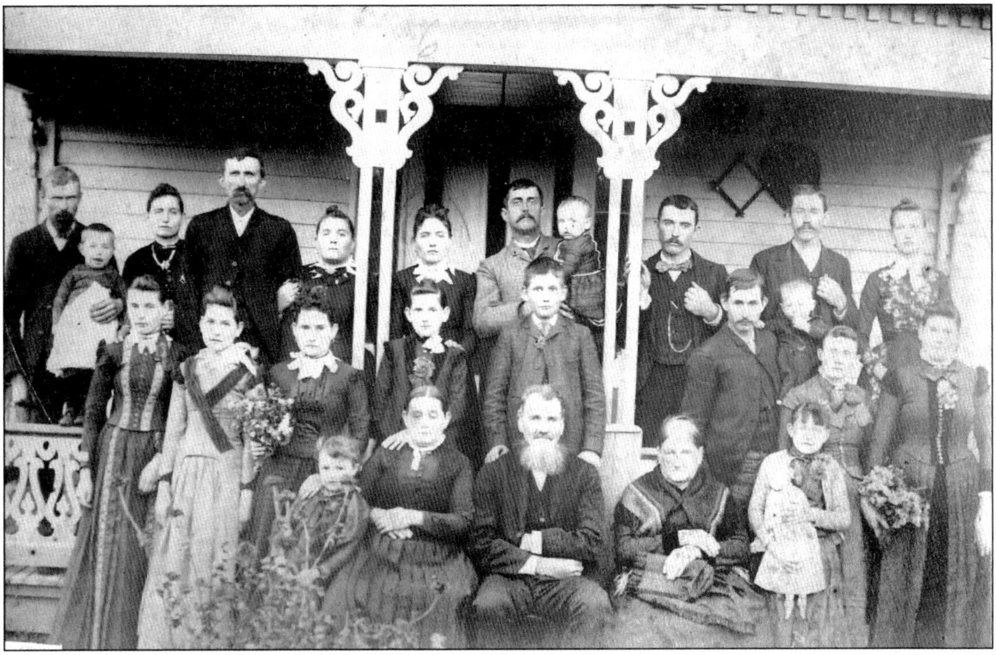

Around 1890, near the Oak Level and Houser Roads, Grandpa Reuben Holmes, his mother, and his wife, Mary, gathered the family for a formal portrait. Shemwell, Fisk, Crockett, Holmes, Travis, Ford, and Breezeel family members also appear. The photographer's writing on the back of the photograph indicates that he traveled from house to house capturing family memories. (Courtesy of Juanita Breezeel.)

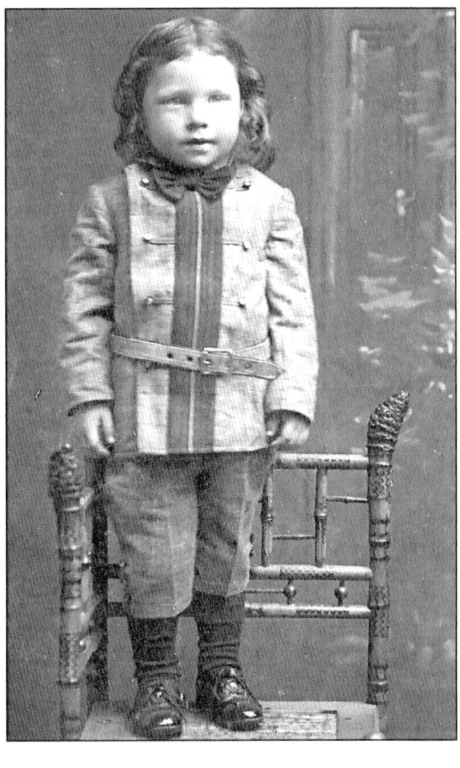

Jodie Joseph Copeland was the eighth child of Jacob Copeland. He was born October 30, 1902, in Harvey. The local doctor implanted a silver dollar in his head where his skull had not closed and told the family he would not live very long. Jodie died on March 14, 1981; he was 78 years old. (Courtesy of Janet Copeland Wallace.)

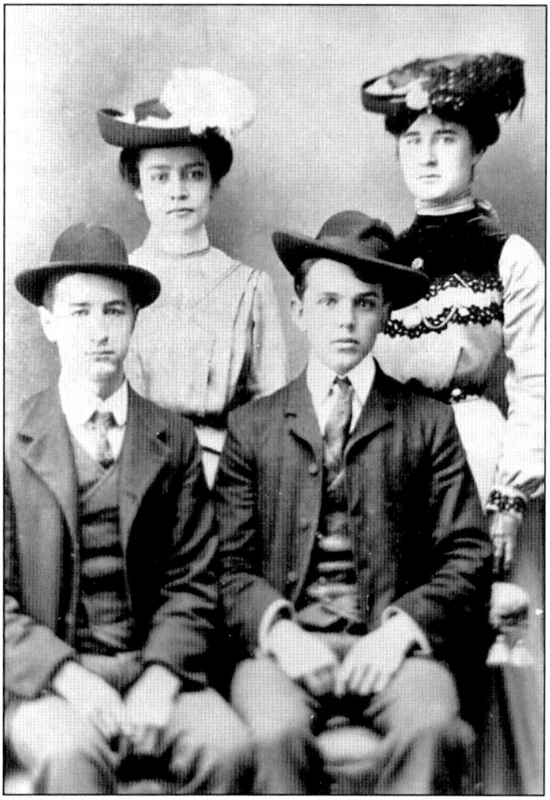

Four young people married on December 22, 1902. Archie McGregor married Euphatear Wood (left). A farming family, they lived near Oak Level and raised three children. John Lee Smith married Nola Mae McGregor (right); they had two children and lived near the McGregors. John farmed and operated sawmills at Oak Level and Aurora at different times. In later years, John was prosperous enough to provide each of his children with 90 acres and a log cabin when they left home. (Courtesy of the Marshall County Genealogical and Historical Society.)

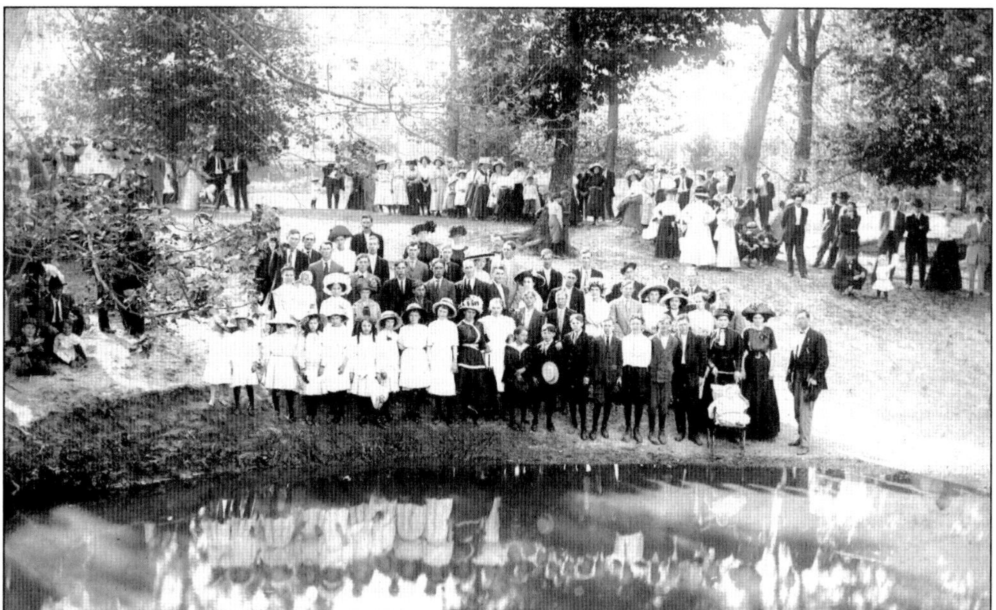

Mass baptisms often were staged at local bodies of water. This one took place in 1906 at Wades Creek. (Courtesy of the Mike McWane family.)

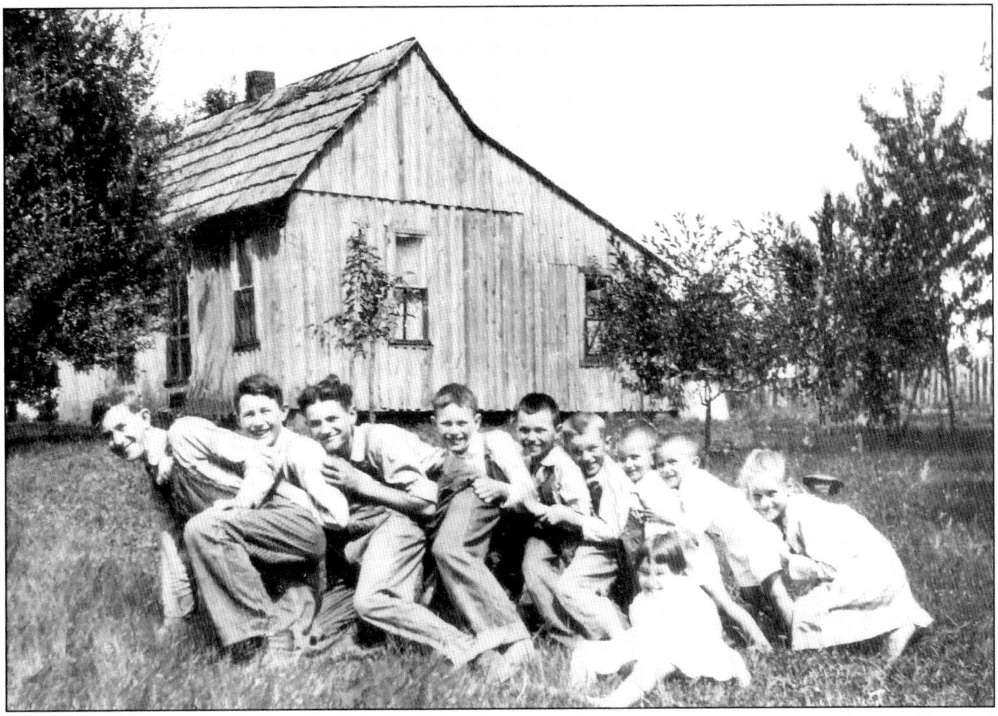

In 1915, Lloyd and Minnie Farmer's house in western Marshall County on Crowell Road hosted a group of relatives. From left to right are (kneeling) Lois and Floyd Reid, Rex Lyles, Arnie and Charles Reid, Othel Barnes, twins Edward and Edwin Reid, and Vergie Reid; (seated in front) Mary Reid. Lois, Floyd, Arnie, Vergie, and Mary were the children of widow Joyce Reid. Rex Lyles was their uncle. Othel, Charles, and the twins were cousins. (Courtesy of Lena Crowley.)

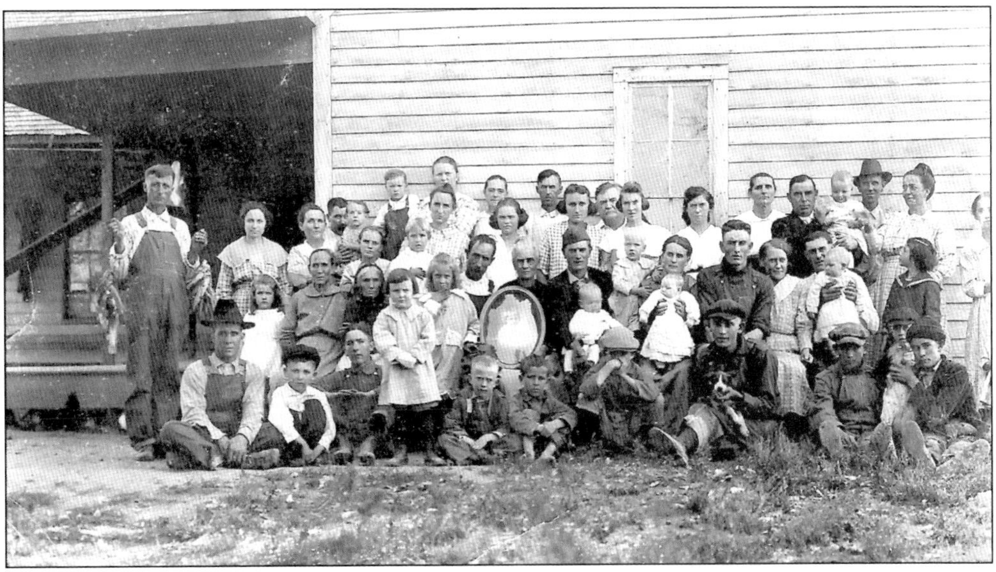

A Smith family gathering in 1916 became an opportunity for a family photograph. As adults, children, and babies gathered beside the house, the portrait of a child was held up so others would not forget one lost in infancy. Otis Edison Smith, on the left, presented his fine catch of fish. (Courtesy of Virginia Smith.)

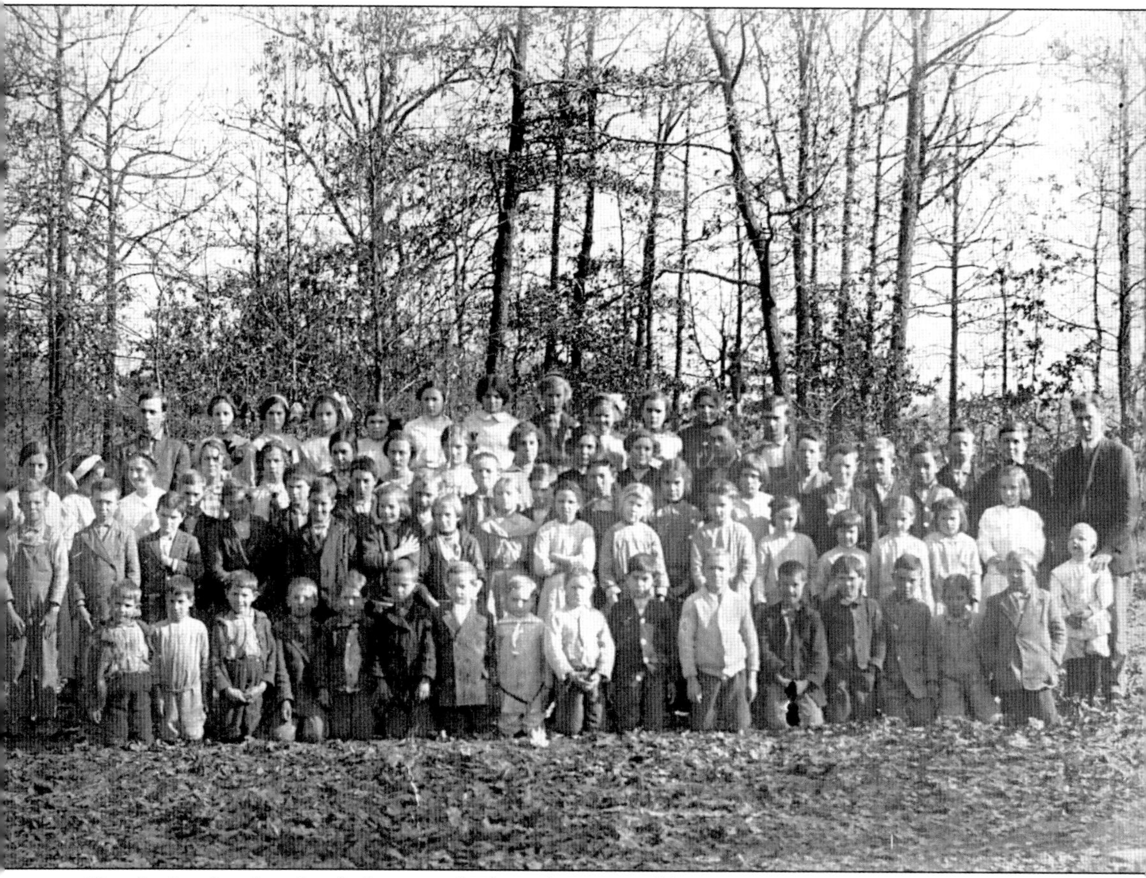

Hundreds of early school photographs have been saved by Marshall County residents. Almost all show the children standing and sitting beside or in front of their school. However, at the New Constitution School, Lovelace Roscoe Shemwell (standing at far right) broke from the norm and placed his students in a grove of trees. Seventy-two students were present. The school was located near Harvey. This photograph was made before World War I, as Roscoe Shemwell was one of Marshall County's fallen heroes of that conflict. (Courtesy of the Marshall County Genealogical and Historical Society.)

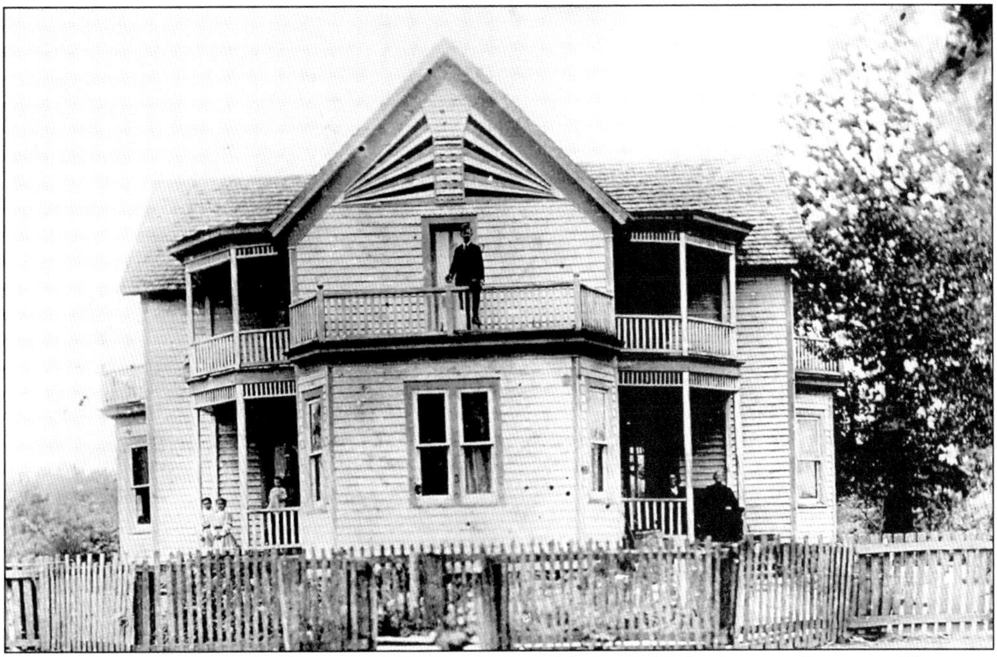

Haven Henson's house had 16 porches. Located in Harvey, the house was home to Haven, a farmer, his wife, Mary, and their family. On the bottom left porch are two young girls and a woman holding an infant. The boy on the center porch posed with his leg over the railing. Sitting on the lower right porch were an elderly woman and another individual. (Courtesy of the Marshall County Genealogical and Historical Society.)

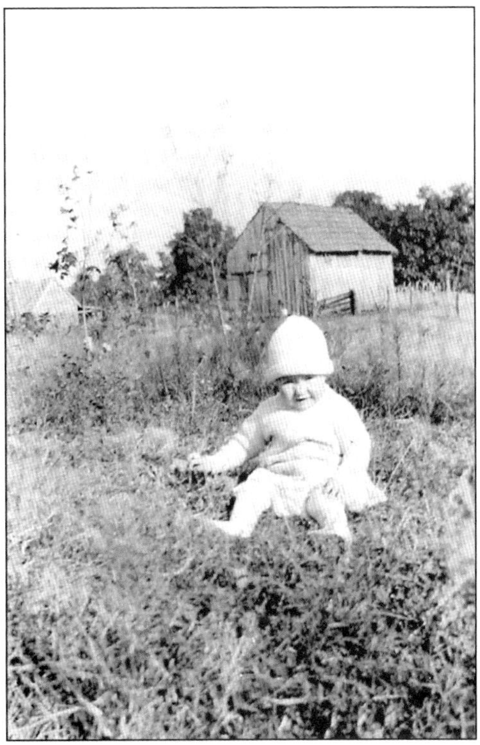

A barn with a shake roof served as a backdrop for Rufus and Gertha Lents to show off their firstborn, Iona Lents. Iona was born on August 12, 1919. (Courtesy of Juanita Breezeel.)

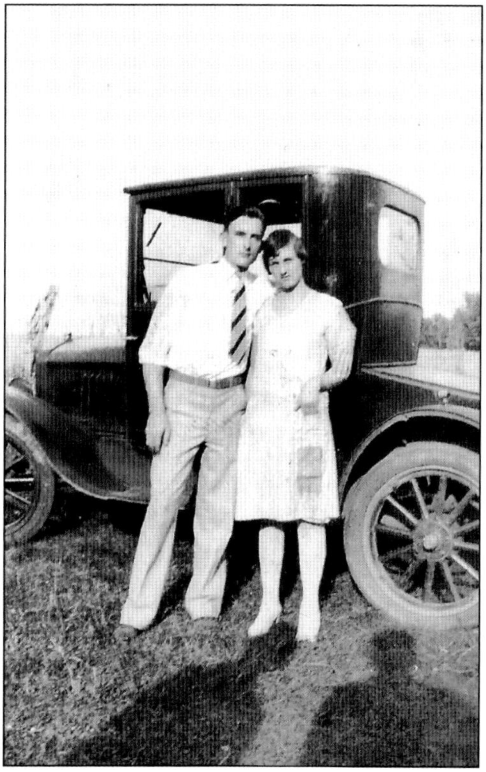

Marie Feezor dated a young man whose name is lost to history, but we know he drove a 1921 Ford Model T, also called a suicide door coupe. Of course, it was black, as all Ford Model Ts were black. (Courtesy of Lena Crowley.)

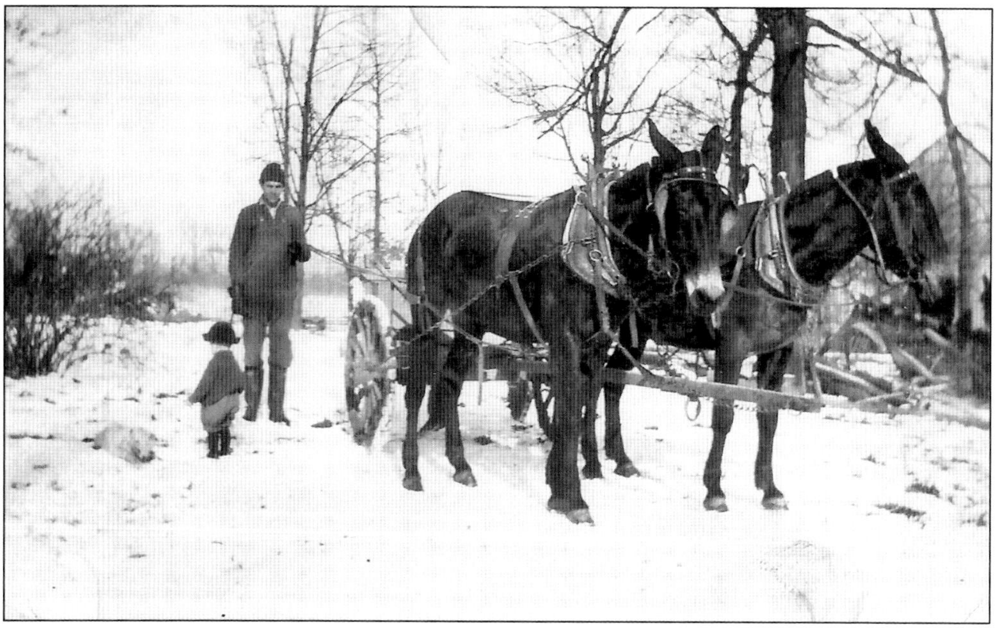

Mules pulled a variety of farm implements including plows, disks, harrows, planters, cultivators, mowers, and reapers. Plowing required the greatest amount of power, often forcing farmers to keep one or two extra mules or horses. The average farmer owned three or four mules or horses. In 1925, Guy Breezeel, an Oak Level farmer, pulled his wagon through the snow with a two-mule hitch. (Courtesy of Juanita Breezeel.)

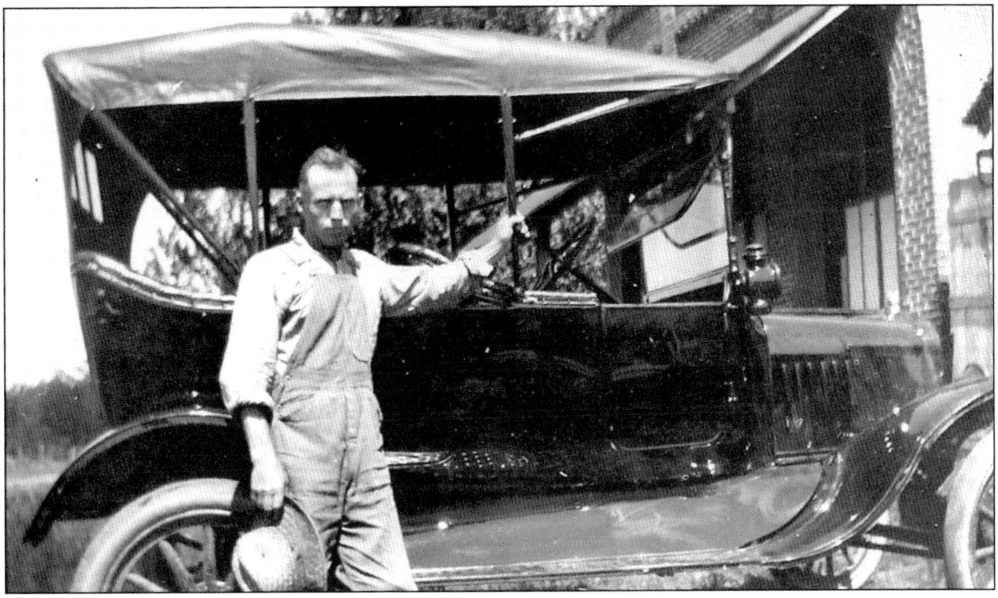

James Ivey was very proud of his 1921 or 1922 Model T Ford automobile. James owed and operated the Ivey store in Harvey. Not long after the Civil War, the store was opened by his father, James Harvey Ivey, for whom the small farming community was named. For years, merchandise was hauled by two-horse wagon from Paducah. The trip took two days, and two trips were made each week. (Courtesy of Beatrice Ivey Cole.)

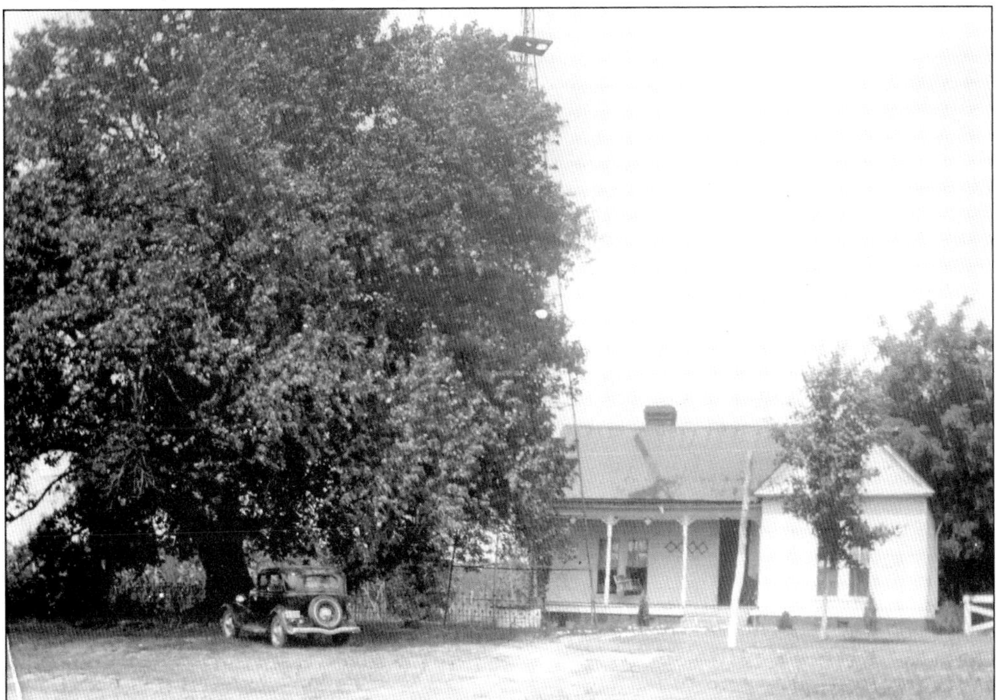

Ed and Millie Ivey's home in Harvey was recognized by the 75-foot-tall windmill in the front yard. Rural families sometimes used windmills to pump water into their homes or fields for irrigation. (Courtesy of Howard C. Ivey.)

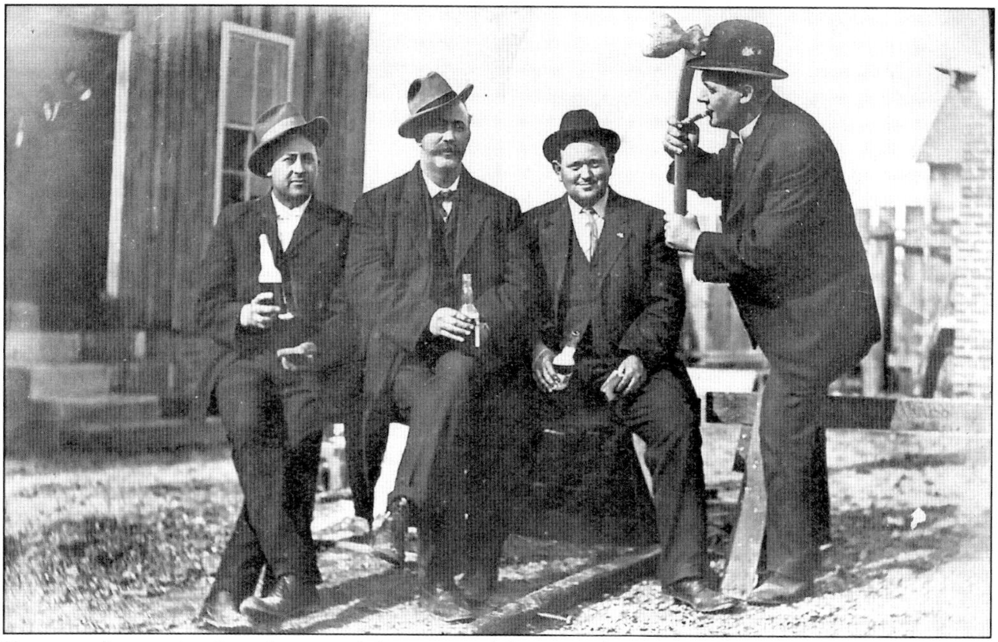

Four gentlemen drinking long-neck beers posed for one of two staged photographs in front of a building located near the store in Harvey. Jim Rickman is second from right. This building served as a "men's social club." (Courtesy of Janet Copeland Wallace.)

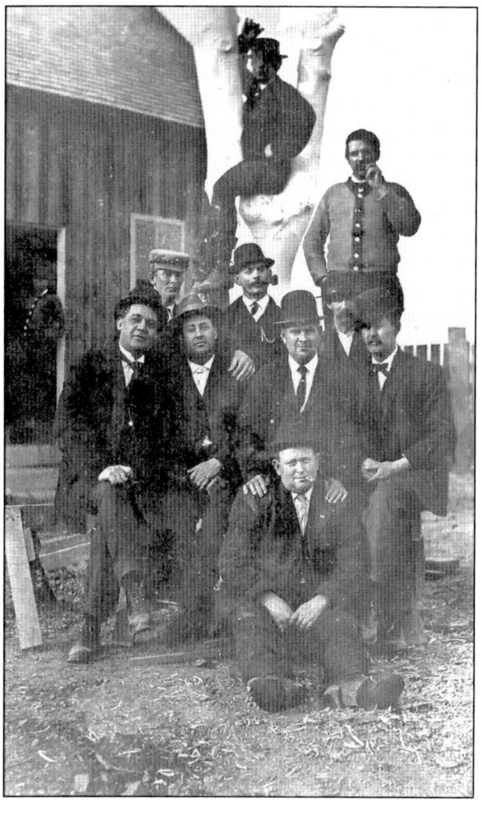

Beer bottles disappeared as the men were joined by other well-dressed gentlemen for this second "staged" photograph. Their antics seem to indicate a degree of interaction that might be found at a social club. Stories about this photograph tell that one of these men is Fred Filbeck of Benton. Other prominent Benton business men are rumored to have been members of the club. (Courtesy of Janet Copeland Wallace.)

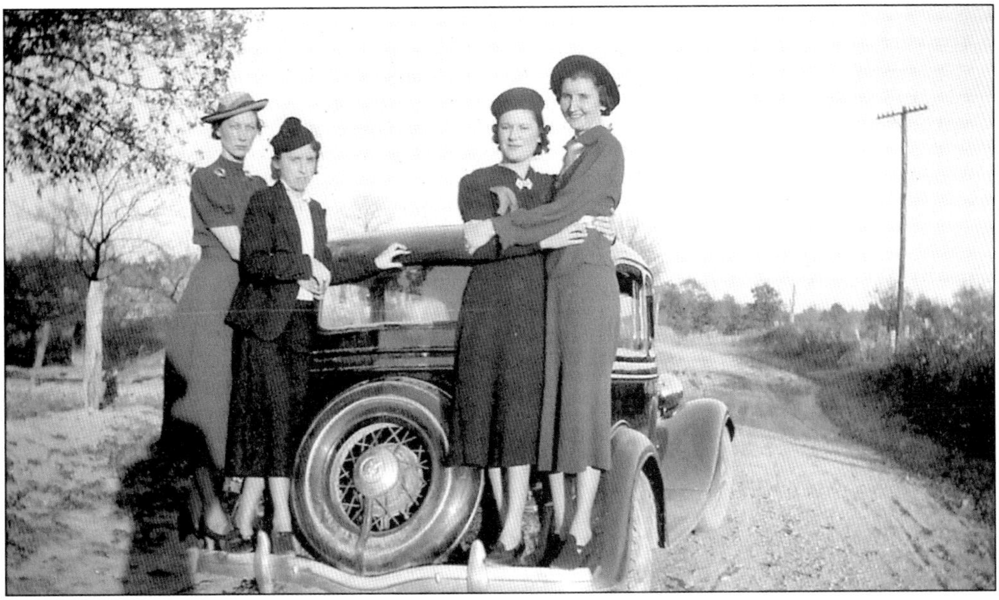

Four well-dressed young women hitched a ride on their way home from the Bethel Baptist Church on the back of a 1933 Ford. From left to right are Genella, Beatrice, Shirley, and Vida. Beatrice and Vida became sisters-in-law. Both attended Murray State College, received teaching certificates, and taught for many years in Marshall County schools. Beatrice's father owned Ivey Store in Harvey. (Courtesy of Beatrice Ivey Cole.)

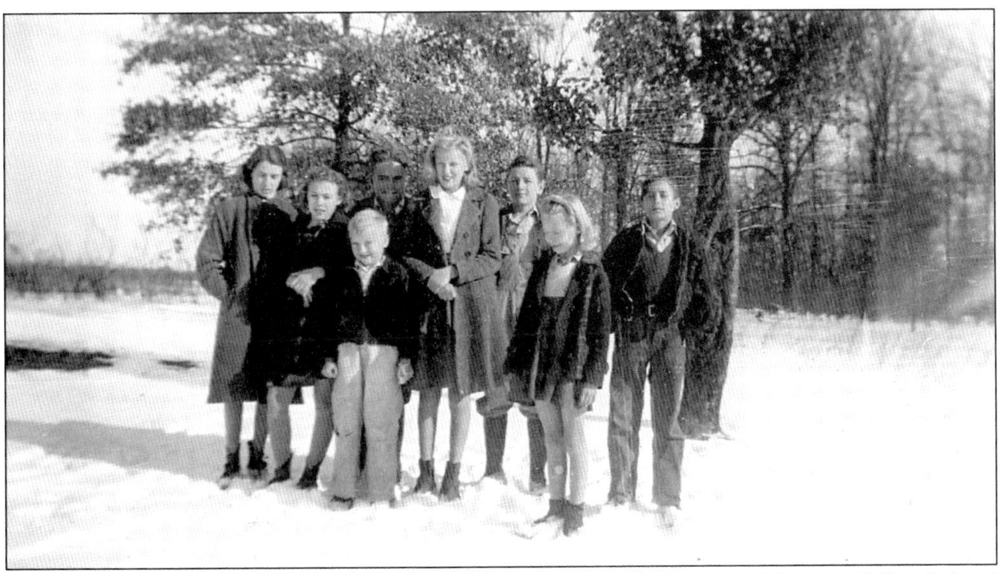

Sometime in the early 1930s, Beatrice Ivey Cole and her students at the Pleasant Valley School enjoyed one of Marshall County's snowfalls. Beatrice's students were Ladonne Thompson, Bill Thompson, Maxine Thompson, Ruth Jean McGregor, Jo Lee McGregor, Earnest Bylerley, and Donald Bylerley. Beatrice later transferred to the Benton elementary school, where she taught second grade for many years. (Courtesy of Beatrice Ivey Cole.)

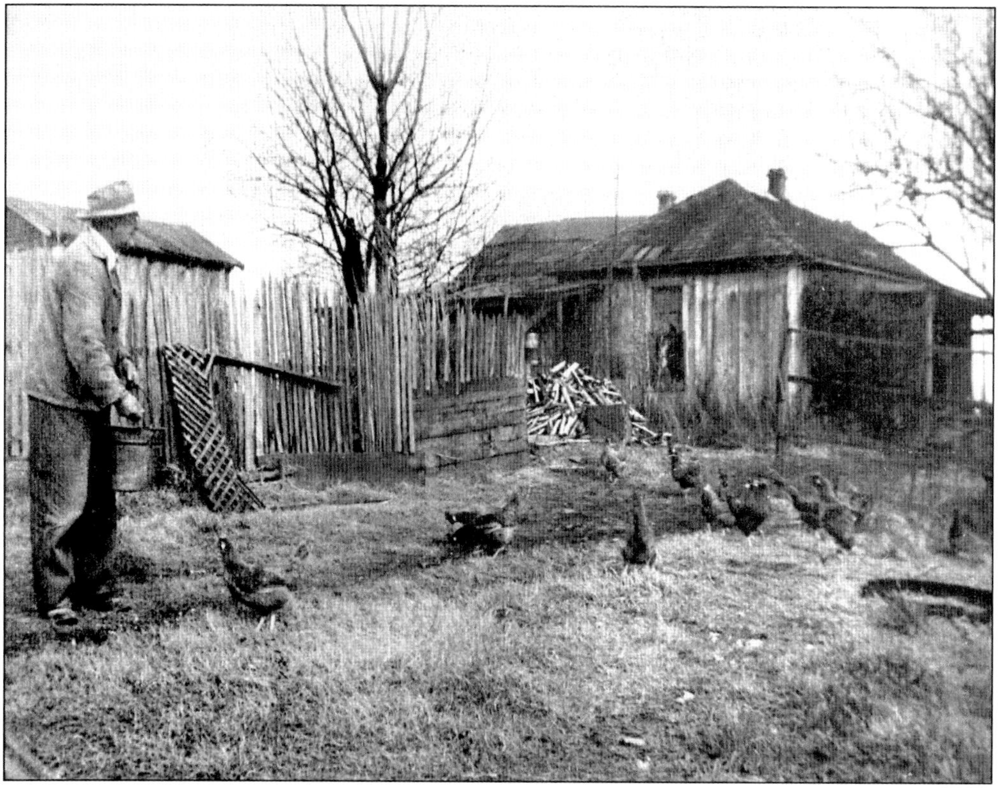

The chickens needed to be fed, so "Pappy" Copeland took on the job. L. L. Copeland lived in Oak Level. Like most county residents, he kept chickens for two reasons, eggs and Sunday dinner, especially if the preacher was coming to the house after church. (Courtesy of Virginia Smith.)

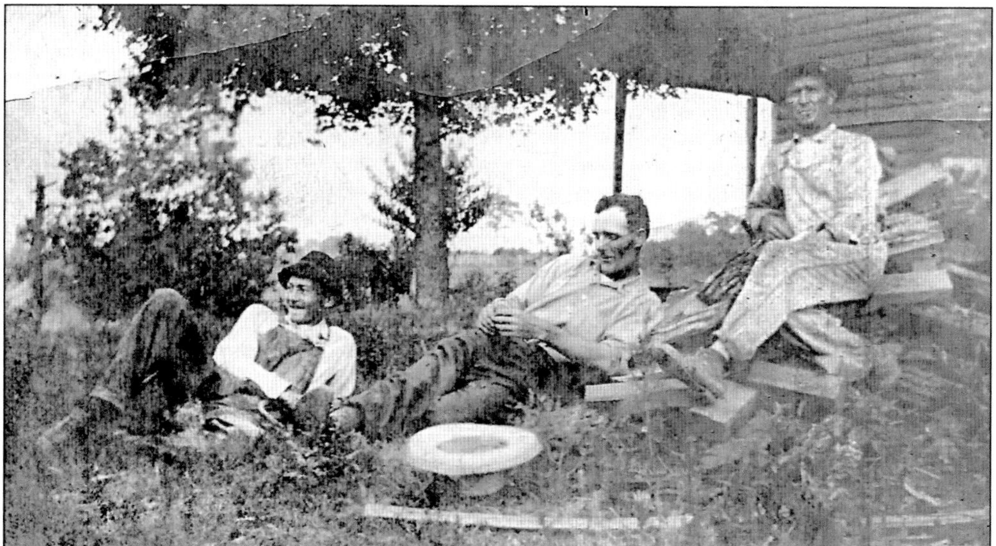

Three Oak Level men relaxed after a hard day of chopping wood. From left to right, Berry Badgett, Avery Parker, and Hollie Copeland, like many men during the early 1900s, had to chop wood for heating and cooking as few Oak Level homes had electricity. (Courtesy of Virginia Smith.)

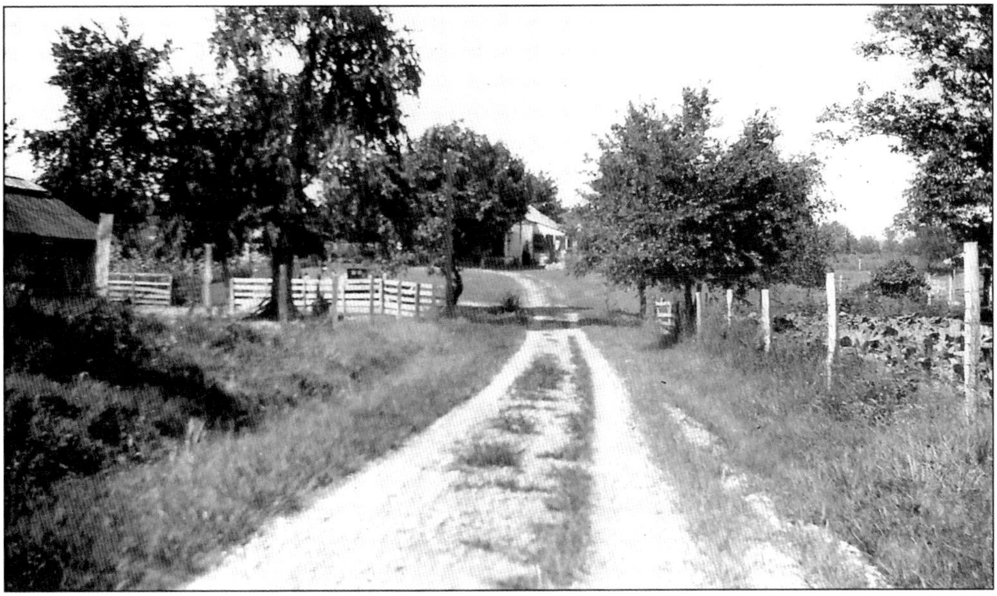

The Great Depression brought some young men and their families back home. Howard Cole tells of leaving Detroit with his parents, Curtis and Ena, and his sister, Marlene, after his father lost his job with the Ford Motor Company in 1931. They purchased the Old Castleberry farm located two miles west of Benton. They traded their Model A Ford for two horses and three wagonloads of corn. The family stayed on the Castleberry farm until the summer of 1935, when they returned to Detroit. (Courtesy of Howard C. Ivey.)

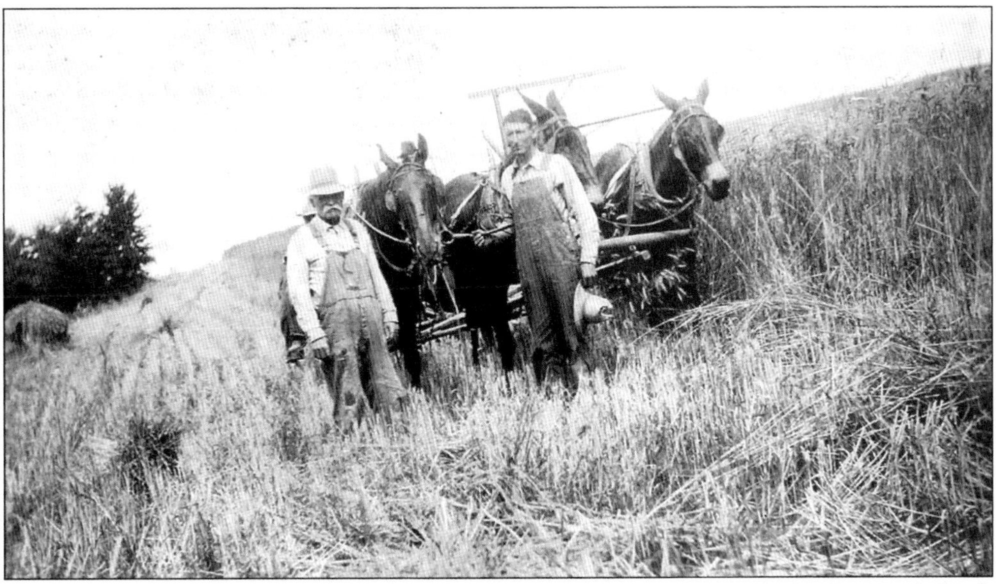

Holding his hat in his hand, "Grandpa" W. D. Cole and Crit McCain worked a three-mule hitch pulling a wheat combine. From the early years of farming in the county and into the 20th century, wheat was the second most important crop grown behind corn. (Courtesy of Howard C. Ivey.)

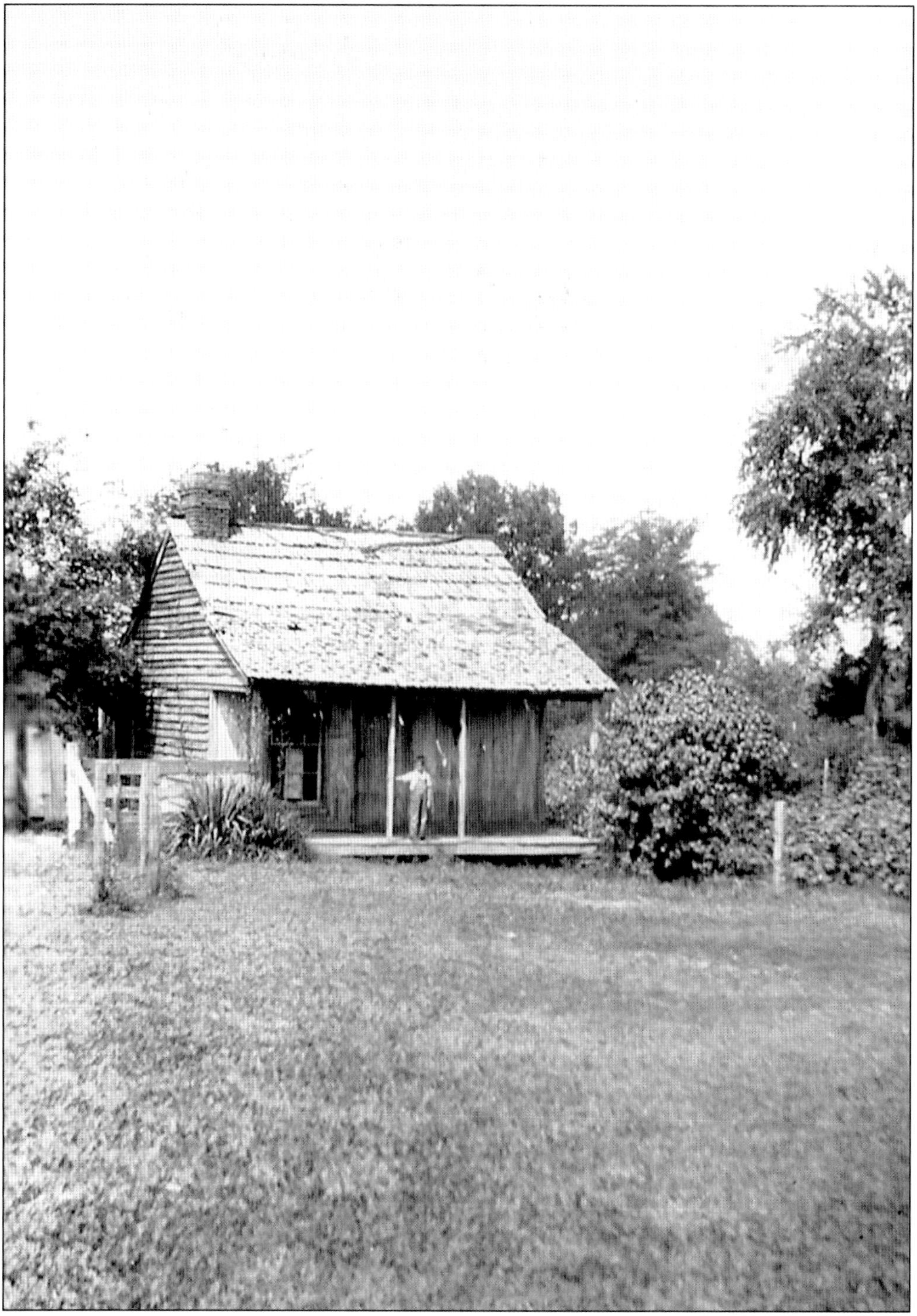

Sharecroppers lived on and worked another man's land for a portion of the crop. This sharecropper's cabin was located on the Old Castleberry farm, west of Benton. Sharecroppers were often furnished with a small house and a garden plot. Their labor provided farmers with the help they needed throughout the year. (Courtesy of Howard C. Ivey.)

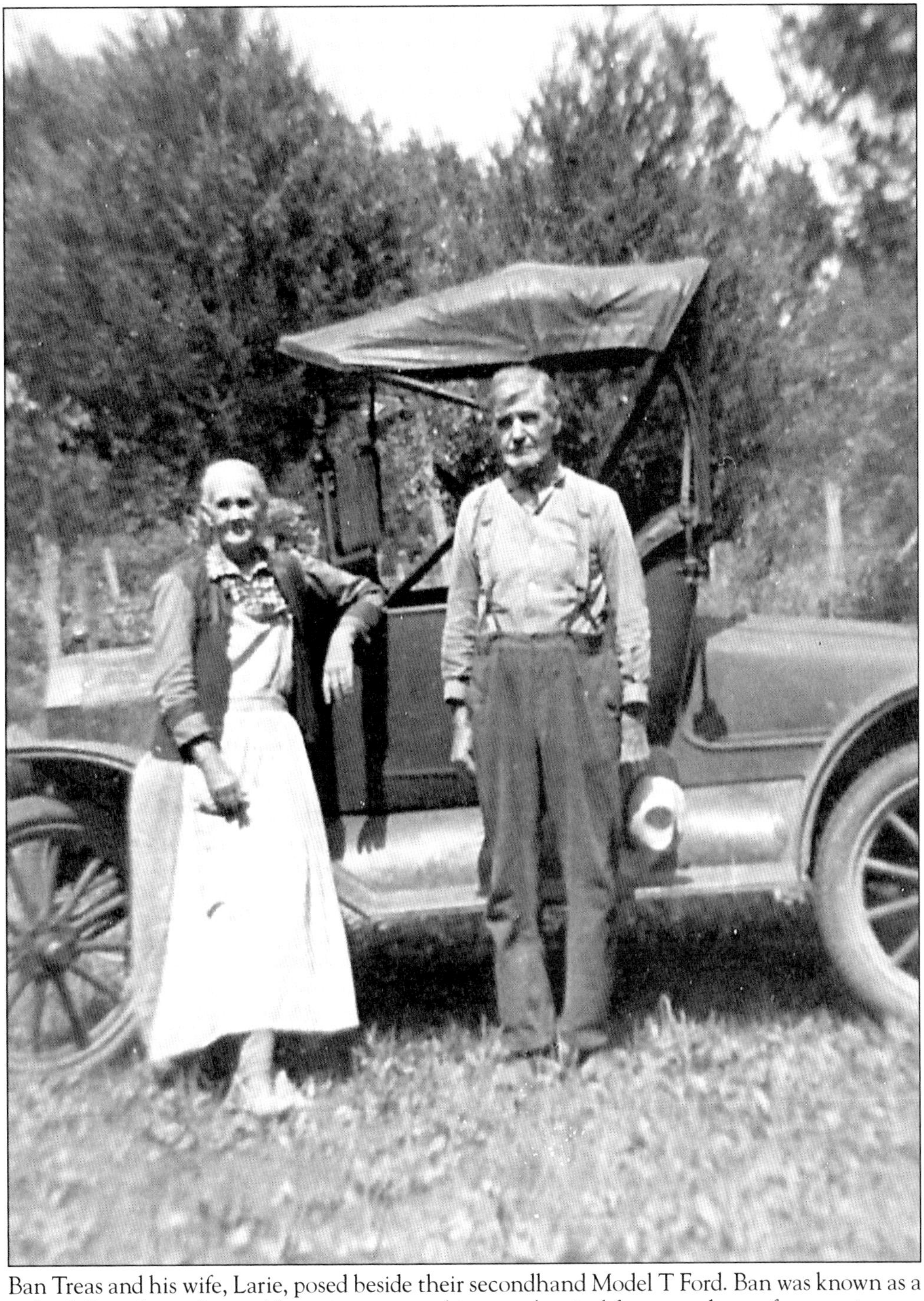

Ban Treas and his wife, Larie, posed beside their secondhand Model T Ford. Ban was known as a jack of all trades, as he could repair most anything mechanical from watches to farm equipment to automobiles. Ban also played the fiddle and would gather with other musicians at the home of Luther Cole. After half an hour of tuning up, they would cut loose with songs like "Orange Blossom Special" and proceed to hold a hoe-down until the wee hours of the morning. (Courtesy of Howard C. Ivey.)

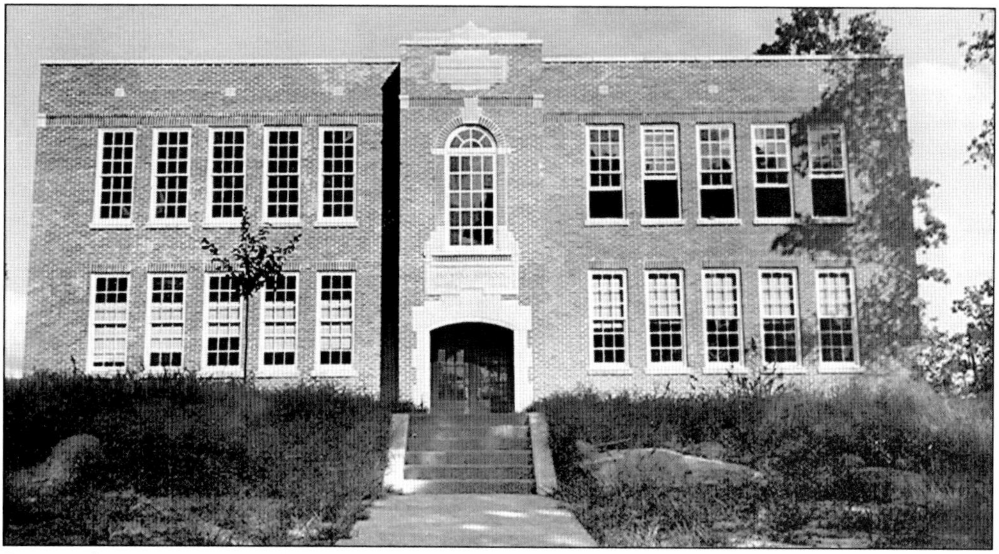

Brewers began a two-year high school in 1920. By 1924, a four-year high school was in place. Like many county schools, all grades attended in one building well into the 20th century, even though separate classrooms by grade level or groups of grades were used. Marshall County residents benefited from several new schools under the Works Progress Administration building program. Construction began on the Brewers School in 1940 and was completed in 1941. (©University of Kentucky, all rights reserved, Goodman-Paxton Photographic Collection, Special Collections and Digital Programs, University of Kentucky Libraries.)

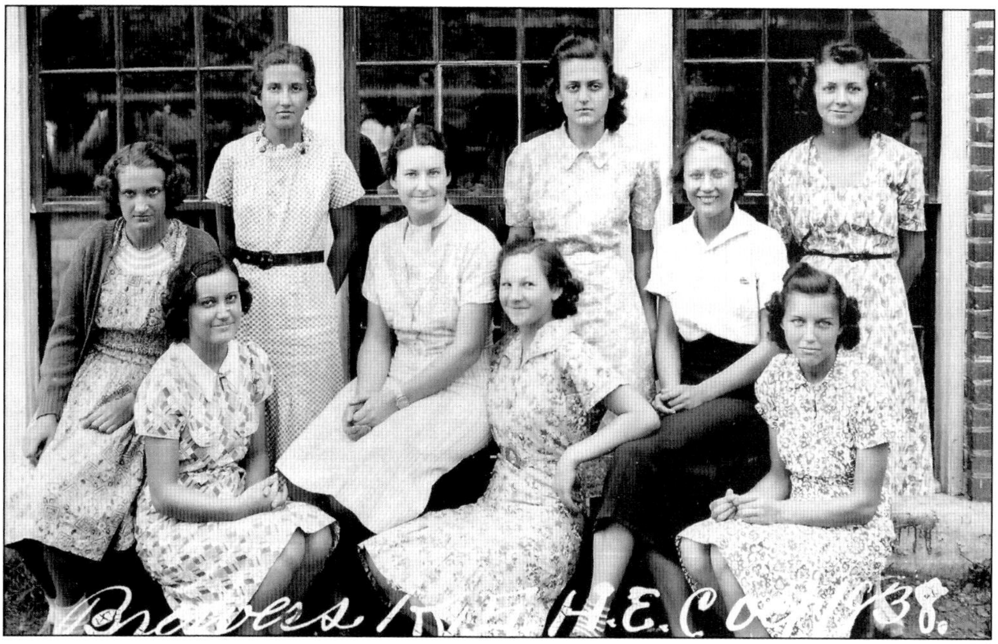

In 1938, a young Elizabeth Harrell, who taught for 28 years in Marshall County, trained these young girls in home economics in Brewers. The class included, from left to right, (seated) Mary Ella Chester, Ina Dell Treas, Elizabeth Harrell, Edith Smith, Lillian Cope, and Martha Brooks Chester; (standing) Ruth Smith, Helen Treas, and Mary Helen Creason. (Courtesy of Elizabeth Harrell.)

Nine
NORTHWEST

Sharpe, Palma, and Possum Trot are all located in the northwestern portion of the county. Some other place names survive, but the villages they were associated with, such as Howard's Grove, Griggstown, Altona, Little Cypress, Scale, Arnettsville, Iola, and Elva, have all but disappeared.

The farming village of Palma had a post office until 1905 and several stores. Sharpe was first known as Oakland and had a post office in J. H. Johnston's general store. Sharpe can boast of the county's first high-school program, started in 1917. It was a two-year program. Possum Trot, considered one of Kentucky's more interesting place names, was spread out for about a mile down the old Calvert City Road. No one really knows how the area arrived at such a name, and everyone in Possum Trot may give you a different answer if you ask.

Altona, on the Tennessee River, north of Calvert City, began near an early ferry service to Smithland. First named Patterson's Ferry, about 50 years later, Anthony Burradel opened a small mercantile business there, and the area became known as Burradel's Landing. The name changed to Altona with the arrival of a post office.

Little Cypress was another early town in northern Marshall County and was founded about 1835. After the arrival of the railroad, a post office was established. The community already had a school and a small store. Many of the men in the area worked at the nearby coke producing plant.

Elva was once a depot on the Paducah, Tennessee, and Alabama Railroad and a shipping point for gravel, railroad ties, and lumber. In the early 1900s, there were also a store, a school, and a telephone exchange. Iola was a flag station on the Paducah, Tennessee, and Alabama Railroad.

Several schools served various parts of the northwestern portion of the county including Coursey (or Canada) and Beechwood, which were located on the road from Calvert to Haddocks Ferry. Griggs (or Griggstown) and Howard's Grove were both southwest of Calvert City. McCain was located southeast of Sharpe. Oak Valley Church of Christ and its school were near Scale. Oak Hill School sat between Little Cypress and the county line.

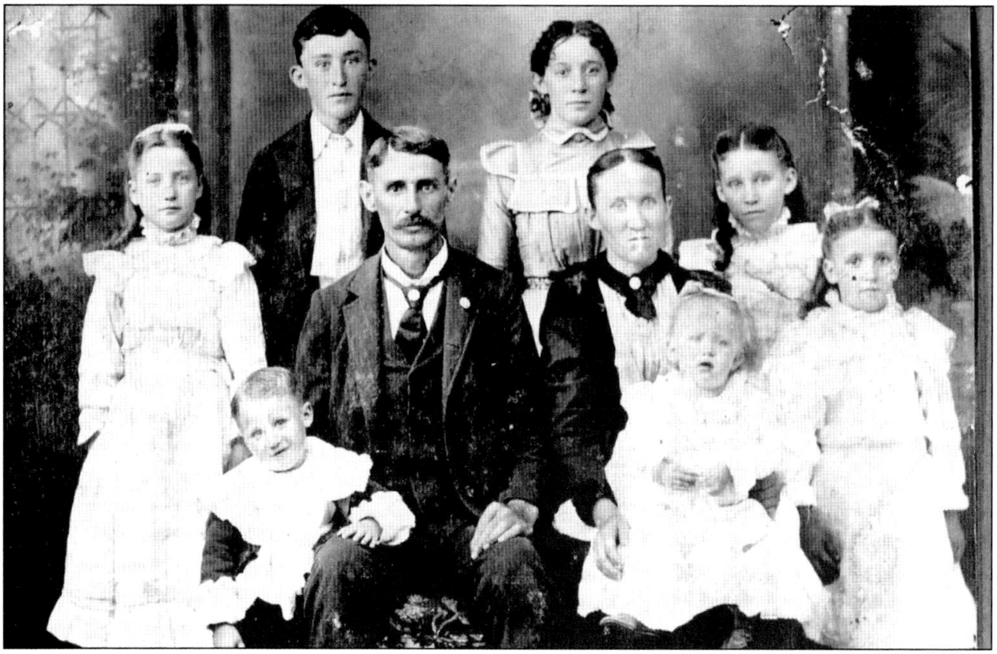

Anathan Noel Vasseur was 32 years old when he married for the second time. He had five children by his first wife—Charlie, Ruby, Minnie Pearl, Emily, and Lillie. Anathan married 22-year-old Mattie Beard in 1894, and by 1900, they had added Augustus and Sallie to the family. This family portrait was taken about 1900 when Sallie was a year old. Vasseur was a farmer and lived off of the Palma Road. (Courtesy of Sherman Powell.)

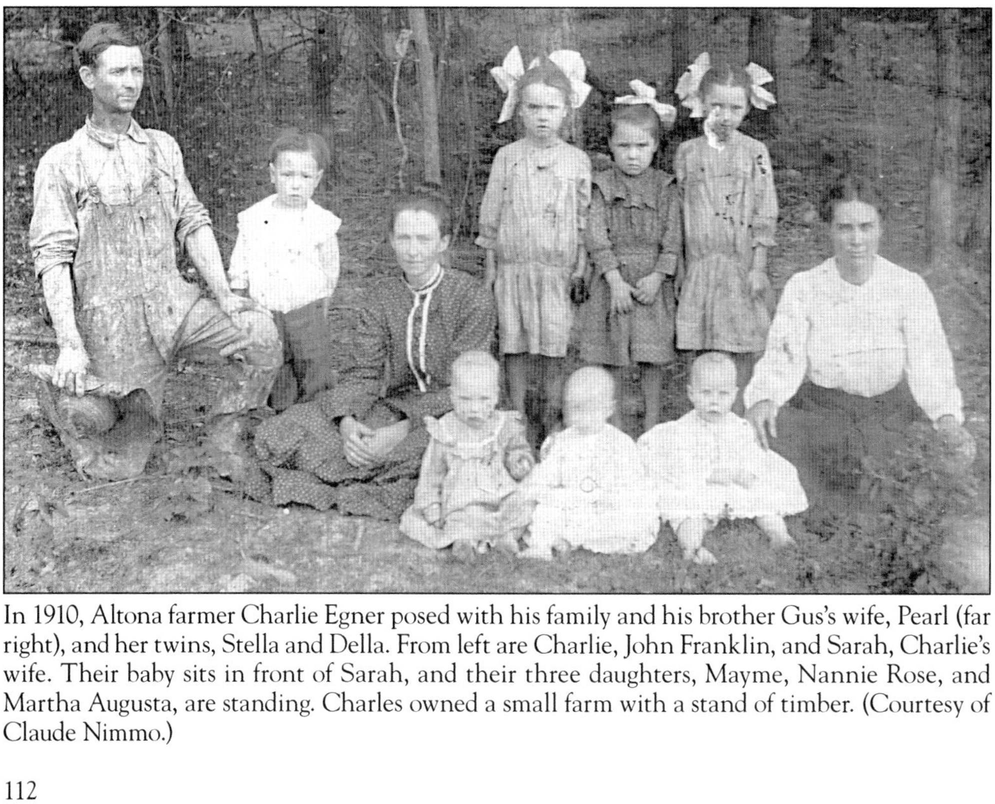

In 1910, Altona farmer Charlie Egner posed with his family and his brother Gus's wife, Pearl (far right), and her twins, Stella and Della. From left are Charlie, John Franklin, and Sarah, Charlie's wife. Their baby sits in front of Sarah, and their three daughters, Mayme, Nannie Rose, and Martha Augusta, are standing. Charles owned a small farm with a stand of timber. (Courtesy of Claude Nimmo.)

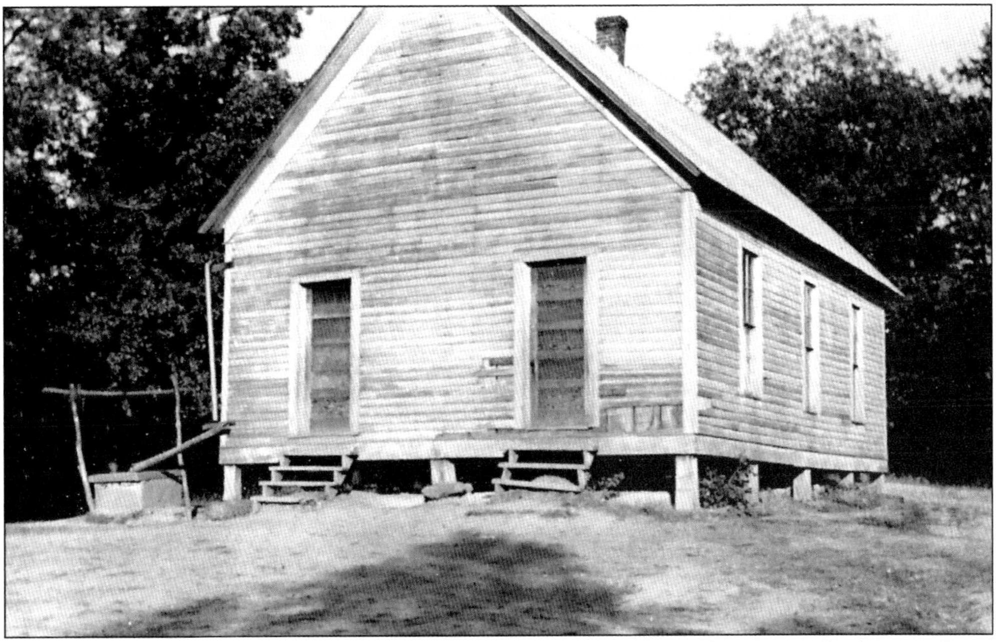

The second Howard's Grove School, 1908 to 1944, had two front doors, one for boys and one for girls. To the left is the cistern; it collected water from the roof and furnished the school with both drinking and washing water. This simple building was an example of the many one-room schoolhouses that once dotted Marshall County. (Courtesy of Elizabeth Harrell.)

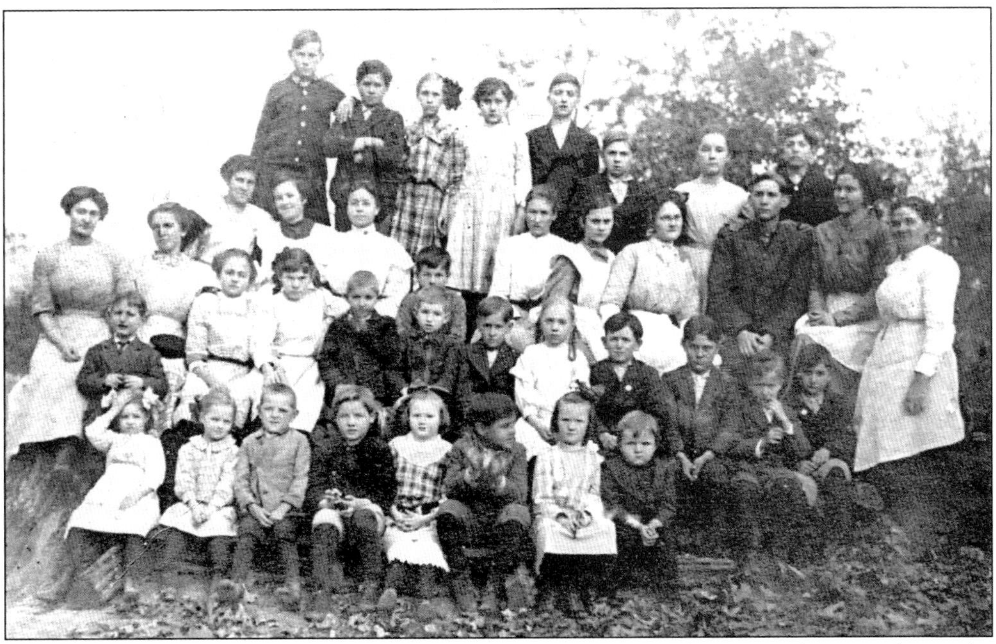

Teaching began at the new Howard's Grove School in 1908. This 1909 photograph may be the earliest one of the students from that school. The original Howard's Grove School opened in 1881 when a new district was formed west of Pleasant Hill and east of Possum Trot. Martha Lindsey gave an acre of ground for the school from the original Howard tract. As the school sat in a wooded grove, it was named Howard's Grove. (Courtesy of Johnny Harrell.)

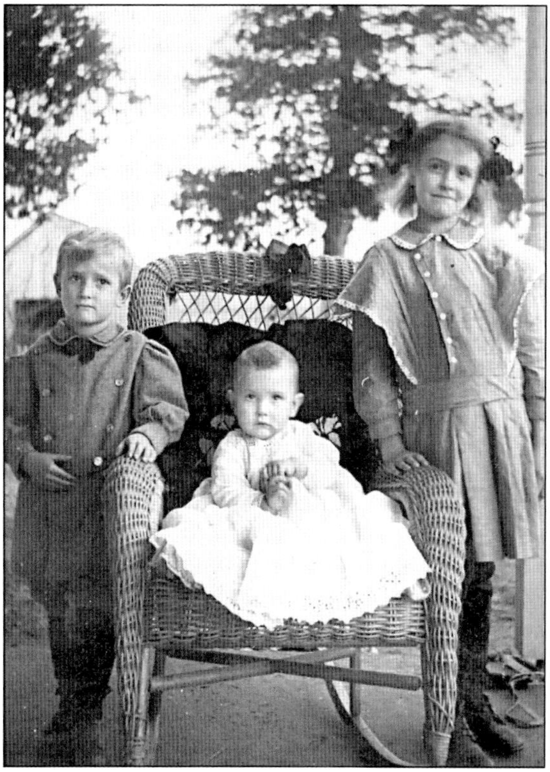

In 1910, Ethel (right), Buford (left), and Buren Powell lived near Calvert City on the farm owned by their parents. Buford, like many Marshall County men, went to Detroit to work. However, Buford fell ill and returned home, where he met and married Bessie Mullinax on October 11, 1928. They had five children. (Courtesy of Alton Powell.)

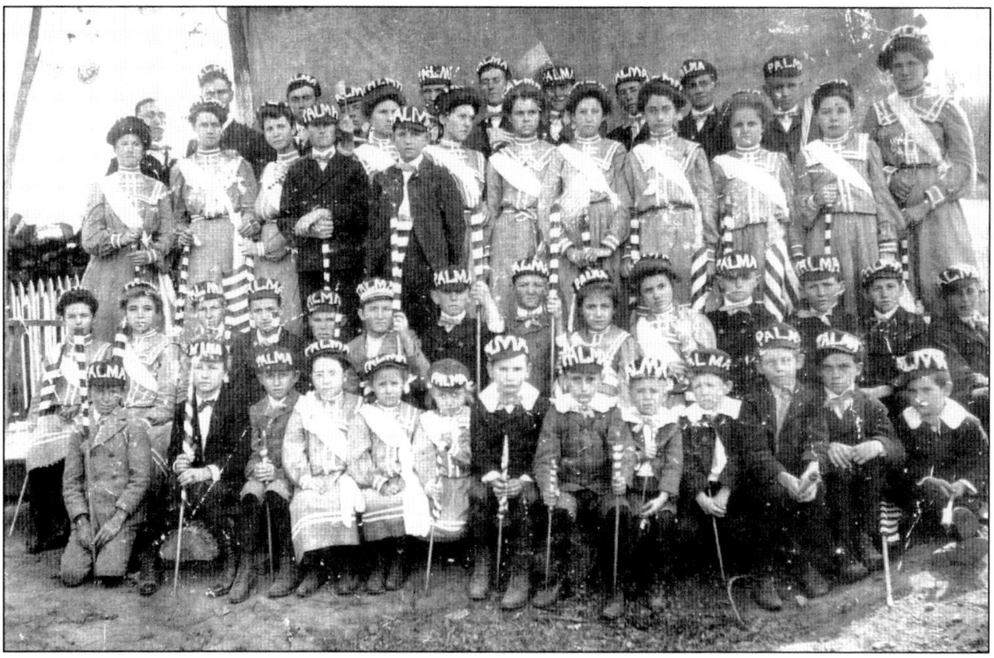

Palma School's teacher Lawrence Irvin Young had his students pull out all the stops for this patriotic photograph. The girls wore identical dresses, and the boys dressed in suits. Everyone sported handmade hats emblazoned with the school's name and furled American flags. (Courtesy of the Marshall County Genealogical and Historical Society.)

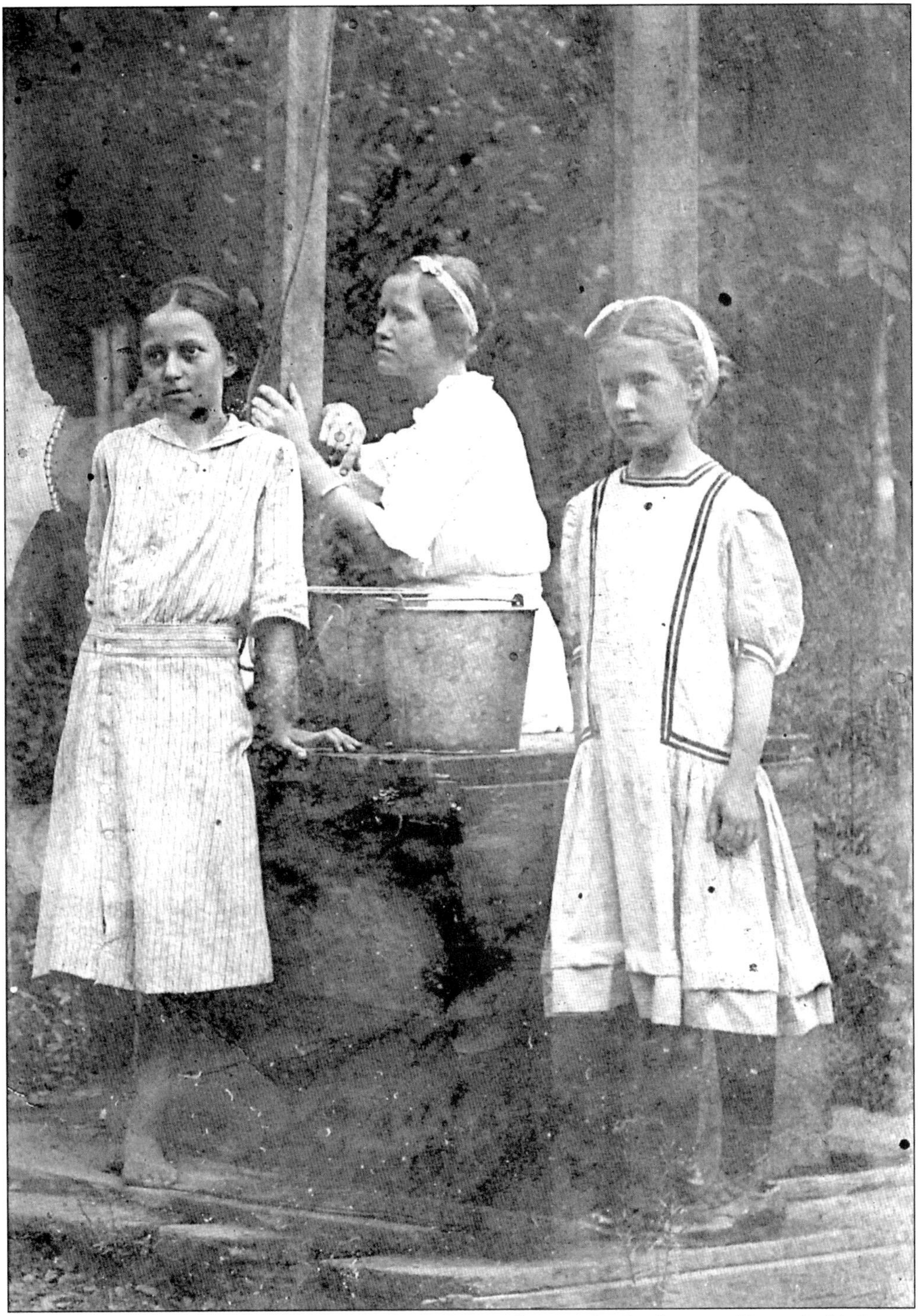

Until the mid-20th century, many homes relied on well water for drinking and household chores. Lee Etta Salyer (right) and her friends were captured drawing water about 1915. This unusual photograph has the faint image of two women in high-collared blouses along its left border. (Courtesy of Lisa Shugers.)

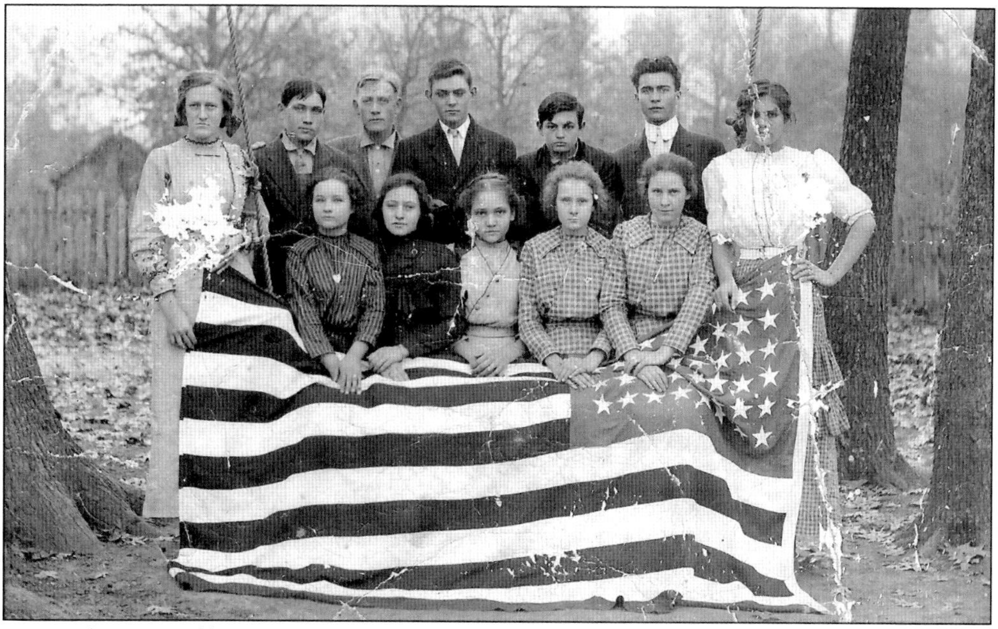

In 1916 during World War I, Saunders Ridge School's older students demonstrated their patriotism by draping themselves in a 48-star American flag for their class picture. Saunders Ridge School was located between Altona and Little Cypress on land donated by Dr. Saunders. Altona's Saunders Ridge School stood on the corner of property owned by Fred Hill where North Star Steel is now located. (Courtesy of Claude Nimmo.)

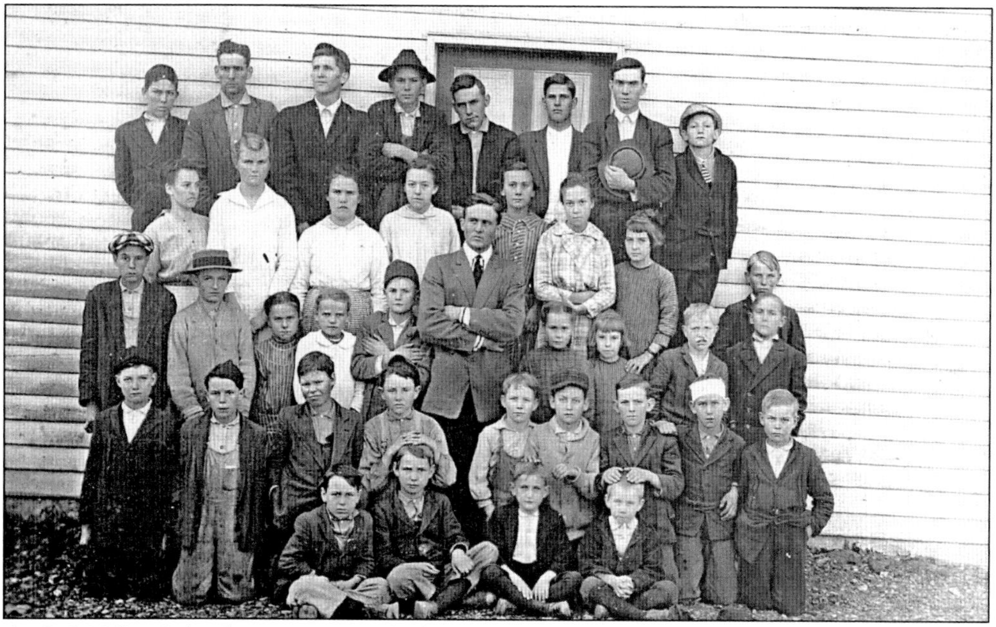

At Oak Valley School in 1918, attitude, hats, and head bandages ruled the day. Teacher Lamar Rose stood in the center. Among the students were 16 named Peck and 5 named Armstrong. Other surnames included 3 Bloomingburgs and 3 Allens. Oak Valley School was associated with the Oak Valley Church of Christ. Oak Valley was west of Scale. (Courtesy of the Marshall County Genealogical and Historical Society.)

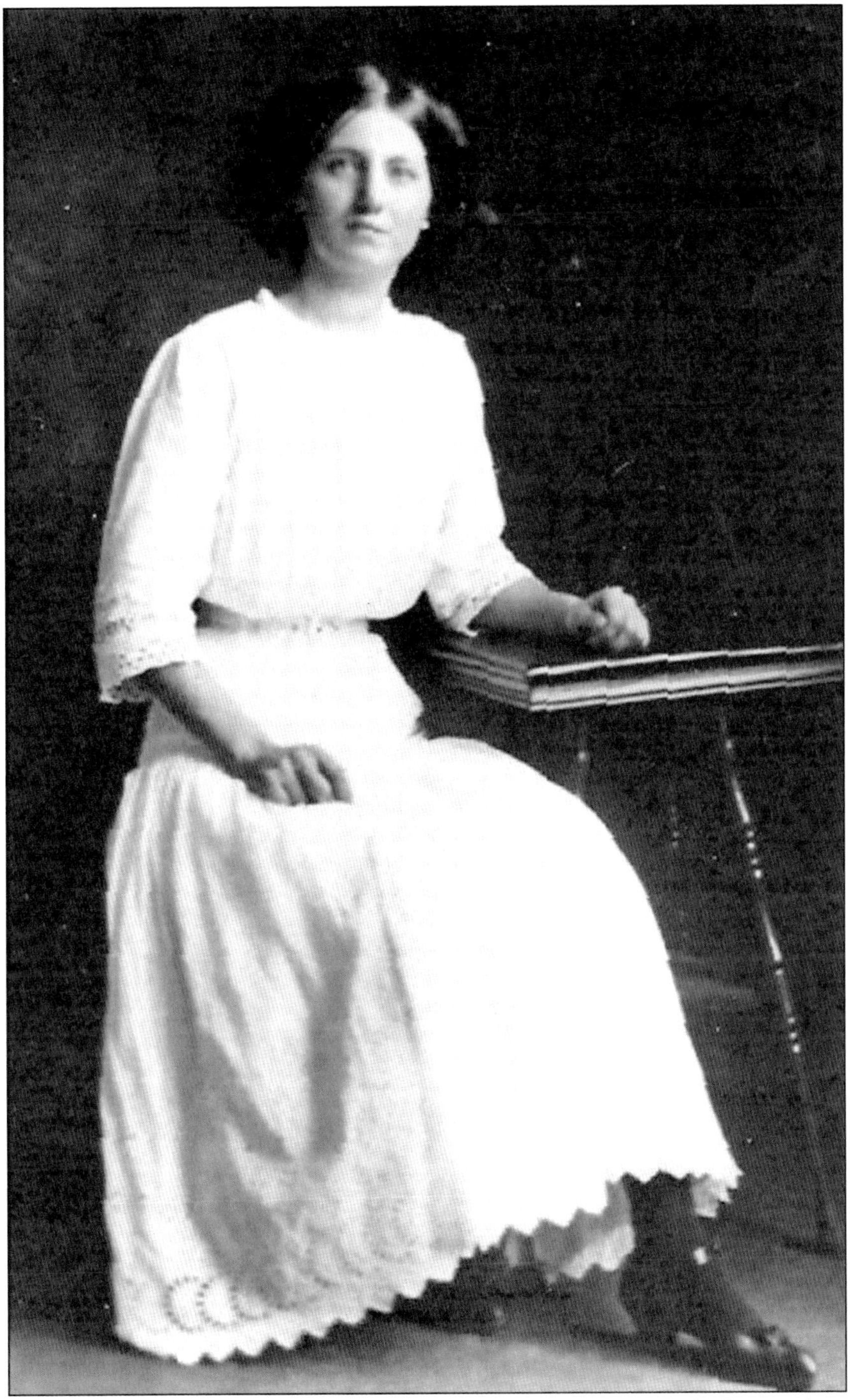

Birder Cintilla Johnston Cain was born on November 2, 1890. She married John Wesley Cain on April 20, 1912. John was from Calloway County but moved to the Griggstown area to work for the widow Mary Johnston Wallace, Birder's aunt, who raised her. Birder and John began married life on the farm she inherited from her father. (Courtesy of the Marshall County Genealogical and Historical Society.)

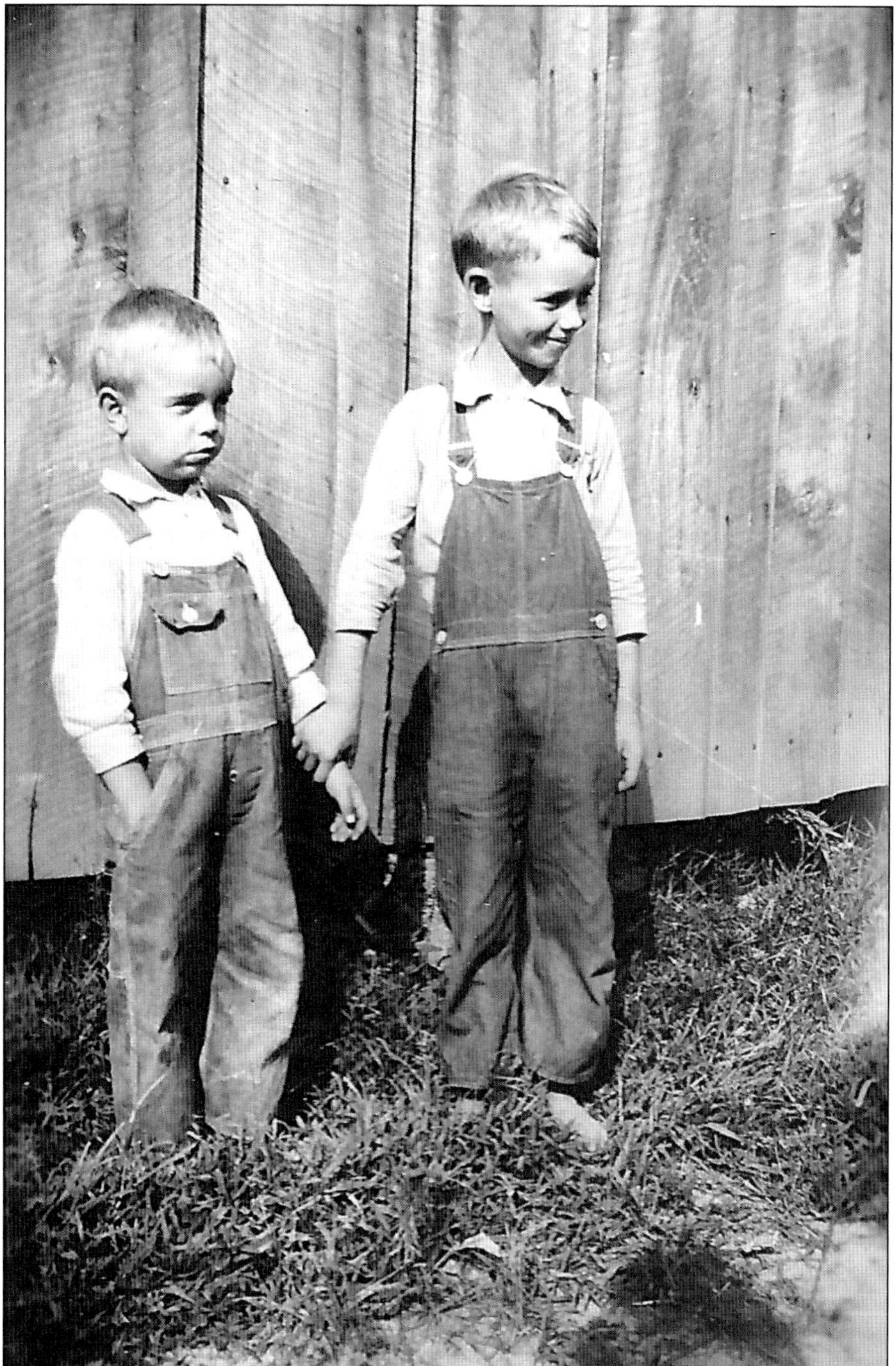

Griggstown boys Elzy Egner and J. D. Smith looked like many farm children of the era. Barefoot, dressed in overalls, and hair cut short, they played, worked, and went to school if their parents believed in schooling. Most parents believed that boys should get an education, even if they only wanted to be farmers like their fathers. However, into the 20th century, many fathers saw little necessity for their daughters to get a complete education. (Courtesy of Virginia Smith.)

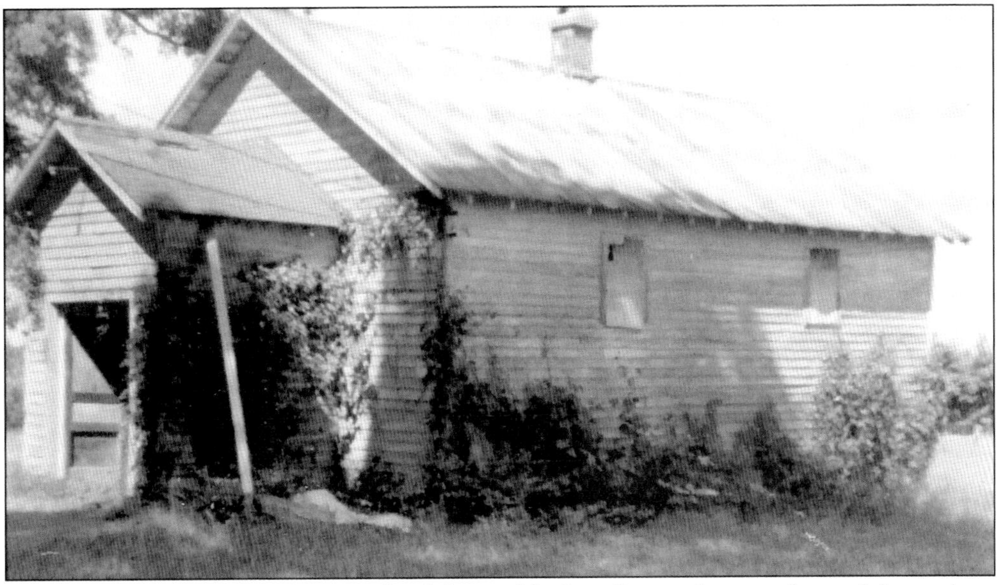

Altona Community Church sat on land donated by Lee Cox and across the road from where North Star Steel is located today. One year after it organized, it became a Missionary Baptist church. The congregation moved to a new building in 1948, and this picture was probably taken soon after. (Courtesy of Natalie Fowler Johnston.)

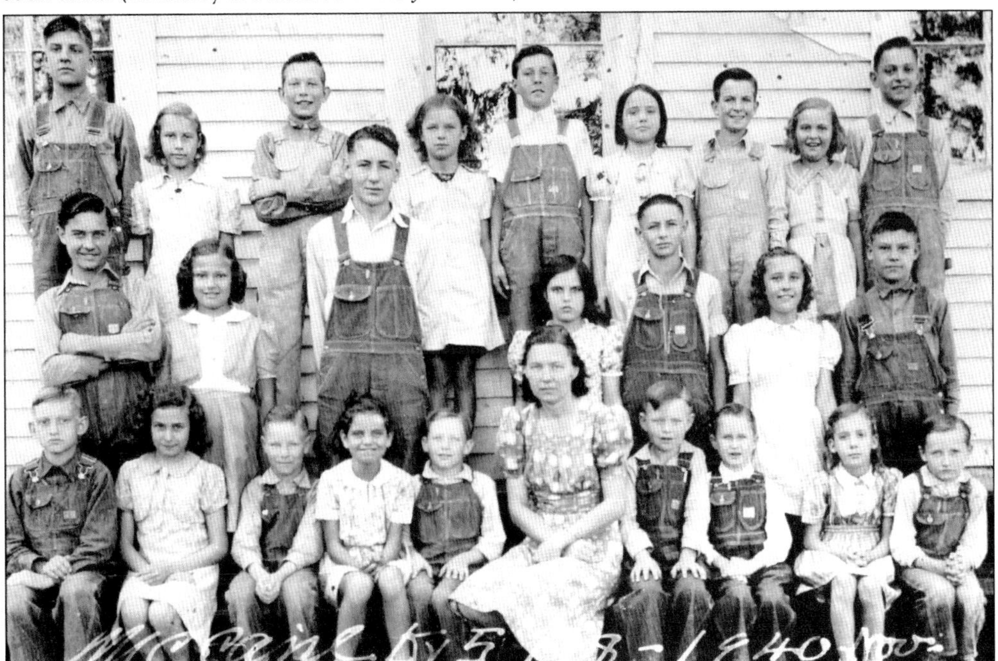

Teacher Curtis Griggs (first row, center) taught at the McCain School, which served western Griggstown for several years. In 1940, boys wore overalls and girls wore dresses to school. Although the photograph is labeled November, the children and their teacher were dressed for warmer weather. Family names in the picture included three Rileys, three Blakneys, three Johnsons, and five Darnells, along with a scattering of Salyers, Baileys, Humphreys, and McCains. (Courtesy of Lisa Shugers.)

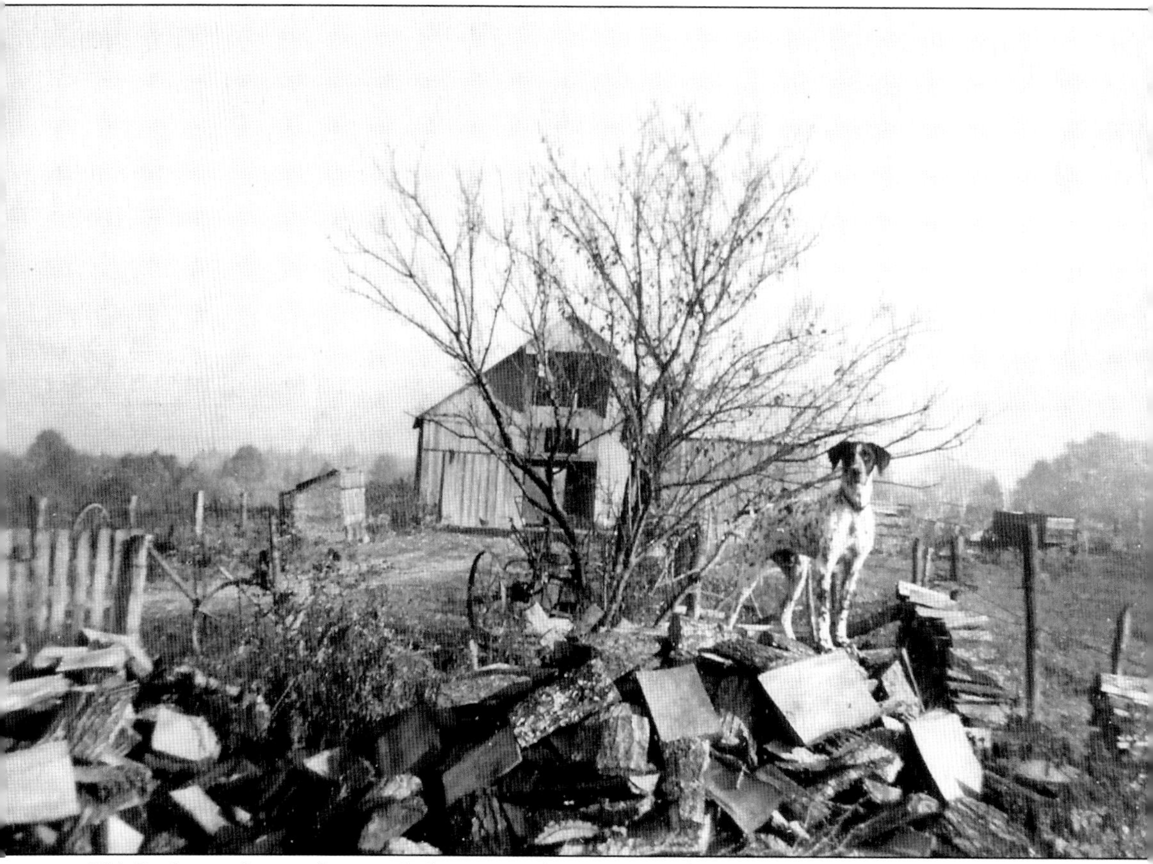

Old Buck stood atop the woodpile to get a better view of his surroundings on the Old Butler Farm. On many a quiet night, county residents could hear the baying of hunting dogs on the scent of a possum or raccoon. The farm was sold to build North Marshall High School, which is now North Marshall Junior High. (Courtesy of Virginia Smith.)

Ten

Kentucky Dam

Several years after the completion of Kentucky Dam, Evilena Filbeck self-published her novel about old Gilbertsville entitled *Gone with the Old River*. Although Evilena changed the names, many of Gilbertsville's residents could be identified among the characters in her story. More importantly, the spirit and soul of Marshall County leapt out from the pages:

> In those days, people moved slower at Gilbertsville. They were more interested in the weather and what their neighbors were doing than what went on in Washington or Frankfort or across the ocean waters. Men had time to lounge on the front porch of Bryant's Store and whittle. They spat tobacco juice, ranted about hard times, Old Hoover and the Republican Administration and prophesied about signs in the sky, like the Northern Lights. They reared back and flipped their long suspenders to emphasize a vital point in conversation. Women wore flowered aprons, burped out loud, had onion breath and flabby stomachs that sagged. . . . Housewives cooked three square meals a day and were old after they reached thirty. Then they lamented about their ailments, gushed over babies, moaned about morals, and eyed young girls with suspicion.

Marshall County of the 1930s kept up with the goings on in the world through radio and newspapers. Yet the people of the county depended upon the same things that they had since they began to settle the area. They relied on the rivers, the land, rain, sunshine, good neighbors, good schools, local doctors, and God. Their lives followed the seasons. Sometimes they left the county, never to return, yet most did. It was home.

The photographs presented previously show the people and the places that fashioned early Marshall County. The following photographs show the beginning of the change wrought by the Tennessee Valley Authority and Kentucky Dam. Nevertheless, if one leaves the main highways of the county and drives the back roads, the past can still be seen both in the land and the people.

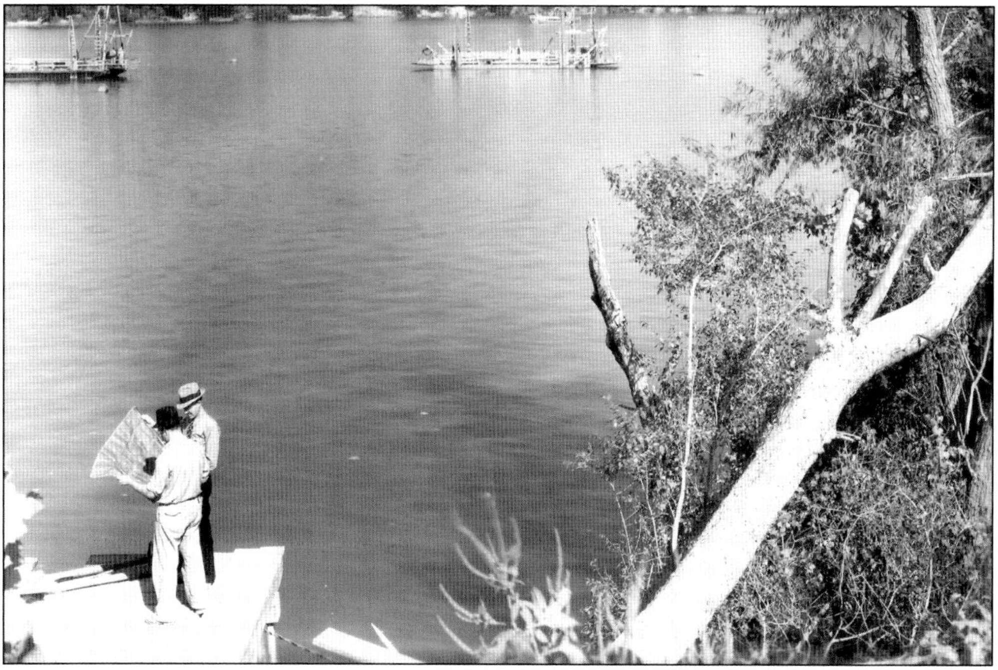

Representative of the TVA arrived in Marshall County in mid-1937 to survey a potential site for a new Tennessee River dam near Gilbertsville. Political action by such men as Luther Draffen of Calvert City and Sen. Alben Barkley of Paducah (the future vice president) secured the location of the dam at Gilbertsville rather than the previously desired location of Aurora. (Courtesy of Bobby Culp and the Tennessee Valley Authority.)

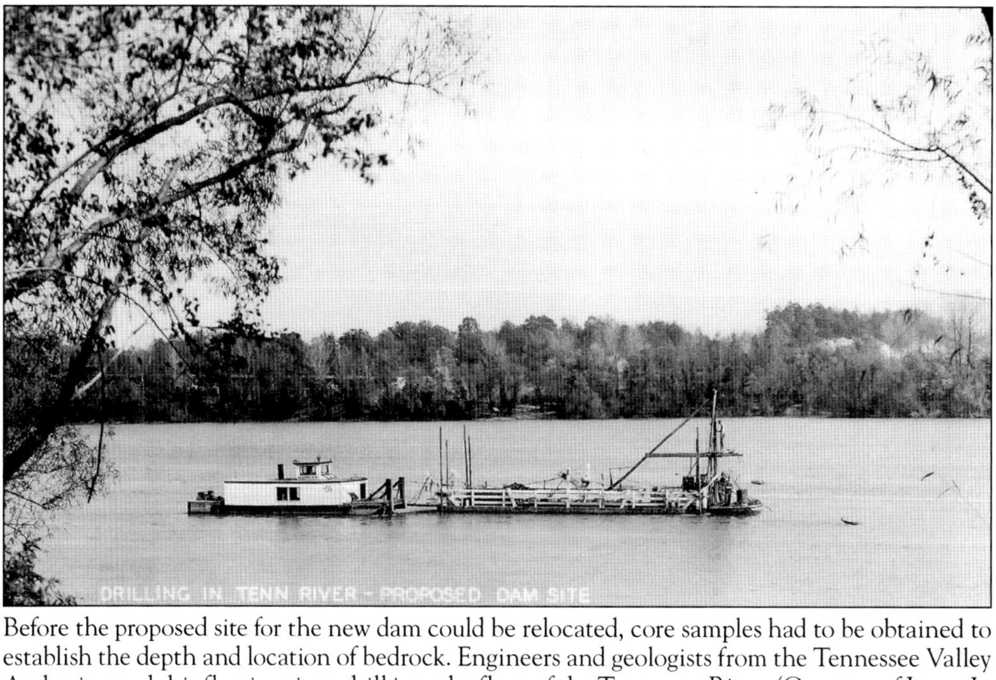

Before the proposed site for the new dam could be relocated, core samples had to be obtained to establish the depth and location of bedrock. Engineers and geologists from the Tennessee Valley Authority used this floating rig to drill into the floor of the Tennessee River. (Courtesy of James L. Draffen and the Tennessee Valley Authority.)

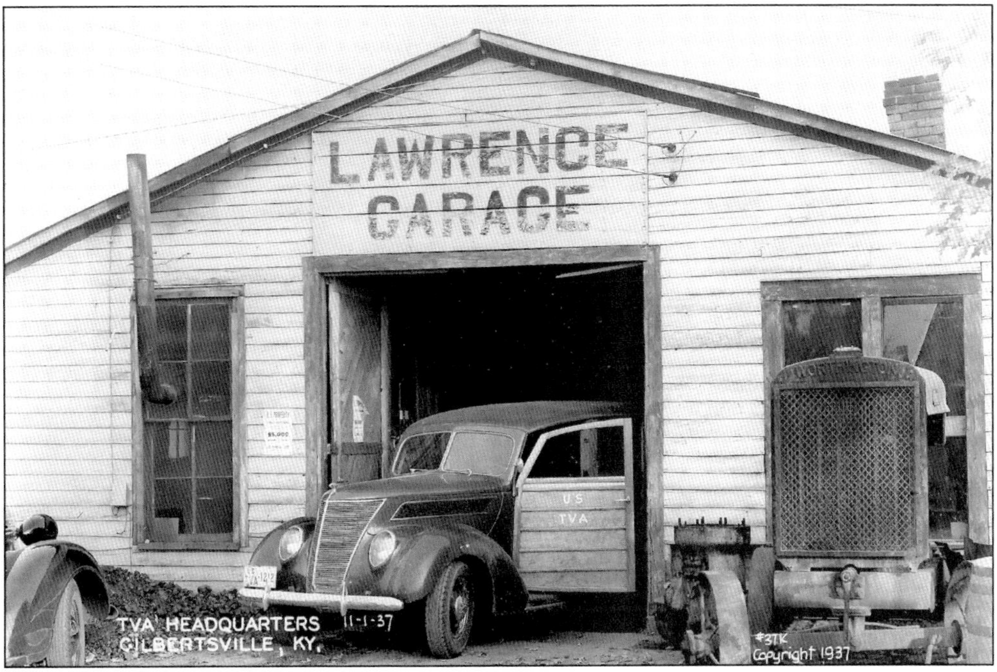

The Lawrence Garage in Gilbertsville was used as TVA Headquarters until more permanent buildings could be constructed. As TVA personnel arrived, they began looking for structures that could fulfill roles as offices and housing. Some residents offered rooms to the visitors; others sold their houses to the TVA. (Courtesy of James L. Draffen and the Tennessee Valley Authority.)

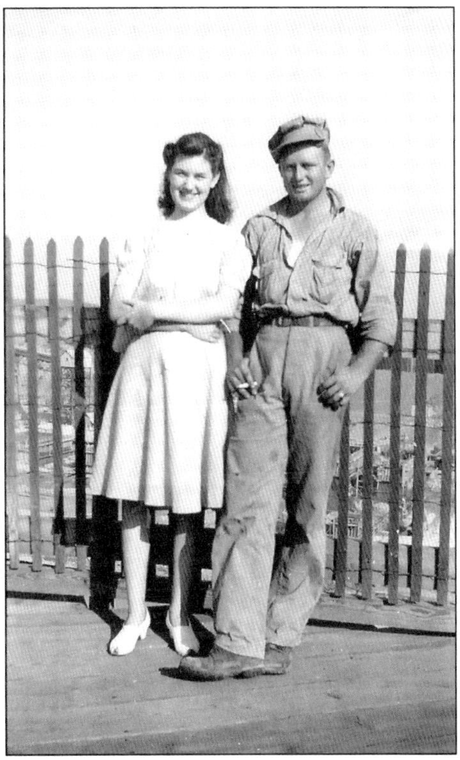

Local men, like Charles Wyatt, a 1938 graduate of Benton High School, found employment with the TVA when construction began on Kentucky Dam. County residents quickly realized the opportunity for well-paying jobs that would provide the local boys and girls with marketable skills. Louise and Charles Wyatt posed with the construction site of Kentucky Dam in the background not long after their marriage in 1940. (Courtesy of Louise Norton Wyatt.)

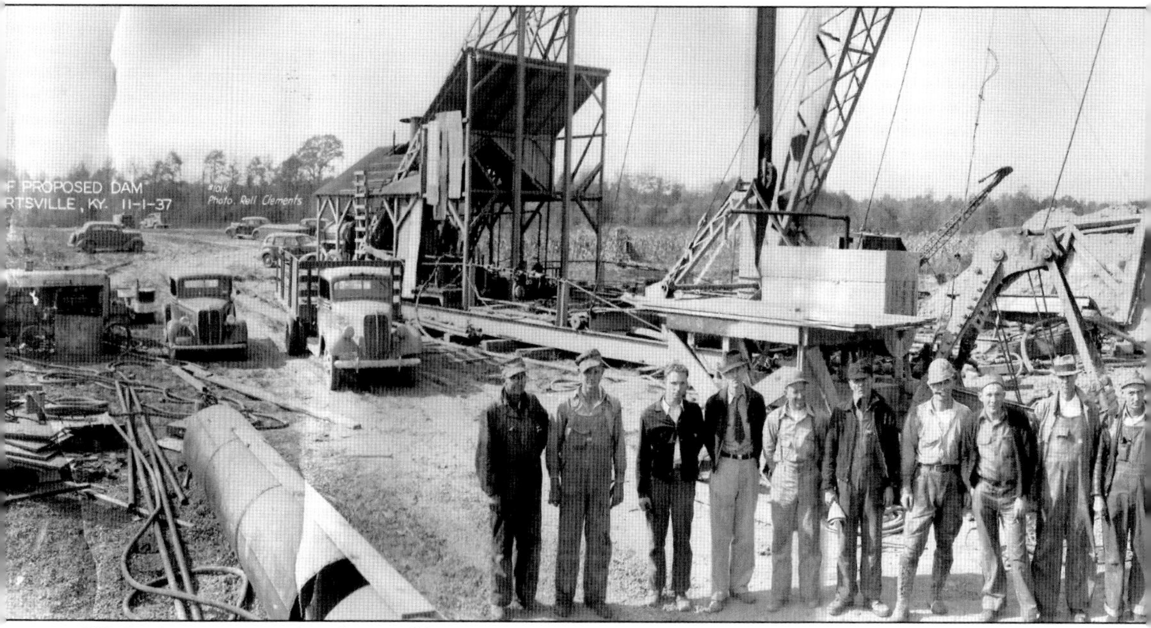

With the support of such notables as soon-to-be vice president Alben Barkley, Sen. George Norris, and Calvert City businessman Luther Draffen, construction began on Kentucky Dam. Senator Norris had waged a 12-year battle for the creation of the Tennessee Valley Authority to build dams on the Tennessee River and its tributaries to control flooding and generate low-cost electricity. It was Senator Norris's influence and knowledge that moved the construction to

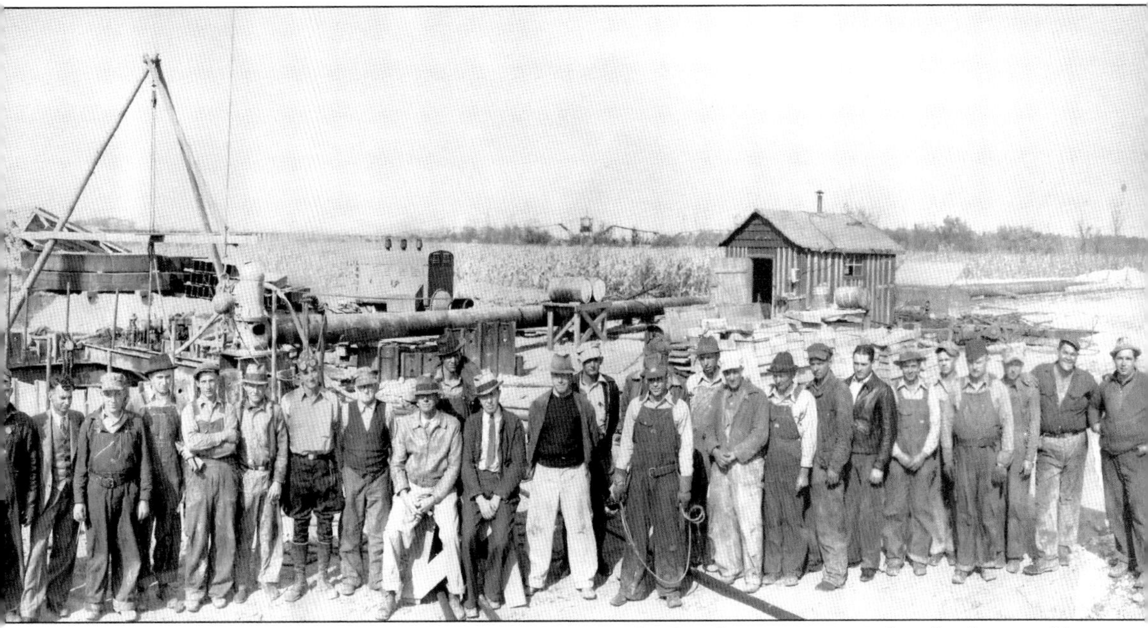

Gilbertsville. According to Draffen, Senator Norris said, "Gentlemen, it is true that the dam could be built on the Tennessee River 75 miles up, and save 10 million dollars, but if that is permitted, it will go down as the biggest blunder the engineers ever perpetrated!" Senator Norris continued to describe exactly where and how the dam should be built. (Courtesy of Charles Brown and Charles Hall.)

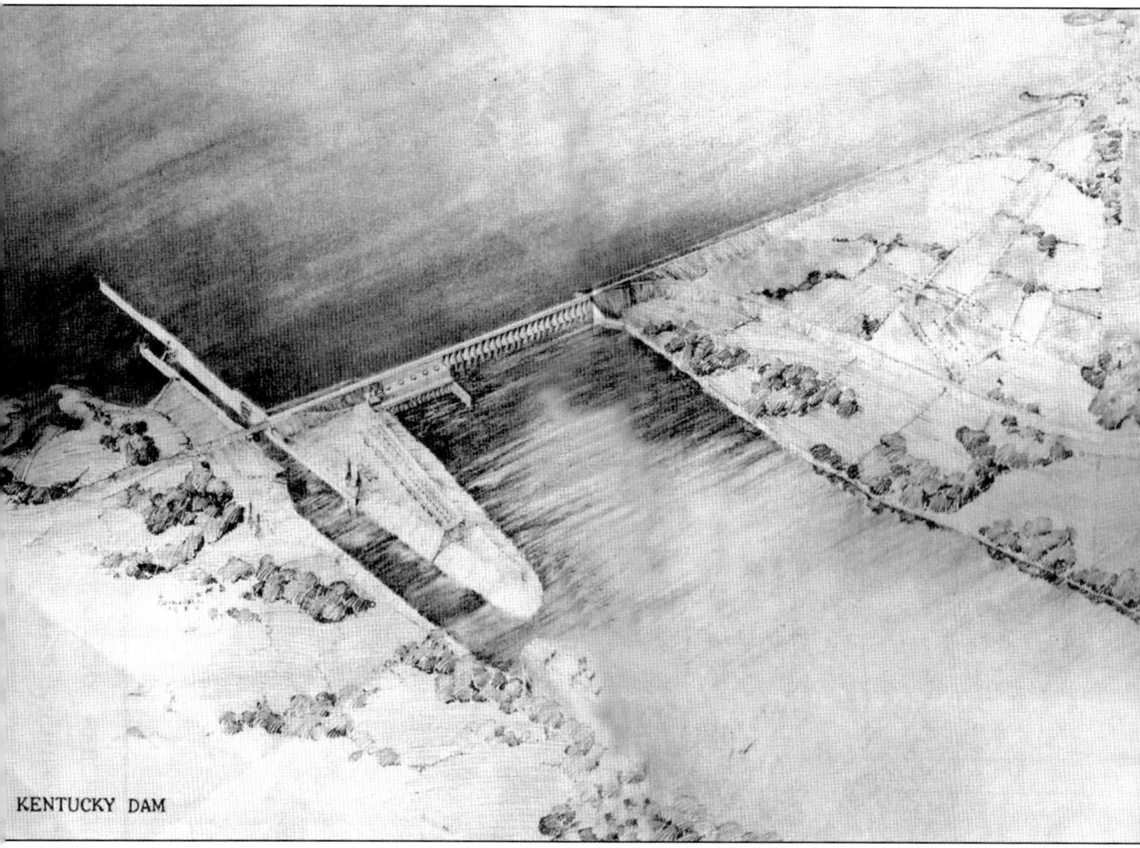

Pres. Harry S. Truman dedicated Kentucky Dam on October 10, 1945. This artist's drawing of the dam was presented in the official guest program for the event. (Courtesy of Rivers Capps.)

REFERENCES

Clark, Thomas D. A *History of Kentucky*. Lexington, KY: The John Bradford Press, 1960.

Collins, Lewis. *History of Kentucky*. Covington, KY: Collins & Company, 1882.

Filbeck, Evilena. *Gone with the Old River*. Calvert City, KY: Evilena Filbeck, 1972.

Hall, Charles H. *The Chemical Century; Calvert City, Kentucky; and Luther Draffen*. Calvert City, KY: Charles H. Hall.

History of Marshall County, Kentucky with Illustrations and Biographical Sketches. Benton, KY: Marshall County Genealogical and Historical Society, 1993.

Ivey, Howard C. *Childhood Memories of My Old Kentucky Home*. Calvert City, KY: Howard C. Ivey.

Kentucky Old Home Journal. Benton, KY: 1898.

Lemon, J. R. *Lemon's Hand Book of Marshall County*. Benton, KY: J. R. Lemon, 1894.

Leon, Lewis Freeman and Edward C. Olds. *The History of Marshall County*. Benton, KY: *The Tribune Democrat*, 1933.